American Culture in the 1910s

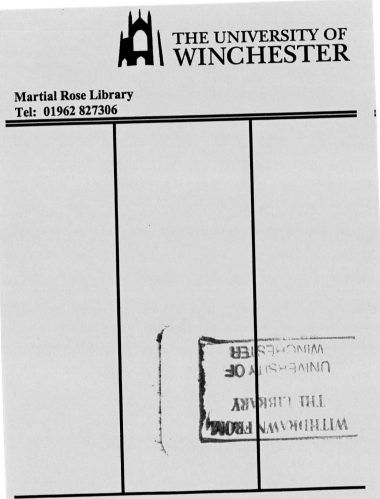

Twentieth-Century American Culture

Series Editor: Martin Halliwell, *Professor of American Studies, University of Leicester*

This series provides accessible but challenging studies of American culture in the twentieth century. Each title covers a specific decade and offers a clear overview of its dominant cultural forms and influential texts, discussing their historical impact and cultural legacy. Collectively the series reframes the notion of 'decade studies' through the prism of cultural production and rethinks the ways in which decades are usually periodised. Broad contextual approaches to the particular decade are combined with focused case studies, dealing with themes of modernity, commerce, freedom, power, resistance, community, race, class, gender, sexuality, internationalism, technology, war and popular culture.

American Culture in the 1910s
Mark Whalan

American Culture in the 1920s
Susan Currell

American Culture in the 1930s
David Eldridge

American Culture in the 1940s
Jacqueline Foertsch

American Culture in the 1950s
Martin Halliwell

American Culture in the 1960s
Sharon Monteith

American Culture in the 1970s
Will Kaufman

American Culture in the 1980s
Graham Thompson

American Culture in the 1990s
Colin Harrison

American Culture in the 1910s

Mark Whalan

Edinburgh University Press

© Mark Whalan, 2010

Edinburgh University Press Ltd
22 George Square, Edinburgh
www.euppublishing.com

Typeset in 11/13 pt Stempel Garamond by
Servis Filmsetting Ltd, Stockport, Cheshire, and
printed and bound in Great Britain by
CPI Antony Rowe, Chippenham and Eastbourne

A CIP record for this book is available from the British Library

ISBN 978 0 7486 3423 1 (hardback)
ISBN 978 0 7486 3424 8 (paperback)

Contents

Figures

Case Studies

Acknowledgements

One of the nice things about projects with such a daunting scope is the number of interesting conversations with other scholars they demand, often from different disciplines. This book would have been much the poorer without input and feedback from Kristofer Allerfeldt, Jo Gill, Helen Hanson, Tim Kendall, Bob Lawson Peebles, Steve Neale, Dan North, Maeve Pearson, Helen Taylor, and Paul Williams at the University of Exeter; from Peter Antelyes, Bill Hoynes, Hua Hsu, Paul Russell, and Karen Robertson at Vassar College; and from Jude Davies, John Fagg, Heather Hutchinson, and Elizabeth Nolan. Students at Exeter, particularly Gavin Smith and my MA class on Cultures of American Modernism, helped me think through aspects of the decade in useful ways. Thanks are also due to my research assistant at Vassar, Jonathan Asen, who did a wonderful job of picking gems from the sometimes trackless forests of 1910s periodicals. Brian and Lou Whalan helped with suggestions and unfailing enthusiasm. This project was wonderfully guided by Nicola Ramsey and James Dale at Edinburgh University Press, and would never have happened without the encouragement and advice of Series Editor Martin Halliwell. I hope my dear friend Grace Cowell will enjoy this book, and I dedicate it to my wife, Lee Rumbarger, who now knows more about the 1910s than she ever thought likely.

Chronology of 1910s American Culture

Date	Events	Visual Art, Photography and Design	Film and Vaudeville
1910	Mann Act passed, preventing the transportation of women across state lines for 'immoral purposes'; becomes known as the White Slave Act. Victor Berger is the first Socialist elected to the United States Congress. Mexican Revolution against President Porfirio Diaz. Boy Scouts of America founded. African American Jack Johnson defeats Jim Jeffries, 'The Great White Hope', to retain heavyweight boxing championship of the world. George Herriman publishes first 'Krazy Kat' cartoon.	International exhibition of pictorial photography, Albright Art Gallery, Buffalo	Florence Lawrence stars in *The Broken Oath* John Randolph Bray patents cel process for animation
1911	Triangle shirtwaist factory fire kills 146 workers in New York City, mostly young immigrant women, and prompts state reform of fire regulations in the workplace. Arizona and New Mexico admitted to statehood. United States Supreme Court breaks up Standard Oil. National Urban League founded.	John Sloan becomes Art Editor of *The Masses* *Sailing*, Edward Hopper's first painting to be sold New York Public Library Main Branch opens, designed by Carrère and Hastings	Al Jolson leaps to Broadway stardom in *La Belle Paree* *Enoch Arden* (Dir. D. W. Griffith)

Fiction and Poetry	Performance and Music	Criticism
Henry James, *The Finer Grain*	Enrico Caruso stars, and Arturo Toscanini conducts, at the New York Met in the world premiere of Giacomo Puccini's *La Fanciulla del West*	Emma Goldman, *Anarchism and Other Essays* Jane Addams, *Twenty Years at Hull House* Theodore Roosevelt, *African Game Trails* *The Crisis,* the house journal for the NAACP, founded, with W. E. B. Du Bois as editor
Edith Wharton, *Ethan Frome* Theodore Dreiser, *Jennie Gerhardt* Frances Hodgson Burnett, *The Secret Garden* W. E. B. Du Bois, *The Quest of the Silver Fleece*	Edward Sheldon, *The Boss* David Belasco, *The Return of Peter Grimm* Irving Berlin, 'Everybody's Doin' It Now', 'Alexander's Ragtime Band' Nat D. Ayer and Seymour Brown, 'Oh, You Beautiful Doll' 1911–12 Abbey Players' tour of the United States	Ambrose Bierce, *The Devil's Dictionary* Frederick Winslow Taylor, *The Principles of Scientific Management* *The Masses* begins George Santayana, 'The Genteel Tradition in American Philosophy'

Date	Events	Visual Art, Photography and Design	Film and Vaudeville
1912	June: After failing to gain the Republican nomination for president, Theodore Roosevelt forms the breakaway Progressive Party. November: Democrat Woodrow Wilson wins presidential election against incumbent Republican William Taft, Roosevelt's Progressive Party and Eugene Debs's Socialists. The *Titanic* sinks on its maiden voyage to New York. Lawrence, MA Textile Strike, involving 23,000 workers.	Arthur Dove's first one-man exhibition, at Stieglitz's '291' Excerpts from Wassily Kandinsky's *Concerning the Spiritual in Art* appear in *Camera Work* 1912–13 John Marin's sequence of watercolours of New York architecture, including the Brooklyn Bridge and the Woolworth Building	Ruling against the Motion Picture Patents Company in Latham loop patent case represents an important legal victory for independent production companies Keystone Pictures Studio opens Harry Houdini pioneers 'Chinese Water Torture Cell' escape Keystone's *A Noise from the Deep*, starring Mabel Normand and Fatty Arbuckle, reputedly pioneers the thrown pie in the face gag Edison's *What Happened to Mary?* pioneers serial film
1913	31 March: A record number of immigrants in a single day arrive at Ellis Island (6,745). Crossword puzzles debut in the *New York World*. Sixteenth Amendment to the Constitution passed, making federal income tax constitutional. Ford opens assembly line. Seventeenth Amendment to the Constitution passed, allowing direct election of senators. Federal Reserve Act. Federal Raker Act allows for the flooding of Hetch Hetchy Valley in Yosemite to provide water for San Francisco.	The Armory Show Opening of remodelled Grand Central Station; completion of Woolworth Building, designed by Cass Gilbert Joseph Stella, 'Battle of Lights, Coney Island' Max Weber, 'Fleeing Mother and Child'	*Traffic in Souls* (Dir. George Loane Tucker)

Fiction and Poetry	Performance and Music	Criticism
James W. Johnson, *The Autobiography of an Ex-Colored Man* Zane Grey, *Riders of the Purple Sage* Harriet Monroe founds *Poetry* magazine Theodore Dreiser, *The Financier* Sui Sin Far, *Mrs Spring Fragrance*	Max Reinhardt, *Sumurun* J. Hartley Manners, *Peg O' My Heart* Rachel Crothers, *He and She* W. C. Handy, 'Memphis Blues'	Mary Antin, *The Promised Land* A. A. Brill, *Psychoanalysis: Its Theories and Practical Application* William James, *Essays in Radical Empiricism*
Willa Cather, *O Pioneers!* Edith Wharton, *The Custom of the Country* Robert Frost, *A Boy's Will* Ellen Glasgow, *Virginia*	IWW co-ordinates Paterson Pageant to rally support for striking textile workers Frederick Weatherly, 'Danny Boy' 1913–14 James Reese Europe's Society Orchestra records eight tracks with Victor; 1914, publishes *Castle House Rag* and *Castle Waltz*	Walter Lippmann, *A Preface to Politics* *The New Republic* founded Ezra Pound, 'Patria Mia' Floyd Dell, *Women as World Builders: Studies in Modern Feminism* Randolph Bourne, *Youth and Life*

Date	Events	Visual Art, Photography and Design	Film and Vaudeville
1914	Telephone lines link New York and San Francisco. America declares neutrality as World War I begins in Europe. Ludlow massacre, as twenty die when state militia attack a striking miners' tent colony in Ludlow, Colorado. Panama Canal opens. Ford institutes five-dollar, eight-hour day. Tampico Affair leads to seven-month US occupation of the Mexican city of Vera Cruz. Federal Trade Commission Act. Provisional Executive Committee for General Zionist Affairs launched in New York, headed by Louis Brandeis.	Clarence White's School of Photography opens Brancusi has his first one-man show in New York, at '291' Edward Hopper, 'Soir Bleu' Marsden Hartley, 'Portrait of a German Officer' First US exhibition of the synchromist painters, including work by Stanton Macdonald Wright	*The Perils of Pauline* (Dir. Louis D. Glasnier; starring Pearl White) *Judith of Bethulia* (Dir. D. W. Griffith) *Cabiria* (Dir. Giovanni Pastrone, Italy) *Gertie the Dinosaur* (Winsor McCay) First appearance of Chaplin's Little Tramp character in Keystone's 'Kid Auto Races at Venice'
1915	Henry Ford develops the tractor. Ku Klux Klan revived at Stone Mountain, Georgia. *Lusitania* sunk by German U-boat, killing 1,198 people, including 114 Americans. US Marines invade Haiti. Victrola phonograph goes on sale.	Francis Picabia and Marcel Duchamp arrive in New York Arthur Dove, 'Plant Forms' Maurice de Zayas opens his Modern Gallery	*The Birth of a Nation* (Dir. D. W. Griffith) *A Fool There Was* (Dir. Frank Powell, starring Theda Bara) Carl Laemmle opens huge Universal City Studios in Los Angeles MPCC prosecuted under Sherman Anti-trust Act Harold Lloyd pioneers his 'Lonesome Luke' character *The Cheat* (Dir. Cecil B. De Mille)

Fiction and Poetry	Performance and Music	Criticism
Edgar Rice Burroughs, *Tarzan of the Apes* Gertrude Stein, *Tender Buttons* Robert Frost, *North of Boston* Margaret Anderson founds *The Little Review* Theodore Dreiser, *The Titan* Sinclair Lewis, *Our Mr Wrenn*	Elmer Rice, *On Trial* *Watch Your Step* (songs by Irving Berlin, performed by Vernon and Irene Castle) Formation of the American Society of Composers, Authors, and Publishers W. C. Handy, 'Saint Louis Blues'	Walter Lippmann, *Drift and Mastery*
Willa Cather, *The Song of the Lark* Charlotte Perkins Gilman, *Herland* Wallace Stevens, 'Sunday Morning' Theodore Dreiser, *The Genius*	Ruth St Denis and Ted Shawn open Denishawn dance school Jelly Roll Morton, 'Jelly Roll Blues' Al Piantadosi and Alfred Bryan, 'I Didn't Raise My Boy to be a Soldier' Sole read-through performance of Scott Joplin's opera *Treemonisha*	Van Wyck Brooks, *America's Coming-Of-Age* Edith Wharton, *Fighting France, from Dunkerque to Belfort* Horace Kallen, 'Democracy versus the Melting Pot'

Date	Events	Visual Art, Photography and Design	Film and Vaudeville
1916	Margaret Sanger opens first US birth control clinic. Woodrow Wilson re-elected president against Republican Charles Evans Hughes under the slogan 'He kept us out of the war'. US munitions exports at $1.3 billion. German agents cause explosion at Black Tom Island, New York, destroying 2,132,000 pounds of munitions – during the Somme offensive. Skirmish between United States and federal Mexican forces at Carrizal. Louis Brandeis becomes first Jewish member of the Supreme Court. Labour leader Tom Mooney controversially convicted of murdering ten people in the Preparedness Day Bombing in San Francisco.	Paul Strand produces his first abstract photographs Georgia O'Keeffe's first exhibition First Norman Rockwell cover (of an eventual total of 321) appears on *Saturday Evening Post* Man Ray, 'The Rope Dancer Accompanies Herself With Her Shadow'; also creates first American Dada assemblage, with *Self-Portrait* Forum Exhibition of Modern American Painters, a key exhibition for American modernist art neglected at The Armory Show Morton Schamberg begins his machine paintings	*Intolerance* (Dir. D. W. Griffith) Famous Players-Lasky merges with Paramount Pictures *20,000 Leagues Under the Sea* (Dir. Stuart Paton)
1917	Last horse-drawn streetcar withdrawn from the streets of Manhattan. 1 February: Germany resumes unrestricted submarine warfare. 1 March: Zimmerman telegraph published, revealing a German offer of alliance to Mexico in forthcoming war with United States. 6 April: United States declares war on Germany. 5 June: Selective service draft begins. 25 June: Espionage Act becomes law. Literacy test added to immigration statutes, as well as immigration being halted from the 'Asiatic barred zone'. Jones Act makes Puerto Rico a territory of the United States. Eighteenth Amendment to the Constitution proposed by Congress. First Pulitzer Prizes awarded.	Society of Independent Artists' Show, which includes Duchamp's 'Fountain' The closure of '291', and last numbers of *Camera Work* James VanDerZee opens his first studio in Harlem Charles Dana Gibson becomes director of the pictorial division of the CPI Charles Sheeler's *Doylestown Sequence* 1917–18, Joseph Stella, 'Brooklyn Bridge'	*The Poor Little Rich Girl* (Dir. Maurice Tourneur, starring Mary Pickford) Buster Keaton's on-screen debut, in *The Butcher Boy Rebecca of Sunnybrook Farm* (Dir. Marshall Neilan, starring Mary Pickford)

Fiction and Poetry	Performance and Music	Criticism
Robert Frost, *Mountain Interval* Ezra Pound, *Lustra* (also begins *Cantos*) H. D., *Sea Garden* Carl Sandburg, *Chicago Poems* Ring Lardner, *You know Me, Al*	First performance of Eugene O'Neill's *Bound East for Cardiff* Susan Glaspell, *Trifles* Diaghilev's Ballets Russes tours the United States Isadora Duncan performs 'The Marseillaise' at the Metropolitan Opera House	John Dewey, *Democracy and Education* Randolph Bourne, 'Trans-National America' Carter G. Woodson founds *Journal of Negro History* Margaret Sanger, *What Every Girl Should Know*
T. S. Eliot, *Prufrock and Other Observations* Edith Wharton, *Summer* Edna St Vincent Millay, *Renascence* William Carlos Williams, *Al Que Quiere!* Mary Austin, *The Ford* Abraham Cahan, *The Rise of David Levinsky*	Théâtre du Vieux Colombier's US Tour George M. Cohan, 'Over There' Original Dixieland Jazz Band's 'Livery Stable Blues' and 'Dixie Jass Band One Step' becomes the first-ever jazz record release Eugene O'Neill, *The Moon of the Caribbees* 1917–18, Princess Theatre musicals by Jerome Kern, P. G. Wodehouse, and Guy Bolton	Joel E. Spingarn, *Creative Criticism*

Date	Events	Visual Art, Photography and Design	Film and Vaudeville
1918	Influenza epidemic kills up to fifty million people worldwide, 1918–20, and at least 675,000 in the United States. January: Woodrow Wilson presents his fourteen points to Congress, outlining his goals for the post-war peace. Summer: initial American troops arrive in Siberia as part of joint Allied force. June: American troops help halt German offensive on Paris at Château-Thierry. September: 550,000 American troops in action in St Mihiel offensive. September–November: 1,200,000 American troops in action in Meuse-Argonne offensive. Eugene Debs sentenced to ten years in jail for sedition. 11 November: armistice with Germany.	Formation of the Provincetown Printers Formation of Whitney Studio Club Lewis Hine dispatched to Europe to photograph for the Red Cross	*Tarzan of the Apes* (Dir. Scott Sidney, starring Elmo Lincoln) *Old Wives for New* (Dir. Cecil B. De Mille) *Shoulder Arms* (starring Charlie Chaplin) *Mickey* (Dir. F. Richard Jones and James Young, starring Mabel Normand)

Fiction and Poetry	Performance and Music	Criticism
Willa Cather, *My Ántonia* Booth Tarkington, *The Magnificent Ambersons* US Post Office burns five hundred copies of *The Little Review* containing sections of James Joyce's *Ulysses*, claiming it is indecent	Frank Bacon and Winchell Smith, *Lightnin'* James P. Johnson, 'Carolina Shout'	First public printing of *The Education of Henry Adams* Henry James, *Within the Rim, and Other Essays, 1914–1915*

Date	Events	Visual Art, Photography and Design	Film and Vaudeville
1919	Eighteenth Amendment to the Constitution ratified, prohibiting the manufacture, sale and transport of alcohol within the United States. It goes into effect in January 1920. February: general strike in Seattle. March: founding of the Third International, or Comintern, in Moscow. June: signing of the Treaty of Versailles. Galleanist radicals explode bombs in eight cities; targets include Attorney General, A. Mitchell Palmer. July–August: race riots in Washington and Chicago. August: Palmer creates the anti-radical General Intelligence division of the Bureau of Investigation, headed by J. Edgar Hoover. September: Boston Police strike; 350,000 steelworkers strike. October: race riot in Elaine, Arkansas; Woodrow Wilson suffers a massive stroke. November: Palmer raids against suspected radicals begin; US Senate refuses to ratify the Treaty of Versailles. December: deportation to the new Soviet Union of Emma Goldman and 248 others suspected of radical activity. Radio Corporation of America founded. 'Black Sox' baseball scandal, as eight members of the Chicago White Sox are banned from baseball for life for attempting to fix the World Series. *New York Daily News*, the first tabloid newspaper, publishes its first issue.	John R. Covert, 'Brass Band'	Foundation of United Artists *The Homesteader* (Dir. Oscar Micheaux) First Felix the Cat films, by Otto Messmer *Broken Blossoms* (Dir. D. W. Griffith)

Fiction and Poetry	Performance and Music	Criticism
Sherwood Anderson, *Winesburg, Ohio* Upton Sinclair, *Jimmie Higgins* Zane Grey, *The Desert of Wheat* Claude McKay, 'If We Must Die'	Actors' Equity strike John Kelette and Jann Kenbrovin, 'I'm Forever Blowing Bubbles'	Waldo Frank, *Our America* Upton Sinclair, *The Brass Check* H. L. Mencken, *The American Language: An Inquiry into the Development of English in the United States* T. S. Eliot, 'Tradition and the Individual Talent' John Reed, *Ten Days that Shook the World*

Introduction

On 1 January 1920, the *New York Times* reflected on the decade just past. It had been a dour and a sober New Year celebration, it reported; the impending implementation of the Eighteenth Amendment and the vigilance of Revenue agents had stripped Times Square of its customary frivolity.[1] Moreover, the events of 1919 had given little cause for celebration. One in five American workers had gone on strike, including a general strike in Seattle and a police strike in Boston. President Woodrow Wilson was still suffering from the effects of a massive stroke in October, with his dream of ratifying the Treaty of Versailles and American leadership in the League of Nations close to collapse. Major cities, including Washington DC and Chicago, had experienced terrible race riots, America's first 'Red Scare' had seen the Attorney General's house targeted by an anarchist bomb, and hundreds of suspected Bolshevik sympathisers had been jailed or deported. As the editorial reflected:

> There were times during 1919 when the era leading up to the war seemed, in the casual retrospect, like some far-off Golden Age . . . Out of a world in which whole nations shivered and starved, we looked back upon a world in which everywhere a mellow plenty smiled. Out of a world of class revolt and the destruction of moral and material values, we saw a world of order and established custom, advancing yearly in wealth and the enjoyment of wealth.[2]

The *New York Times* has not been alone in seeing the Great War as effecting a seismic change in American society and culture, with several influential early cultural historians labelling 1917 a year which saw the end of a certain kind of 'American innocence'.[3] For example, Henry May's path-breaking 1959 work *The End of American Innocence: A*

Study of the First Years of Our Own Time, 1912–1917 located these
years as the juncture between the Victorian and Modern eras, a rupture
he saw as so dramatic that the earlier era came to seem like 'a world
so foreign, so seemingly simple, that we sometimes tend, foolishly
enough, to find it comical'.[4] Indeed, if decades are sometimes awkward
units to deploy for the purposes of periodisation, the 1910s seem to
pose a particular challenge; a recent *Observer* feature on 'Why We
Love History in 10-Year Chapters' commented that 'Nobody has ever
written a book on the 1910s', as 'the presence of a world war in one
half of the decade rather breaks it up.'[5] Erroneous as that statement
is – there have been books on the 1910s, though not many – the fact of
the war has made the 1910s much less utilised as a unit for historical
periodisation than the 1920s, 1930s or 1960s, for example.

There is certainly little disputing that the war changed American
culture enormously. It cemented the United States as the world's
economic superpower and produced the first 'American moment' in
world affairs, which arrived as American armies proved decisive in
their first-ever campaign in Europe and Wilson was briefly the global
visionary proposing a new world order in his campaign for the fourteen points at Versailles. The war set back the European economy by
eight years and advanced the US economy by six – establishing the
United States as both the world's leading economy and creditor.[6] It
altered majority American views: about international commitments
and cultural exchange, including immigration; about progressive
reform and the responsibilities of the state; about the function of publicity and persuasion in the public sphere; and about individualism
and socialism. Culturally, it was the defining historical event for a new
generation of artists and writers: Ernest Hemingway, John dos Passos,
e. e. cummings, F. Scott Fitzgerald, Gertrude Stein and William
Faulkner all saw wartime service (albeit of markedly different kinds).
A generation of African American writers and musicians accompanied the great black migration from rural South to urban North,
and Hollywood cemented its economic and cultural hegemony over
global film production as the European industry collapsed. All this
makes the 1910s a period of disruption and change, and one far from
inevitable as a unit of analysis.

A second problem with periodising the 1910s is the looming cultural presence of the 1920s. So ingrained is the mythology of the 1920s
that the 1910s has often served as its straw man, a decade of dryness
(in more ways than one) *avant le deluge*. Isabel Leighton's 1949 edited
collection *The Aspirin Age: 1919–1941*, even took the hangover as the

defining symbol of the era; but typifying the 1920s as an era of overindulgent consumption had been initiated by the first important cultural history of the 1920s, *Only Yesterday* by Frederick Lewis Allen.[7] He prefaces his account by contrasting the situation of what he calls 'a moderately well-to-do couple of Cleveland or Boston or Seattle or Baltimore' in 1919 with what their lives were like in 1929. His fictional Mr and Mrs Smith of 1919 drive primitive cars; they believe that prohibition will improve the character of the nation; they have never heard of companionate marriage, crossword puzzles, confession magazines, or radio broadcasting. Mrs Smith wears dowdy fashions with her long hair, and would never dream of smoking a cigarette, drinking at a bar, or wearing make-up. The caricature of the 1910s which this suggests – a pre-modern and naive decade, anterior to the holy Fitzgeraldian trinity of leisure, technology and sexuality which made the 1920s roar – is still a key part of how it is remembered in popular terms.

Both these issues present problems – or at least intriguing obstacles – for this project of periodisation. It is surely the balance, however, between the tumultuous changes in America between 1917 and 1920 and the strength of the connections between the two halves of the decade that make the 1910s such an arresting period to consider. Most cultural historians – including May and Allen – stress this pattern of continuity as well as rupture; even the *New York Times* editorial of 1920 suggested that perceiving the days before 1917 as a golden age was a 'casual view' because, to the alert observer, there was a 'serpent in that garden'. Certainly, the earlier half of the decade did not lack conflict: seeking the presidential nomination in 1912, Theodore Roosevelt had warned Americans that 'we stand at [the] Armageddon' of an impending class war, and a bitter textile strike that year in Lawrence, led by the radical Industrial Workers of the World, made many think this was far from hyperbole. In the first half of decade the United States military had been involved in imperial adventures in Haiti, Mexico, and the Philippines. Modernism was established in American visual and literary arts before 1914; both the Armory Show and Gertrude Stein's writing of *Tender Buttons* pre-dated wartime hostilities. So, too, did hallmarks of mass culture's complex relationship with consumer consumption: Hollywood, the dance craze, and Ford's assembly line. Influential cultural historians, such as Warren Susman and T. J. Jackson Lears, describe a development operative throughout the period – a change from a production-based economy to a consumerist one that configured important shifts in how identity and subjectivity were understood and experienced.

Susman famously called this the change from subjectivities defined through notions of character to a view based in personality, a shift which placed emphasis on self-fulfillment, leisure and consumption rather than on work as the primary mode through which the self would be socially understood. For Lears, modern America was characterised by a psychological recoil among middle-class American from 'a culture evaporating into unreality' and weightlessness – a recoil which increasingly sought therapeutic remedies that could guarantee a return to 'authentic' experience. These remedies substituted 'therapies of abundance' for 'therapies of scarcity' and, as he notes, although many historians have seen this as a move towards 'liberation', therapists and social engineers tended to urge 'that "liberated" impulses be channeled into "constructive" purposes: not only the consumption of goods . . . but also the re-creation of mind and body for more efficient service in factory and office'.[8] Work by Kathy Peiss on how working-class women experienced leisure in the period shows that public and commercial entertainment spaces such as the amusement park and the public dance hall were incredibly popular, partly because they allowed women to engage in new cultures of sexual experimentation and freedoms away from parental and familial control – and all well before the 1920s.

All three historians, therefore, offer a corrective to seeing the 1920s as a decade of dramatic transformation, identifying it instead as a decade of the *acceleration* of consumer consumption and its attendant social and psychological forms, rather than its originary moment. Certainly, the icons and the mechanics of consumption were a staple features of the 1910s, features encouraged and disseminated through the expansion and consolidation of a truly national mass culture in magazines and the cinema. The advertising space in 'slick' large-circulation magazines such as the *Saturday Evening Post* was taken up with ads for new model Fords and Cadillacs; the literature of the decade is just as transfixed by motoring (and by motor accidents) as that of the 1920s. Car registration leapt from around half a million in 1910 to eight million by 1920, in an industry which employed 200,000 workers by the decade's close.[9] Such growth was partially enabled by the assembly-line production which Ford had pioneered in Dearborn in 1913, following the protocols of Frederick Winslow Taylor's *The Principles of Scientific Management* (1911) – which aimed to eliminate the 'awkward, inefficient, or ill-directed movements of men' in the workplace through time-and-motion studies, and by allocating single, simple repetitive tasks to well-paid assembly-line workers.[10] This boom partially underwrote the dramatic growth of American gross national product (GNP) from $35.3 billion in 1910 to $91.5 billion in 1920. As early as 1913, magazines were declaring it 'sex o'clock' in America; film stars, commercial dance halls and jazz were all features of American life by 1920. Signature achievements of modern architecture, such as the old Pennsylvania Station, the Woolworth Building, the revamped Grand Central Station and the Panama Canal, began to change American perceptions of both urban and continental space. What Stephen Kern identifies as the technological invention which had the greatest effect on the perception and experience of space – the telephone – was growing ever-more prevalent: 1910 saw over a million phones in America, and the first transcontinental line was opened in 1914.[11] Rapid urbanisation meant that the 1920 census was the first to record a majority of Americans living in urban areas, although this point was probably passed in 1914. Those urban areas were increasingly electrified, served by rapid public transport systems and replete with large entertainment districts (by 1917, 24 per cent of all American dwellings had electricity, compared to just 8 per cent in 1907).[12] Moreover, the trope of articulating new decades through images of new women – a technique Allen uses to begin his seminal history, as we have just seen – was being criticised as a tired strategy even in the 1910s. As Edna Kenton testily remarked in 1916, horrified reactions to 'New Women' were hard to take seriously when 'New Women' had been around for at least thirty years.[13]

Progressive Culture

Challenging stark distinctions between the two decades is, therefore, an important move, primarily to undermine narratives of the 1920s as the period when the cultural implications of exceptional consumption suddenly became apparent. Yet general differences do exist between the periods, and nowhere more so than in their approach to the ideas and aesthetics of reform. The 1910s represented the pinnacle of the Progressive Movement, the term given to a broad coalition of social reformers who drove through a series of legislative and infrastructural reforms necessary for the management of an increasingly complex urban, industrial, bureaucratic and corporate society. As Robert Wiebe has discussed, these reforms accompanied the shift from America being essentially a series of 'island communities' – isolated from one another by weak communication, governed by local autonomy and administered largely informally – to a centralised system typified by national formulation of public policy, managerial government and the specialisation and accumulation of knowledge.[14] Not necessarily affiliated with either of the two traditional parties (although there were Progressives in both) the movement drew much of its energy from voluntary organisations, from a cadre of newly professionalised disciplines and from women – all frequently informed with a zealous sense of high purpose. As W. E. B. Du Bois, who had himself trained in the new discipline of sociology, put it in his novel *The Quest of the Silver Fleece*:

> There were carelessly gowned women and men smart and shabby, but none of them were thinking of clothes nor even of one another. They had great deeds in mind; they were scanning the earth; they were toiling for men. The same grim excitement that sends smaller souls hunting for birds and rabbits and lions, had sent them hunting the enemies of mankind: they were bent to the chase, scenting the game, knowing the infinite meaning of their hunt and the glory of victory . . . These people were not only earnest, but expert.[15]

Progressivism has attracted a huge historical literature which has disagreed on the composition, objectives and origins of the Progressive Movement – whether it was grassroots or a technocracy; its relationship to liberalism, conservatism, and socialism; how it related to sectional political traditions; and the importance of labour and agrarian movements to the tenor of its reformist zeal.[16] Given the diversity of its interests and aims, some have questioned the use of a singular label at all. Most agree, however, that the reforming crusade of a new middle class was central to the movement, a social class that Michael McGerr has recently estimated at 20 per cent of the population in 1900.[17] This class was composed of a series of newly professionalised and effectively regulated professions, including doctors, lawyers, public educators, social scientists and corporate bureaucrats. During these years, universities increasingly provided these professions with institutionalised disciplines and formal entry requirements; such indicators of prestige meant that 'the exceptional vitality of the new middle class derived in large measure from the very personal benefits its membership bestowed'.[18] Membership of professional organisations boomed while, at the other end of the middle-class scale, millions of Americans moved into white-collar clerical work. As David Nasaw notes, between 1880 and 1910, the number of typists and stenographers in the United States had leapt from 5,000 to 300,000, while the overall clerical workforce rose from 160,000 to more than 1.7 million.[19]

As well as changing leisure and cultural practices – these workers tended to finish work at 5 p.m. and have enough wages to go out to public entertainments in the evening, which led to the development of a new culture of urban nightlife – this swelling and increasingly powerful class also took hold of the country's political agenda. For McGerr, the Progressive programme coalesced around several objectives including conservation, ambitions to reign in corporate trusts and ease the growing class conflict in American life, to improve education and child welfare, a commitment to female suffrage, a stress on racial segregation, and prohibition. In doing so, McGerr makes the broad argument that 'Progressives . . . intended nothing less than to transform other Americans, to remake the nation's feuding, polyglot population in their own middle-class image.'[20] This ambition sought to displace an upper-class emphasis on individualism, leisure and pleasure as the pre-eminent focus of social existence, and to eradicate a working-class emphasis on mutualism and socialism. Instead, Progressives stressed duty, the regulation and moderation of consumption, and a model of social interaction that several Progressive theorists referred to as 'association' and 'social solidarity'.

Progressive achievements in the 1910s were considerable – constitutional amendments alone provided for directly elected senators in 1913, which curtailed the power of party machines and business interests to appoint senators; the establishment of a graduated federal income tax and inheritance tax; and the franchise to women in 1920. The Eighteenth Amendment, enforcing nationwide prohibition, was passed in 1919; this followed a decade of individual states and counties mostly in the West and the South opting to go dry. In 1911, a long-running Federal anti-trust suit finally broke up John D. Rockefeller's Standard Oil, an action which 'would stand as the most famous court-ordered breakup of a corporation until American Telephone and Telegraph, almost eight decades later'.[21] In 1913, Wilson's Federal Reserve Act improved the US financial system by centralising finance, providing flexible currency and better regional banking, and boosting the availability of credit – moves designed in part to avoid panics such as the crisis of 1907.[22] A radical revision in attitudes to public health saw infant mortality fall by two-thirds between 1885 and 1915; the number of high school students and staff doubled in the decade.[23]

Politically, Progressivism became a mainstream mantle which candidates adopted to woo an electorate they believed was impatient for reform. This was particularly evident in the presidential election of 1912, when Theodore Roosevelt left the Republicans to form the breakaway Progressive Party – only to lose to the Democrats under their most formidable progressive, Woodrow Wilson.[24] This also cemented the Republicans under William Taft as the party of big business and small government, and 'introduced a conflict between progressive idealism . . . and conservative values' which would be replayed in many subsequent twentieth-century elections (and some twenty-first-century ones).[25] Yet Taft was clearly the loser between Roosevelt's promise of a 'New Nationalism', and Wilson's platform of a 'New Freedom', both of which promised tighter regulation of the trusts and an expanded role for Federal government. Although Wilson won easily, the public desire for change was most evident in the vote for Eugene Debs, the Socialist candidate; at over 900,000 votes and 6 per cent of the total, it was a greater share than any Socialist vote before or since in a presidential election.[26] As the final chapter of the book will discuss, it was not until the war that Progressivism reached its peak, with measures such as the Federal control of commodity prices and the nationalisation of the railways – measures that conservative Republicans did much to position themselves against in the 1920s.

Culture was an indispensible vehicle for mobilising the informed civic consent through which Progressives sought to effect social change. This positioned culture's role as both informative and asso-ciative, fostering a sense of identification within, and responsibility towards, a social collective. Progressive cultural products from the 1910s form many of its most distinctive achievements: the child labour photographs of Lewis Hine; the utopian feminist manifesto *Herland* (1915) by Charlotte Perkins Gilman; Upton Sinclair's exposés of the American coal and newspaper industries in *King Coal* (1917) and *The Brass Check* (1919) respectively; Mary Antin's best-selling immigrant autobiography, *The Promised Land* (1912); *The Crisis* – the magazine of the newly constituted National Association for the Advancement of Colored People (NAACP); and *The New Republic* magazine, launched in 1914 by two of the decade's most influential journalists and intellectuals, Herbert Croly and Walter Lippmann. Although these differed in many respects from one another, they shared some common features: a faith in the impartial, professionalised, expert view; a belief in social models of progress and improvement (be they economic, racial, or political) which often carried a utopian spirit; a distrust of monied elites and capitalist oligarchy; a faith in a middle-class readership capable of being swayed by rational and by emotive methods of persuasion; a focus on social cohesion and collective responsibility; and a desire to ameliorate extremes of inequality. Much of this radiated out from Progressivism's particular interest in education, best exemplified in the work of the pragmatist philosopher John Dewey. In his landmark *Democracy and Education* of 1916, he argued for the inevitable reliance of a functional democracy on education, as democracies could flourish only through their citizens' 'voluntary disposition and interest' – instrumentalised practices that education alone could inculcate. Yet, for Dewey, education informed a more expansive notion of democracy than mere voluntarism, one which epitomised the progressive ideal of 'association': 'A democracy is more than a form of government; it is primarily a form of associated living, of conjoint communicated experience.'[27]

Histories of this cultural moment balance these utopian inclinations with Progressive imperatives towards class narcissism, class hegemony or class formation. Some have seen Progressive cultural interest in the working class not as an attempt to forge representational forms of sociality, but as part of an agenda of middle-class formation at a moment when middle-class cultural norms and practices were new and uncertain – and which consequently sought to distance and marginalise aristocrats and labourers 'in an attempt to establish and solidify the moral territory of a bourgeois center'.[28] Moreover, Progressives worried over the sphere of public discourse wherein they sought to carry out their informed persuasion, and wondered whether capitalist democracy as it was currently practised was really the best mechanism for putting expert, reasoned policy into practice. Such disquiet was fuelled by the events of World War I; as the newly cynical Lippmann gloomily put it in his fierce critique of the American public sphere *Public Opinion* of 1921, the answer was technocratic formation of public opinion, as 'representative government . . . cannot be worked successfully, no matter what the basis of election, unless there is an independent, expert organization for making the unseen facts intelligible to those who have to make the decisions'.[29]

Lewis Hine's Child Labour Photographs

As Lippmann's dim prognosis suggests, culture's key role as an agent of the moral suasion which drove Progressive reform was attended by a number of internal contradictions. Probably the most complex negotiation of these cultural politics of Progressivism in the 1910s is to be found in Lewis Hine's photographs for the National Child Labor Committee (NCLC), produced between 1907 and 1917. The committee had been formed in 1904, and was just one aspect of the Progressives' focus on children. The era witnessed many campaigns to improve the funding for public education, and to make it compulsory; campaigns to reshape and increase children's leisure, including agitation for more public playgrounds (many staffed with playground assistants to govern and regulate the types of games children could play); and moves to establish a juvenile court system.[30] Few of these reforms could take effect if children were at work, however, and in 1910 labour statistics showed that 18.4 per cent of ten- to fifteen-year-olds were in employment. Although state reform of labour laws progressed through the 1900s, the campaign for a federal law on child labour underwrote Hine's creation and distribution of his photographic archive for the NCLC.

Hine himself had a long background in education within various Progressive institutions. He worked in the early 1900s in the Ethical Culture School (ECS) in New York, was well versed in Progressive educational theory by writers such as John Dewey and Ella Flagg Young, and received a master's degree in pedagogy from New York University in 1905. By that time, he had begun to recognise the role photography could play in education; his first project, photographing recent immigrants at the processing centre on Ellis Island, was designed so that his pupils at the ECS 'may have the same regard for contemporary immigrants as they have for the Pilgrims who landed at Plymouth Rock'.[31] He left teaching in 1907 to begin work with the NCLC and, in the next ten years, accumulated more than five thousand negatives of children at work in at least eighteen states; Vicki Goldberg reports that in some years he would travel in excess of fifty thousand miles by train and car in search of images.[32] He photographed children as young as five, at work as newspaper sellers on the streets of America's major cities, in textile mills in the South, in canneries and in oyster shelling, in glass factories, in fields performing agricultural labour, and in coal mines. Often he would have to lie about his intentions to gain access to the workplaces he wanted to photograph, posing variously as a Bible salesman, industrial photographer, or as a postcard salesman just to escape the suspicions of factory bosses or foremen; and he knew the exact distance from the ground of his coat buttons to ascertain children's heights and ages.

Hine called this 'detective work', and presented his photos in an extraordinary range of conjunctions of photograph and text designed to persuade and inform across a variety of public forums and publications – a range including 'photo montage, photo-story, photo mosaic, picture essay, centerfold, centerfold pull-out, accordion fold-leaflet, post card, and Time exposures'.[33] This dissemination of the photographic image in the service of a Progressive political agenda was far from the rapidly developing idea of how 'art photography' should be produced, displayed and received; as Alan Trachtenberg notes in his influential distinction between the photographic practices of Hine and Alfred Stieglitz, Hine 'saw himself not as an individual genius breaking convention but as a working photographer performing a certain kind of cultural (and political) labor; he focused his work not on the photograph in exhibition but on the published image – not the single photograph as fine print (its tonal values intact), but the reproduced image within an ensemble of images and words'.[34]

Hine's outrage at the often harsh and dangerous conditions the children he conversed with and photographed is clear, but just how effectively he mediated the disparity between his status as a middle-class, salaried, professionalised social worker and the disempowered children he photographed remains a point of contention. For Trachtenberg, Hine's work at its best employs an aesthetic of 'sociality', as he 'attempted to enter his pictures into the internal experience of his audience, to awaken in them an imaginative response which would issue in a revised identity, one which now acknowledges the imagined voices of his pictured workers as part of one's essential social world'.[35] In contrast, the art historian George Dimock sees Hine as producing an aesthetic whereby the working children of his photographs are positioned as pathologised and aberrant victims, in tacit contrast to middle-class ideals of childhood as resolutely non-economic and domestic.[36] Indeed, this goes to the heart of the moral and cultural imperialism McGerr sees at the heart of the progressive project: working-class subjects of their reforms often rightly recognised this impulse as designed to eradicate not only the most exploitative aspects of the American workplace, but also to bulldoze working-class cultural and social practices which often nurtured a distance from middle-class norms. Dimock goes on to suggest that Hine's current canonical status perhaps unconsciously reinforces a troubling politics of middle-class spectatorship, whereby contemporary viewers relish being established as 'enfranchised, adult viewers situated in imaginary relations of dominance vis-à-vis these "victims" of industrial capitalism. Our experience of these images may include, perhaps, the fantasy that we can "save" (or have "saved") those children.'[37] Such questions illustrate the irresolvable tensions of Progressive culture: the desire to ameliorate the brutalities of industrial capital coexisting with a residual tendency to pathologise the working class; and the desire to represent suffering as an engine for reformist action without acknowledging the pleasures of voyeurism, paternalism, or moral self-satisfaction that such representation can involve.

Moreover, another limitation to these cultures of persuasion was the ease by which they could be – and were – co-opted into the persuasive exigencies of the consumer market. Hine's photoessays, survey exhibits, and innovative combination of text and image in the service of the campaign to introduce tighter child labour legislation look different when placed against the growing uptake of photography by advertising: indeed, Hine himself quoted approvingly a businessman's statement that 'advertising is art; it is literature; it is invention. Failure is its one cardinal sin' in one of his most eloquent discussions of what he called Social Photography.[38] The reformist function of the cultural products of the Progressives, in several cases, became part of the swiftly developing cultures of persuasion which would

shape both World War I propaganda and the boom in advertising and public relations of the 1920s. Similarly, the Progressive utopian impulse could be transformed into a consumer vision of futurity, the so-called 'capitalist realism' so favoured by American advertising of the twentieth century. This 'capitalist realism', as Northop Frye remarked, was 'a kind of sentimental idealism, an attempt to present a conventionally attractive or impressive appearance as an actual or attainable reality'.[39] This helps explain historian Richard Tedlow's famous remark that 'Publicity, the hope of the Progressive Era, became propaganda, the scourge of the twenties.'[40] The legacy of Hine's archive therefore suggests the limits of cultural practice as provoking political reform: even the largely ineffectual Keating-Owen Child Labor Act of 1916 was ruled unconstitutional by the Supreme Court two years later, and a robust Federal labour law on child workers did not appear until 1938.

Figure I.1 Lewis Hine, 'Small Newsie Down-Town', St Louis, 1910. From the Records of the National Child Labor Committee, courtesy of the Library of Congress, LC-USZ6-632.

New Women

Similar tensions resided within the decade's feminist activism, although this did not prevent its enormous legislative success; what historian Richard McCormick calls the 'astoundingly fertile confluence of feminism and Progressivism' was everywhere apparent in the decade.[41] Women formed a substantial component of the reforming, professional middle class: by the early 1910s, 15 per cent of all doctorates awarded in the United States went to women (the figure was 9 per cent in the early 1950s).[42] After a period in the doldrums, the women's suffrage movement was revitalised in these years – often drawing on British models of public protest, but also sustained by a grass-roots network of women's clubs, settlement houses, and temperance campaigners for their support. Organisations such as the Women's Trade Union League, the National Consumer's League, and the Woman's Christian Temperance Union helped the cause and, by 1917, the National American Woman Suffrage Association was the biggest volunteer organisation for American women with two million members.[43] An effective strategy had been state-by-state campaigning, which ran in parallel with a demand for a Federal constitutional amendment; by 1913, nine states had allocated women full voting rights, with partial rights existing in twenty-nine more. (These campaigns were often opposed by brewing interests, which encouraged successful suffrage campaigns to help pass state and county-level prohibition statutes.) The day before Wilson's inauguration in 1913 five thousand women had marched in favour of suffrage in Washington; by 1917, under the pressure of war, suffragists were picketing the White House, and a further seven states allocated women the vote.[44] Wilson endorsed the principle of female suffrage a year later.

Feminist energies spun off from this core in a number of directions, and among the most influential was the settlement movement. By 1910 there were four hundred settlement houses in America's cities, functioning as centres for local social support and locally based political activity across a broad platform of issues; activism included lobbying to improve education, public health, municipal hygiene, childcare provision and immigrant assimilation. The most famous of America's settlement leaders, Jane Addams, was a national political figure who had drawn up much of Roosevelt's social welfare plans for his 1912 platform, and even nominated him for the Progressive candidacy in 1912.[45] She emphasised both the practical and the ideological side of her Chicago settlement; as she noted in her autobiography *Twenty Years at Hull-House*, 'From the first it seemed understood that we were ready to perform the humblest neighborhood services. We were asked to wash the new-born babies, and to prepare the dead for burial, to nurse the sick, and to mind the children.'[46] Yet, the broader role of the settlement was its insistence 'on the unity of life, to gather to itself the sense of righteousness to be found in its neighbourhood, and as far as possible in its city; to work towards the betterment not of one kind of people or class of people, but for the common good'.[47]

Addams was also active in the women's trade union movement, helping to organise the Women's Trade Union League – an organisation dedicated to improving women's position within the national labour movement (the American Federation of Labor was at best indifferent and at worst hostile to female membership) and also to lobbying for protective legislation in the workplace. Their cause was assisted by the public outcry over the tragedy of the Triangle Shirtwaist fire in 1911 which took the lives of 146 women, mostly young and many of them immigrants, working in sweatshop conditions for the Triangle Shirtwaist Company in Washington Square, New York. Working on the top three floors, with only one fire escape and with many of the doors locked to prevent workers leaving early, once the fire broke out few had any chance of escape. The owners of the company, found not guilty of manslaughter, paid only $75 per death in a civil suit; but a commission appointed by the state governor to investigate the fire led to thirty-six reforming laws in the state labour code.[48] Other feminist activism focused on the temperance crusade, which made much of the damage that alcohol and the saloon did to the home. A smaller feminist contingent focused on campaigns for 'birth control'. The leading figure here was Margaret Sanger, a New York former nurse, who coined the term; beginning in 1912 she published a series of articles entitled 'What Every Girl Should Know', which appeared in the Socialist *New York Call* and dealt with information on contraception. In 1916 she opened the first birth-control clinic in the United States, only for it to be raided by police nine days later. Regularly arrested for breaching obscenity statutes (the Post Office had declared as radical even the term 'birth control'), she was forced to flee to Europe in 1914 to avoid prosecution; her husband was tried and convicted instead. Frequently inundated by letters from working-class women telling of exhaustion from perpetual childbearing, domestic abuse and sexual unhappiness, it is unsurprising that Sanger's cause was also adopted by left-wing feminists as part of the decade's trenchant and broad critique of patriarchal laws and customs. The anarchist feminist Emma Goldman, deported in 1919 during the period of most intense persecution of such radical vision, summed up the scope of this analysis:

> Emancipation should make it possible for women to be human in the truest sense. Everything within her that craves assertion and

activity should reach its fullest expression; all artificial barriers should be broken, and the road towards greater freedom cleared of every trace of centuries of submission and slavery.[49]

Charlotte Perkins Gilman, *Herland* (1915)

First-wave feminists in the decade disagreed over a number of issues: the function of women in the public sphere; the connection between socialism and feminism; the role of sexuality, consumption and personal pleasure in a progressive feminism; and, as the decade wore on, the connections between feminism and pacifism. Many of these tensions are implicit in one of the decade's most arresting feminist texts, Charlotte Perkins Gilman's utopian novel *Herland*. Somewhat of a maverick, Gilman was known primarily as an independent-minded lecturer promulgating her own brand of socialist-eugenic feminism. She even refused the label 'feminist', preferring 'humanist' – a tag indicating her view that female liberation was essential for the liberation of the entire species.[50] Utopian fiction was a key vehicle for her political polemic; she wrote three utopian novels in her career, with *Herland* representing the wittiest and most widely discussed of these since its reprinting in the 1970s. With one eye on Edward Bellamy's socialist Utopia of 1888, *Looking Backward*, and one on the novels of imperial romance and jungle adventure of H. Rider Haggard and Edgar Rice Burroughs, Gilman's novel presents the spectacle of a hidden country in the South American jungle occupied solely by women which is 'discovered' by three American male explorers.

Cut off from the rest of the world for two thousand years in a country the size of Holland, the three million inhabitants of Herland have produced a model society devoid of warfare, social inequality, disease and deprivation. They reproduce parthenogenetically, and their religion and whole social system revolve around their valorisation of motherhood; in the words of Moadine, one of the tutors who instructs the explorers on the ways of Herland, '"The children in this country are the one center and focus of all our thoughts. Every step of our advance is always considered in its effect on them – on the race. You see we are *Mothers*," she repeated, as if in that she had said it all.'[51] It is also a society of perfect collectivism: children are reared collectively, all business and agriculture are collective, and personal desires are subsumed to the common good so unthinkingly that personal desire is virtually unimaginable. As Ann Lane notes, Gilman 'understood as did no critic before her that the home was the primary location of inequality for women', and so Herland's women have no fixed homes – and no kitchens (all food is vegetarian and prepared communally).[52] The women are strong, fit, well educated, and dressed both uniformly and practically. 'These women aren't *womanly*,' growls Terry, the most misogynist of the three explorers; and, according to his own lights, right he is.[53]

As Van – the narrator – perceives, however, 'those "feminine charms" we are so fond of are not feminine at all, but mere reflected masculinity

– developed to please us because they had to please us'.[54] These ideas go back to Gilman's most important book, *Women and Economics* (which appeared in 1898, and which – as Lane observes – Gilman was accused of perpetually rewriting in her subsequent work).[55] Of principal importance was her observation that the human race is marked by an 'excessive sex distinction', caused by the fact that 'with us an entire sex lives in a relation of economic dependence upon the other sex, and the economic relation is combined with the sex relation'.[56] Women's economic dependence on men has led them to become 'over-sexed', in Gilman's words; they overemphasise sexual difference in order to attract the partner necessary for their economic subsistence. This also has meant that human traits of innovation, expertise, intelligence and, above all, rationality have been annexed as masculine traits. With the power relations of patriarchal society reversed, however, Gilman deploys her sharp sense of satire to demonstrate how much 'femininity' is configured by powerlessness. As Sandra Gilbert and Susan Gubar observe, the men in *Herland* 'become petulant, irritable, jealous, vain of their physical appearance, and rivalrous for approval, as Gilman humorously diagnoses the faults ascribed to her own sex as symptoms of a disease called marginalization'.[57]

Herland originally appeared serially in Gilman's periodical *The Forerunner*; she personally wrote every line of every issue of the thirty-two-page magazine which appeared monthly between 1909 and 1916. She also wrote all the adverts, only endorsing products she herself used and approved of. As Elizabeth Nolan has noted, this placed her at odds with a new generation of feminists more excited than she by the liberatory possibilities of personal desire; this was expressed not only in their differing attitudes towards consumer culture and advertising but most pointedly in their attitudes to sex and sexuality.[58] In this Gilman shared the view of Jane Addams who, in 1930, criticised the postwar generation, tartly remarking that 'self-expression and self-development and determination to secure a new freedom in sex relations seems [*sic*] at moments to absorb the entire reforming energy of the young' – an energy which had led them to focus on 'liberty for the individual' rather than for the collective.[59]

As contemporary feminists often note with disapproval, *Herland* is sexless, and its women recoil from any notion of sex for pleasure rather than procreation.[60] To Ellador, Van's wife, such a notion seems 'against nature', and *Herland*'s eugenic programme of improvement encourages any woman who exhibits a sexual sensuality not to have children.[61] This vision of sexuality as racial atavism mirrored Gilman's view of its place in the contemporary feminist struggle; as McGerr notes, she 'warned that sexual freedom was an "indulgence" that could become the basis for women's further oppression in the future'.[62] In contrast, the new generation of feminists saw things differently. As Margaret Anderson, the editor of the radical literary little magazine the *Little Review*, put it: 'Until we become conscious that there's something very wrong with our attitude towards sex, we'll never get rid of the hard, tight, anaemic, metallic woman who flourishes in America as nowhere else in the world.' Seeing sex as being at the core of a broader agenda of liberation, she asked 'How can we prevent these crimes against love and sex – how put a stop to human waste in all its hideous forms – if we don't recognize the new idealism which means not to deny?'[63] The 'cult of youth' launched in the 1910s by figures such as Anderson asserted women's right to sensual pleasure, and frequently embraced elements of the marketplace which seemed capable of providing it. Such assertions underwrote a generational schism over the issue of personal pleasure which provided much of the hostility to the progressive spirit as the decade proceeded; for Anderson, the 'Victorian type' which 'recognizes the sex impulse only as a means to an end' was no serious concern of hers: it 'belong[ed] to the past too definitely to be harmful'.[64]

Socialism and the Left

Feminists were not the only ones who critiqued Progressives for underestimating the importance of pleasure in human life, and for idealising the rational citizen in a way that downgraded or pathologised the importance of desire to the human personality. Socialists often saw Progressive moves to regulate social and cultural activity – whether through the prohibition movement, or the censorship and morality campaigns which targeted most forms of mass culture in the decade – as little more than class-based cultural imperialism. Moreover, they criticised Progressives for their reluctance to countenance alternatives to capitalist economic models, just as they worried that this more moderate programme of reform would siphon off their political support.

Socialism thrived in the decade partly because of the miserable conditions of labouring people: although diminishing working hours and increases in wages progressed apace, life remained both harsh and precarious for many. Periods of economic downturn, such as occurred in 1914 with the sudden global economic crisis prompted by the European war, threw many workers into hardship; during the winter, national rates of unemployment stood at 11.5 per cent.[65] Many working-class men could not earn enough to feed themselves, let alone a family; in Chicago in 1910 the average worker in an abattoir earned only 38 per cent of the income necessary to support a family of four.[66] Women and children were forced into the workplace in such conditions, and such low wages meant that bitter strikes and industrial conflict remained features of American life, racking the decade even before the surge of labour activism in 1919.

Opinions differed over how to deal with this antagonism between

capital and labour in the decade. Eugene Debs, leading the Socialist
Party of America, shied away from the Marxist view of society and
the principle of revolutionary change. Instead, he valorised the spirit
of 1776 and Christian brotherhood – as well as democratic reform –
as his models for building a classless society.[67] This bore some fruit;
in 1912, amid what papers referred to as a 'rising tide of socialism',
1,150 Socialists held elected office in thirty-six states and 325 towns
and cities.[68] Even less willing to countenance radical solutions was
the biggest union umbrella organisation, the American Federation
of Labor, under Samuel Gompers. Focusing on skilled workmen in
trade unions, they largely ignored the plight of unskilled workers,
rigorously excluded African Americans, and lobbied for immigration restriction. By the 1910s, the AFL had carved out a comfortable
relationship with the Democratic Party but, with a membership of
three million in 1917, it was able to wield considerable influence. The
most radical organisation of the decade, however, was the Industrial
Workers of the World – or the Wobblies, as they were often known.
Committed to forming a superunion of the entire working class,
and also to a revolutionary model of political change, the IWW's
constitution began with the statement that 'the working class and
the employing class have nothing in common'.[69] They terrified

Figure I.2 Political satire in *The Masses*: John Sloan, 'After the War, a Medal and Maybe a Job',
1914. Cabinet of American Illustration, courtesy of the Library of Congress, LC-USZC4-12974.

middle-class America and, partly for that reason, the IWW inspired millions of unskilled workers and recent migrants, especially in the tough conditions of Western mines and forestry camps. It was the IWW that took the leadership of the bitter textile strike in Lawrence, Massachusetts, in 1912 – a moment which 'marked the crest of [its] prewar power', and it would be they who bore the brunt of the crackdown on organised labour during the war years.[70]

The Masses Magazine

The Industrial Workers of the World supplied much of the energy for the vibrant intellectual culture of the left in the decade, but the pre-eminent forum for espousing a broadly conceived vision of radical social change was *The Masses* magazine. It endorsed the aesthetics as well as the politics of revolution, embracing feminism, free love, sections of the modernist movement in art, campaigns for better birth control information, anti-imperialism, and a rejection of US involvement in World War I. Led by two charismatic editors Max Eastman and Floyd Dell, and enlivened by their star reporter, John Reed, Eastman described *The Masses* as offering a 'mixture of proletarian revolt with revolt against the genteel tradition'; it declared itself 'against rigidity and dogma wherever it is found'.[71] For Dell, it stood for 'fun, truth, beauty, realism, freedom, peace, feminism, revolution'.[72]

In all this it represented the most significant cultural product of the remarkable collaboration of social, political, and artistic radicalism in the pre-war era of the decade, one that had its spiritual and intellectual home in Greenwich Village. The ideas of Bergson, Freud, Darwin and Marx found regular space in their pages; irony and wit were as common as the stolid Marxist language of class struggle. They were supporters of Sanger's campaign for birth control, and Dell produced a series of articles entitled 'Feminism for Men' which argued that feminism was necessary for male freedom as 'the bravest things will not be done in the world until women do not have to look to men for support'.[73] Dell was also at the forefront of the decade's popularisation of Freud, undergoing analysis in 1917 with Dr Samuel Tannenbaum, a popular figure in Greenwich Village radical circles (and who advocated visiting prostitutes for his more repressed clients).[74] The magazine was partially financed by what Eastman called the 'rebel rich', the 'skeleton in our revolutionary closet' – including the salon hostess and *Über*-village figure Mabel Dodge.[75] They printed literary work by Sherwood Anderson, Carl Sandburg, and Louis Untermeyer; the magazine was famous for its political cartoons by John Sloan, George Bellows, and Robert Minor. Such a heterogeneous concoction meant that contradiction was as rife as its programmatics were hazy, but that missed the central point of *The Masses*: its contention was that contradiction, a healthy interest in new ideas, and non-conformism were necessary for a much-needed overhaul of politics and the public sphere.

The link between an aesthetic and a politics of exhilarating novelty and youth was most evident in *The Masses*'s involvement in the Paterson silk strike of 1913. There, 25,000 workers under the leadership of the IWW had struck for better wages, union rights and an eight-hour day. The strike closed three hundred mills, but a nationwide news blackout had left the strikers desperately short of funds and support. After investigating the strike and being thrown into Passaic Jail, John Reed – along with Dodge, IWW president 'Big' Bill Haywood and Margaret Sanger – organised a pageant dramatising the events of the strike to take place at Madison Square Garden. This occurred on 7 June in front of a crowd of 15,000, most of them workers, with many more people locked out. Played on a stage designed by Robert Edmon Jones – who would be closely involved with the Provincetown Players – the thousand players, mostly workers from Paterson, acted out the mass arrests, the funeral of a strike martyr, and an IWW rally addressed by Haywood.

The Paterson Strike Pageant, as it became known, dramatised the successes and the failures of this broad coalition. It was covered by all the New York newspapers; and as the radical critic Randolph Bourne observed, though he found it 'Crude and rather terrifying', 'it stamped into one's mind the idea that new social art was in the American world, some-thing genuinely and excitingly new'.[76] For historian of the IWW, Patrick Renshaw, it was 'perhaps the supreme example of the kind of dramatic propaganda gesture at which the Wobblies excelled'.[77] Yet the pageant lost money, and was criticised from both the left and the right. It reinforced the frequent critique that *The Masses* was written *about* the working class rather than *by* or *for* them, especially because of its frequent focus on personal, aesthetic and sexual liberty – an agenda which offended many working-class activists who thought it either immoral or distracting. (Testily responding to a suggestion from Village poet Harry Kemp that he deliver his oratory more stirringly, Haywood had snapped 'I'm not running this strike for Greenwich Village.')[78] It was also ultimately ineffectual: the strike failed, and many IWW members in Paterson were sacked.

The other major significance of *The Masses* was the manner of its demise. From the outset of the world war in August 1914, the magazine had seen it as a 'nationalistic war', one which distracted from its 'loyalty to a struggle that is vaster and more freighted with the world's future than a war between nations'. It had backed Wilson's electoral platform in 1916 – that he had kept America out of the war – and predicted that 'war is the destroyer of liberty' on the eve of American entry in April 1917.[79] This proved prophetic, and soon they were crusading against coercive American war policy. Eastman's 'Conscription for What?' in July 1917 ridiculed Wilson's pronouncement that the draft was not conscription but rather 'selection from a nation which has volunteered in mass', and averred that the nation had not volunteered at all – predicting 'that some of the brave among these free will conscientiously object to this deed of violence against their elementary liberties'. This included Eastman himself, who described as an 'act of tyranny, discordant with the memory even of the decent kings' the government's act of conscription without publishing their war aims.[80] After the Espionage Act of June 1917, which penalised material viewed as obstructing the war effort, such writing ran the risk of being adjudged illegal. Consequently, the August *Masses* was banned from the post; by the September number, Reed was decrying the 'blackest month for freemen our generation has known', and the 'hideous apathy [with which] the country has acquiesced in a regime of judicial tyranny, bureaucratic suppression and industrial barbarism'.[81] Red-baiting Postmaster General Albert Burleson had seven *Masses* contributors, including Dell and Eastman, arrested for conspiring to obstruct enlistment. Although the jury was deadlocked, and the defendants freed in April 1918, others in similar situations were not so fortunate. Along with hundreds of others from the IWW and the Socialist party, Haywood and Goldman were jailed and, following the passage of the draconian Sedition Act in 1918, the situation worsened – the most prominent victim being Debs, sent down for ten years for declaring that the 'subject class has . . . nothing to gain and all to lose' from the war – 'especially their lives'.[82] In such circumstances *The Masses* was finished – just one of eighteen radical magazines Burleson closed in a crackdown which did much to destroy the coalition of socialist and aesthetic radicalism that typified large sections of pre-war avant-garde American culture.[83] As the final chapter will demonstrate, the force of state power evident in the first American Red Scare, combined with the dogmas of the Bolshevik revolution, did much to push these versions of radicalism apart in the postwar era. By 1926, Dell had abandoned his modernist sensibilities for a doctrinaire Marxism; once the champion of a broadly conceived freedom, in the light of the 'Russian experience' he now believed that '"freedom" is merely a bourgeois myth'.[84]

The energy of *The Masses* was symptomatic of American journalism in the decade, which in quantity and influence would not be surpassed in the nation's history. Some 2,200 daily English-language papers existed in the United States in 1910, along with four hundred foreign-language and special-interest dailies; together, they had a circulation of around 22.4 million. Fourteen thousand more papers appeared in weekly editions and, in 1913, the leading weekly magazine, the *Saturday Evening Post*, sold almost two million per issue.[85] Metropolitan dailies battled for circulation, none more so than Joseph Pulitzer's *New York World* and William Randolph Hearst's two New York Journal papers. They fought over the most popular comic strips, where full-colour printing served as a technological showcase; a fierce legal battle took place over Rudolph Dirks's 'The Katzenjammer Kids', and Hearst also sued Bud Fisher over defecting with his wildly popular 'Mutt and Jeff'. There were frequent concerns over editorial bias and quality: Pulitzer instituted a fact-checking bureau in 1911 at the *World*, partly in response to an increase in complaints about the 'yellow journalism' that had dominated the previous decade; and, in 1919, Upton Sinclair published *The Brass Check*, a reflection on his twenty-year involvement in journalism and an exposé of what he saw as its prostitution to big business. Advertising bought in 66 per cent of the major papers' revenue by 1914, and extensive syndication – as well as chain owners, such as Hearst, E. W. Scripps and Frank Munsey – put decisions over much of the content in America's press into the hands of a few powerful individuals.[86] Nonetheless, African American, socialist, and foreign-language papers flourished to a large extent outside of these controls, as did influential journals such as *The New Republic* and *The Nation*, revamped in 1917.

Sharing that sense of fierce independence, and distinctive even in a decade of larger-than-life figures in journalism, was H. L. Mencken. Straight talking, irreverent and iconoclastic, in his editorials at the *Baltimore Sun* and literary criticism in *The Smart Set*, where he worked with the equally waspish drama critic, George Jean Nathan, he demonstrated the range of what he proudly identified as his prejudices. He distrusted politicians, reformers and censorious puritans; he revelled in poking his uniquely acerbic style of fun at his two most famous neologisms, the booboisie and the Bible Belt. His statement that 'I am strongly in favour of liberty and I hate fraud' identified his two governing ideas; they informed his campaigns against prohibition, as well as against the New York Society for the Suppression of Vice's targeting of Theodore Dreiser, his favourite contemporary American novelist.[87] He was not shy, however, of chastising Dreiser for his sloppy approach to the American language: he himself wrote of the painful search for 'the perfect word', rewarded by 'the constant joy of sudden discovery, of happy accident'.[88] Like Orwell after him, he knew the political insidiousness of the empty phrase, whether it was from advertisement or president. In one of his sharpest attacks of the time (and after he had faced intense public censure for his pro-German sympathies in the early part of World War I), he lambasted Wilson for his 'transparent contradictions, [his] gaudy processions of mere counter-words, [his] so vast and obvious a nonsensicality'. For Mencken, language was politics, and so was laughter – and any attempt to prohibit, dilute or obfuscate either of them was an assault on American constitutional democracy. What was so terrifying about Wilson's 'vaporous and preposterous phrases', he felt, was that 'for a long while anyone who laughed was in danger of the calaboose'.[89]

Early Modernism

Mencken, who professed to have 'no more public spirit than a cat', shared a distrust of Progressives and socialists with an emergent group of modernists in the decade, a group whose commitments to radical individualism and aesthetic experimentalism had little to do with a view of culture as the instrument for manufacturing political consensus.[90] The first decade of modernism in the United States, the 1910s saw a radical change in the aesthetics and in the institutions of its most ambitious and experimental cultural practitioners. In fine art, photography, dance, music, theatre and poetry, Americans followed the lead of the modernist movement in Europe to produce work that was formally experimental and often confusing or disjointed; that destabilised well-established traditions of perspective such as realism, representationalism, or harmony; that took artistic inspiration from cultures or objects disdained as crude, primitive or banal by what was referred to as 'the genteel tradition'; and that loudly announced its deliberate difference from the kinds of culture most people enjoyed and appreciated.

It was part of modernism's unparalleled skill in self-mythologisation to couch this agenda in the terms of a war with the prevailing middle-class moral and cultural consensus (Margaret Anderson, for example, called her memoir of founding the *Little Review* 'a war story'). As scholars such as Richard Hofstadter and Henry May have noted, Progressive thought was characterised by a desire to conserve, or even restore, elements of the past. This conservatism, especially pronounced in moral and cultural terms, was shared by the 'cultural custodians' of the middle-class artistic institutions that had grown up in the late nineteenth century: America's great art galleries, its large-circulation magazines, its opera houses, its book publishers. Accordingly, modernism's imperative to 'make it new' flourished by necessity in a range of new forums. Small art galleries, such as Alfred Stieglitz's '291' in New York, pioneered the showcasing of European modernist art and the best of America's experimental artists and photographers. New 'little' theatre companies, disconnected from the major booking circuits, nourished a new commitment to expressionism, experimentalism, and a theatre of contemporary social concerns. New 'Little Magazines' with small circulations, such as *Poetry*, *The Little Review*, *Others*, *The Glebe*, *The Soil* and *The Seven Arts*, printed innovative new poetry and fiction, and disseminated the ideas of modernism's key intellectual figures. And salons – orchestrated by figures such as Walter and Louise Arensberg and Mabel Dodge in New York, and Margery Currey and Floyd Dell in Chicago – were carefully constructed social gatherings designed to facilitate stimulation (of all kinds), contradiction, debate, brilliance, and productivity. Salons in Europe – hosted by Leo and Gertrude Stein in Paris, and Ezra Pound in London – facilitated such international dialogue on the other side of the Atlantic. Certain modernists were celebrated for their skills in conversation, which became as valued a form of intellectual production as paintings or novels: Gertrude Stein, Jane Heap and Stieglitz were particularly venerated for their ability to converse. Dodge herself became a self-declared 'Species of Head Hunter', seeking out 'Heads of things, Heads of Movements, Heads of Newspapers, Heads of all kinds of people'.[91] In Janet Lyon's words on the salon, 'the development of modernism was inconceivable without these embodied circulations of art', which represented 'an unusual intersection of public discourses and intimate interiority'.[92]

Frequently, such modernists decided to position themselves at the fringe of – or above – the social scene, rather than engage with the political machinery of reforming it. Ezra Pound, for example, instructed his own books both to 'ruffle the skirts of prudes', but most of all to 'go to practical people . . . Say that you do no work/and that you will live forever.'[93] Such a view was anathema to Progressives: Walter Lippmann complained about modernists' 'divine impatience with method in an inspired enthusiasm for the result'; and Jane Addams proclaimed that the function of art was

> to preserve in permanent and beautiful form those emotions and solaces which cheer life, make it kindlier and more comprehensible, lift the mind of the worker from the harshness of his task, and, by connecting him with what has gone before, free him from a sense of isolation and hardship.[94]

Modernists, by contrast, frequently stressed intensity rather than solace; novelty rather than continuity or permanence; individualist iconoclasm rather than collectivism; and rich experience rather than social melioration.

As many critics of the decade have understood, the tenor of early modernism's radicalism often resided in its fusion of unorthodox aesthetics, politics and personal style – a fusion sometimes best communicated by anecdote. (Some of the best include Margaret Anderson leading the entire staff of the *Little Review* to live in tents on the shore of Lake Michigan one summer to save all the rent money for bringing out the magazine; Vachel Lindsay's status as a 'hobohemian', tramping across the Midwest with his 'Rhymes to be Traded for Bread' as his only currency at farmhouses; and Marcel Duchamp and John Sloan climbing to the top of the Washington Square arch to declare Greenwich Village an independent and free republic.) Underneath such behaviour was the recognition, if somewhat vaguely conceived, of a point made by Robert Wiebe – that the networks and compartmentalisation of 'national progressivism had been predicated upon the existence of the modern corporation and its myriad relationships with the rest of American society. Chronologically, psychologically, this network had come first.'[95] The passion with which modernists frequently sought to disengage from both those networks could easily veer into an elitist disdain for both bourgeois conformism and for 'the masses' – especially recent immigrants and the mass-produced and market-driven elements of American culture that increasingly relied upon a cross-class appeal. Yet avant-garde positions were also not without their inconsistencies. Modernist aloofness often belied an anxious sense of modernists' own irrelevance, an anxiety evident in the often shrill cynicism many expressed towards the social scene, and in the frequently brash assertion of their own heroism and importance. Moreover, as T. J. Jackson Lears observes, 'under a twentieth-century regime which multiplied wants and sanctioned total gratification, the avant-garde cult of self-fulfilment sometimes only exaggerated the culture it set out to repudiate'.[96]

The sharply drawn cultural divisions which modernists identified and often fostered paralleled the tendency of cultural critics of the time to identify the American social sense of hopelessly bifurcated. Randolph Bourne's *Youth and Life* (1913) – one of the clearest early calls for a 'cult of youth' – saw this split as generational, with a conservative older generation aghast at a new spirit in American middle-class youth, with 'its social agitation, its religious heresy, its presumptive individuality, its economic restlessness'.[97] Even more influential was Van Wyck Brooks's *America's Coming-Of-Age* (1915), which rejected his earlier faith in the ability of technocracy and industrial progress to form a unified culture, diagnosing instead a crippling split in American life which was inimical to any notion of nourishing community and vital personality. Adopting the language of phrenology, he saw this division as between what he termed 'highbrow' and 'lowbrow': 'on the one hand a quite unclouded, quite unhypocritical assumption of transcendent theory ("high ideals"); on the other a simultaneous acceptance of catchpenny realities'. This resulted in 'Desiccated culture at one end and stark utility at the other [which has] created a deadlock in the American mind,' a division between business and culture, pragmatics and aesthetics, which he traced to America's Puritan intellectual heritage.[98]

Brooks's notion of a bifurcated America had been influenced by George Santayana's 1911 address 'The Genteel Tradition in American Philosophy', which decried the effect of the 'genteel tradition' in American cultural and philosophical life. As Brooks would do, Santayana saw a problematic division between 'The American Will' and 'the American Intellect', a split between a masculine, business spirit of 'aggressive enterprise' and a feminine, philosophical 'genteel tradition'.[99] For Henry Adams, whose influential and profoundly reflective spiritual, political and cultural autobiography *The Education of Henry Adams* appeared in an expanded edition in 1918, the divisions were just as acute. In the most famous section of the autobiography, he is struck by the exhibit of a dynamo at the Paris Exposition of 1900, seeing it as an example of a powerful, masculine, (and highly American) new force in modern life – and one absolutely discontinuous with the earlier feminised, spiritual and religious force which had built the societies and infrastructure of Europe. Just one of several critics who saw America as less able to resist the social ravages of industrialism owing to its lack of a long-established and tenacious pre-industrial culture, he lamented that the energy which had built the Louvre and Chartres Cathedral represented 'the highest energy ever known to man, the creator of four-fifths of his noblest art . . . and yet this energy was unknown to the American mind'.[100]

Cultures of Nationalism

As several cultural historians have observed, these bifurcations were frequently framed in gendered terms – women were variously linked with a rarefied and meliorist form of high culture, with the spirituality of old Europe, and also frequently with the energies of a developing mass culture. That this is so gives one indication of why intellectuals from the time (including Brooks, Santayana and Adams) identified Walt Whitman as a uniquely suggestive figure for how to mend American divisions. He appealed because of his stress on sexuality – and also sympathy – as the key mediating mechanisms for unifying disparity and assuming association across gendered, racial, sectional and class divides. His fulminations against the capitalistic excesses of the Gilded Age, his commitment to an expansive and spiritualised notion of democracy, his working-class affinities and his formal experimentalism also seemed to bridge American bifurcations through what Brooks called a 'middle tradition', in which 'the hitherto incompatible extremes of the American temperament were fused'.[101] Moreover, he was championed as what Mencken called an 'invader of the public decencies', a forerunner of the anti-Puritanism so characteristic of the time.[102] Implicit in all this was Whitman's potential as a great *national* figure, one providing what Brooks termed a cultural 'focal centre' which indicated 'that secure and unobtrusive element of national character . . . [which provides] a certain underlying coherence and background of mutual understanding'.[103] Even modernist poets, who loathed Whitman's seeming disregard for craft and concision, saw him this way: in 1913 Ezra Pound announced he had 'detested' Whitman for 'long enough', and suggested that as 'we have one sap and one root—/Let there be commerce between us.'[104] Mencken, too, advanced a cultural nationalism that drew from Whitman's (and Twain's) appetite for the muscularity of American vernacular speech. His desire to move American culture decisively away from what he felt was a stultifying Anglophilia was clearest in his *The American Language: An Inquiry into the Development of English in the United States* (1919), a project that defined and celebrated the particularities of American English which he would return to over the course of his career.

These attempts to articulate a new cultural nationalism were widely echoed in intellectual circles in the decade, although paradoxically this nationalism was often developed in dialogue with international intellectuals. Photographer Alfred Steiglitz's growing sense of cultural nationalism developed while helping to create New York as an international centre for Dada in conjunction with figures such as Francis Picabia and Marcel Duchamp; and Waldo Frank's cultural nationalist manifesto *Our America* (1919) was written at the request of the *Nouvelle Revue Française*, which wanted a book on 'Young America' for a French readership. New magazines such as *The Seven Arts* saw young intellectuals such as Frank, Brooks and Randolph Bourne articulate new visions of American culture, even as they also ran pieces on 'Young Spain', 'Youngest Ireland' and 'Young India'. Robert Coady's lively manifesto for American art in his little magazine *The Soil* was perhaps the most pugnacious argument for this nationalist approach to culture, as well as the most eager to embrace the artefacts of mass culture and American industry. Yet, even his vision was articulated in the terms of international dialogue, asserting that

Traditions are being merged, blood is being mixed. Something new, something big is happening here.

An Englishman developed the Bessemer Process and we built our skyscraper. A Dane married a Spanish-African and Bert Williams sings 'Nobody.' We've dug into the soil and developed the Steam Shovel, we play ball and we box. . .

Our art is, as yet, outside of our art world. It's in the spirit of the Panama Canal. It's in the East River and the Battery. It's in Pittsburgh and Duluth. It's coming from the ball field, the stadium and the ring.[105]

This revived concern with national identity and national culture was just part of the broader anxiety over these issues in American political and social life. Politically, this sentiment was closely linked to the widening sphere of US continental imperialism; American troops invaded Mexico and Haiti in the 1910s (remaining in the latter until 1935) as well as permanently occupying the Panama Canal Zone. Troops were still fighting guerrillas in the Philippines, and protecting US access to Chinese markets, more than ten years after the United States had nominally freed the islands from Spanish rule. Moreover, concerns over national identity and patriotism regularly returned to the issue of immigration and ethnic assimilation, concerns which ratcheted into the xenophobic hysteria of the war years.

As the historian Matthew Frye Jacobson has recently argued, the growing imperialism of American foreign policy at this time and its handling of mass immigration are two sides of the same coin. Indeed, he observes that 'American integration into the world economic system in this period exposed a rather profound dependence on foreign peoples as imported workers for American factories and as overseas consumers of American products,' a situation which produced a political culture 'characterised by a paradoxical combination of supreme confidence in US superiority and righteousness, with an anxiety driven by fierce parochialism'.[106] Between 1901 and 1910, almost nine million immigrants arrived in the United States; the subsequent decade saw close to six million, a figure which would have been much larger had not the war intervened. In 1910, 14.7 per cent of the population had been born overseas. These were different migrants from the typical nineteenth-century influx; rather than hailing from Ireland, Germany and Scandinavia, these new migrants were largely from eastern and southern Europe, and many of them were Jews fleeing persecution and poverty. This difference stoked nativist fears;

white supremacists and 'hard line' eugenicists, such as Madison Grant in his *The Passing of the Great Race* (1916), subdivided the racial category of white into Nordic, Alpine and Mediterranean to argue that this immigration was racially distinctive from, and inferior to, 'old stock' Americans. Consequently, Grant argued that these new Americans threatened the biological capital that had produced American identity and global power. Others voiced concerns over the importation of socialism, over the rapid change in the linguistic and social make-up of American cities, and over the effect of seemingly limitless supplies of cheap unskilled workers on American wages. In the West, fears about the 'Yellow Peril' attended Japanese migrants, and everywhere debate raged about how America should deal with cultural and racial plurality. As Timothy Prchal observes, four models emerged for how to deal with immigration: restriction, assimilation, the melting pot, and cultural pluralism.[107] If nativists like Grant argued for immigration restriction of the kind that occurred in the 1920s, figures such as Theodore Roosevelt pushed hard for an assimilationist position – envisioning an 'unhyphenated America', where divided national loyalty was tantamount to 'moral treason'. (Initially he saw the 'solution' to this as a broad welfare programme for new immigrants; later in the decade it turned to a more strident and protectionist nationalism.)[108] In contrast, cultural critics such as Horace Kallen and Randolph Bourne promoted forms of cultural pluralism – Bourne suggesting the formation of a 'trans-national America', which rejected the idea of the melting pot and what he called a 'premature and sentimental nationalism', in favour of an 'attempt to weave a wholly novel international nation out of our chaotic America'.[109]

Recent migrants also participated in the debate and, indeed, became ever more prevalent in the cultural life of the nation. Jewish entrepreneurs and entertainers were increasingly important in the emerging film industry, the popular music industry and the vaudeville stage. Hollywood studio bosses, such as Carl Laemmle and Adolph Zukor (and the legendary Hollywood make-up artist, Max Factor), as well as entertainers such as Al Jolson, Sophie Tucker and Irving Berlin, were all naturalised Jewish Americans who had been born overseas. Immigrant intellectuals, such as the anthropologist Franz Boas, challenged the racialist hierarchies which underpinned much nativist sentiment, arguing instead for a cultural relativism that refuted evolutionary explanations of cultural and ethnic difference. Also noticeable was the rise of Jewish women of letters such as Anzia Yezierska and Mary Antin. Antin gained considerable fame as a champion of immigration through her best-selling autobiography *The Promised Land* (1912), which charted her move from Tsarist and anti-Semitic tyranny in Russia to life as a college graduate in the United States. The book informed her active public career, as she published widely and lectured to large audiences on how her own story of assimilation, success and patriotic devotion to America was proof that immigration was a national resource rather than a burden.[110] Antin favoured a model of assimilation rather than cultural pluralism – her autobiography's famous first sentence proclaimed 'I was born, I have lived, and I have been made over' – but she also stressed what John Higham characterises as 'the doctrine of immigrant gifts' in arguing for the future value of immigrants' economic, intellectual and perhaps even cultural contributions to America:[111]

> What if the cross-legged tailor is supporting a boy in college who is one day going to mend your state constitution for you? What if the rag-picker's daughters are hastening over the ocean to teach your children in the public schools? Think, every time you pass the greasy alien on the street, that he was born thousands of years before the oldest native American; and he may have something to communicate to you, when you two shall have learned a common language.[112]

As with much else, however, it was the increasingly aggressive and homogenising force of wartime nationalism that set the tone of the immigration debate by the decade's end. This was partially a response to the demographic size of potentially divided loyalties: in 1917, 4.6 million people in the United States had been born within the boundaries of the Central Powers, to say nothing of Irish and Jewish Americans understandably ambivalent about fighting in support of Imperial Britain and Tsarist Russia.[113] After being vetoed once by Taft and twice by Wilson, an immigration restriction bill – which insisted migrants pass a literacy test – passed in February 1917, a measure which set the precedent for the tougher restrictive legislation of the 1920s.

Immigrants were not safe from the violent end of America's racial politics. Italians, Germans and Jews were lynched in the decade; the anti-Catholic paper *The Menace* had a peak circulation of 1.5 million in 1915; and in that year a reformed Ku Klux Klan dedicated itself to opposing Catholics and immigrants. During the war, vigilante groups such as the American Protective League targeted immigrants in their campaigns to coerce national loyalty, a phenomenon that became increasingly ugly and anti-Semitic in the Red Scare of 1919.

This, however, paled in comparison to the conditions for African Americans at the time. What amounted to a racial pogrom in East St Louis in 1917 killed thirty-nine black Americans, and the Red Summer of 1919 saw race riots targeting black communities in major cities across the country – including Chicago, Washington, Longview and Knoxville. In that year alone, seventy-seven African Americans were lynched, some of them in military uniform, and eleven of them by being burned alive, even as elsewhere black regiments were being welcomed home as heroes. As one black newspaper reported, 'For valor displayed in the recent war, it seems that the Negro's particular decoration is to be the "double cross"'.[114]

These events capped what had been a terrible decade in race relations in the United States. Segregation statutes continued to go on the legislative books in many states; disenfranchisement, sharecropping, poverty, peonage and a total racial bias in the legal system were facts of life in the South. The election of Wilson – the first southerner in the White House since the Civil War – was indicative of a southernisation of national attitudes to race which was deeply inimical to African American freedoms and opportunity. African Americans continued to be barred from most labour unions and, in the North, segregation was routinely applied in many public facilities (despite being technically illegal in many states). In culture African Americans had little access to Hollywood, the large-circulation magazines or mainstream theatre, and yet all of these (as well as a large slice of the advertising industry) regularly featured distortions and stereotype based in traditions of blackface minstrelsy, representations which continued to be extremely popular and lucrative.

The decade did see a shift in African American political activism and demography, however, which would play an increasingly important role over the next thirty years. The year 1915 saw the death of Booker T. Washington, president of the Tuskegee Institute in Alabama who, for twenty years, had been the most high-profile black political leader in America – and who had promoted a strategy of vocational education, remaining in the South, and accommodation to segregation and white southern political power. With his death, that mantle of leadership passed to W. E. B. Du Bois, one of the century's most prominent American intellectuals. He had announced his differences from Washington in his 1903 collection, *The Souls of Black Folk*, stressing the need for a more combative attitude to segregation, the importance of university and professional education for developing a powerful and politically active black middle class (which he dubbed the 'talented tenth') and forcefully denouncing the centrality of mate-rialism in American political life. In 1910 he was one of the founder members of the National Association for the Advancement of Colored People (NAACP), an organisation with an interracial board of direc-tors and a decidedly middle-class, progressive flavour; its favoured tactic of juridical activism made it central to the Civil Rights struggle over the next sixty years. Du Bois served as the editor of *The Crisis*, the house journal of the organisation – which gave him a prominent outlet for his impassioned, incisive and often rhetorically purple analyses of American racial politics. As he stated in its initial number, the editorials would be committed to 'the rights of men, irrespective of color or race, for the highest ideals of American democracy, and for reasonable but earnest and persistent attempt to gain these rights and realize these ideals'.[115]

This shift in political tone was assisted by what became known as the Great Migration, as hundreds of thousands of African Americans left the rural South, where their parents or grandparents had been slaves, to move to northern cities. They were pushed by southern violence, political impotence, the increasing reluctance to hire blacks in artisan trades, poverty and the boll-weevil that devastated southern cotton crops from 1898 onwards. Even for whites, the South was the economic laggard of the nation, with little industrialisation, ill-funded education and low wages; and many of them migrated in this period as well. African Americans were pulled north by the jobs that opened up in Northern cities as the war cut off European immigration; between 1910 and 1920, the black population of New York City rose by 66 per cent, of Chicago by 148 per cent, and of Detroit by 611 per cent.[116] These jobs were frequently unskilled labour in manufacturing industries, such as Chicago's meat-packing houses and steel industry, Detroit's burgeoning motor-car industry, and the service jobs that attended them. As they moved to the North, black Americans founded the great black districts of northern cities that formed the ground for so much cultural and intellectual life in the century. Harlem and Chicago's South Side became consolidated as black districts in the 1910s, and this provided new audiences and focus for the development of cultural and intellectual institutions. The *Chicago Defender* was widely circulated in the South, and gave potential migrants advice and encouragement about moving north (so much so that local officials in the South, worried over the loss of their cheap labour, often sought to ban it). The National League on Urban Conditions Among Negroes (later renamed the National Urban League) was formed in New York

City in 1911 to assist migrants, to train black social workers and to conduct research into migration and urban conditions; by 1918 it was operative in thirty-one cities. In 1915, Carter G. Woodson founded the *Journal of Negro History*. More demotically, black musicians, blues musicians and jazz artists travelling north established a vibrant urban music culture transplanted from its southern roots. This all paved the way for the efflorescence of black culture in the 1920s known as the New Negro Renaissance; from 1923 the Urban League produced *Opportunity*, one of the most important journals of the Renaissance, and Woodson's work underpinned the new interest in African historicism that animated much 1920s black culture. Northern cities also allowed for more militant, mass organisations to flourish, such as black nationalist Marcus Garvey's Universal Negro Improvement Association. By the end of the 1910s, the phrase 'The New Negro' was widely current, connoting urbanism, radicalism and a new form of black masculinity that was revitalised by war experience and unwilling to tolerate racial slights or degradation. As the young editors of the black socialist magazine *The Messenger* announced, the New Negro was committed to 'education and physical action in self defense'; and he was 'the product of the same world wide forces that have brought into being the great liberal and radical movements that are now seizing the reins of political, economic and social power in all of the civilized countries of the world'.[117]

The Messenger's editors were right to declare that the war had changed American society and politics dramatically – even if they misjudged in what direction that shift had occurred. As the final chapter will demonstrate, it dampened many Progressives' idealistic hopes about the function of culture in the public sphere. The sheer size and coerciveness of the wartime state made the localised, voluntary grass-roots politics and cultural dialogue which had underpinned much of what made the 1910s distinctive seem hopelessly miniscule and ineffectual.[118] It saw an assault on civil liberties and a rampant nativism that did much to shut down the expansive and diverse public sphere that had nourished that distinctiveness. Progressive faith in association and individual rationality was diminished by the effects of government propaganda conducted on an unprecedented scale, propaganda which fanned the latent xenophobia and anti-intellectualism in American public life. As Randolph Bourne, one of the champions of such organic community and dialogue, famously declared in 1918, 'war is the health of the state'.

Conclusion

This book will often return to the story of how the institutional organisation of culture in wartime consolidated trends in the 1910s towards the nationalisation of culture and the homogenisation of tastes, and also how it took the Progressive vision of culture as associative and meliorative in the direction of propaganda and coercion in a way few could have foreseen. At the same time, the war destroyed many fragile coalitions between political and aesthetic radicals, as well as the tone of blithe individualism that their work often presented. Three contrasting visions and ambitions for culture marked the decade – (1) the associative, civic and often technocratic vision of the Progressives; (2) the market ambitions of a nationalising and expanding mass-culture industry; and (3) the oppositional and experimental spirit of modernism. The pressure of the war saw fierce conflicts between these visions, as well as setting their respective courses for the 1920s.

This will be explored most fully in the final chapter, on the Great War and American culture, after the preceding chapters set out how these different visions were manifest in a variety of cultural forms. Chapters 1 (on film and vaudeville) and 4 (on performance and music) examine the 'trustification' of the cinema, vaudeville and theatre, all forms which functioned through a centralisation of finance and decisions about content – decisions that often sought to smooth over sectional differences in national tastes and which increasingly sought to appeal to an expanding middle class. Chapter 4 also examines how the increasing middle-class engagement with public entertainments was also a feature of dance and music, one particularly manifest in the 'dance craze' of the 1910s. In contrast, modernism was an animating force in the visual arts, poetry, art dance and theatre, one that often rejected an appeal to a bourgeois centre through an aesthetics of dislocation or difficulty. Chapters 2 (on visual art and photography), 3 (on fiction and poetry) and 4 trace the development of modernism in the decade in these various media, with a particular focus on the fruitful, but often conflicted, relationship with European modernism – and also how modernism sought to engage with the aesthetic and psychological implications of rapid urbanisation and technological change. Finally, the conclusion considers the legacies of the decade to American culture in the twentieth century and beyond – particularly the nostalgia which its compelling mix of utopianism and irreverence, vernacular and elite, expansion and exclusion, still serves to evoke.

Chapter 1

Film and Vaudeville

If the 1910s was a decade of cultural transition, then nowhere was that transition as rapid or as wholesale as in the film industry. By 1920, and largely developed over the course of the decade, the major elements of what film historians have termed the 'Classical' Hollywood cinema were in place. With the exception of comedy, the financial and popular successes of the industry were now feature length instead of the one or two reels customary in 1910; and from barely having a majority market share in the United States in 1910, the American film industry was now the largest in the world. The majority of the major studios which still dominate the industry had not only come into being but had begun the monopolising industrial structure of 'vertical integration', consolidating control of the apparatus of film production, distribution and exhibition. The formal and narrative elements of the films those studios produced had gelled into a style of remarkable consistency. This prized narrative unity; an avoidance of ambiguity in character, motivation or resolution; and an editing style based on 'techniques of continuity and "invisible" editing'.[1] The star system had burgeoned into a social and economic phenomenon; uncredited in films and customarily paid $5 to $10 a week in 1907, by 1916 film actors could earn salaries of up to $1,865 a day.[2] And rather than appealing primarily to an urban, working-class audience, cinema had widened its appeal to the middle classes; total weekly audiences almost doubled from the twenty-six million who had attended in 1910. As the chapter will discuss, these dramatic developments – in audience, the form of film, its national economic significance and its impact on the culture of celebrity – not only changed the nature of films and film-going in the decade, but also had thoroughgoing connections with the entirety of American performance culture, particularly vaudeville and the 'legitimate' theatre.

Film Audiences and Exhibition Space

At the start of the decade, most urban film-going Americans saw their films in nickelodeons. (Rural and small-town audiences formed an important market for films but were initially served by travelling shows in often makeshift venues.) Nickelodeons, which were usually small, poorly ventilated and cheaply run venues – often utilising old storefronts, with wooden benches for seating and a sheet of muslin for a projection screen – were then nearing the end of their extraordinary vogue, which had begun in 1905. Estimates vary but, at their peak year of 1908, there were approximately eight thousand nickelodeons nationwide; in Indianapolis in 1908, for example, there were twenty-one, only three years after the city's first one opened. For a nickel, one gained admission to a theatre playing a programme on continuous loop. Usually with only one (hand-cranked) projector, the nickelodeons covered the changing of reels – or merely mixed up the programme – with vaudeville acts, 'illustrated songs' (projected slides accompanied by a local singer who performed in-house) or illustrated lectures. Westerns, melodrama and slapstick comedy were all popular, and 'daily changes' saw the programmes alter each day. The audiences were typically working class, were often immigrants and contained many children; on occasion nickelodeons even aggressively marketed their services as providing cheap, secure (and entertaining) childcare. As Roy Rosenzweig has noted, in 1912 in Worcester, Massachusetts, a labour report noted the average weekly leisure budget for local working-class families ran to twenty cents. In such circumstances the cinema – cheaper than other cheap amusements such as vaudeville, ten-cent melodrama or even saloons – had a decisive advantage, even if one discounts the enthralling nature of the films to these early audiences.[3] But enthralled they were, and not as passive consumers of escapist fantasies, as cultural elites often charged (Young American architectural critic Lewis Mumford, for example, damned the cinema as a form of 'spiritual masturbation' which gave 'jaded and throttled people the sensations of living without the direct experience of life'.)[4] Instead, as Steven Ross notes, 'life inside these theaters was filled with talking, yelling, fighting, singing, and lots of laughter. Movie theaters were places where people could recapture the sense of aliveness that had been lost in the regimented factories of the era.'[5]

The cinema was often referred to at this time as the 'workingman's academy', and a survey of cinema audiences in Manhattan in 1910 found that 72 per cent came from the blue-collar sector, 25 per cent from the clerical workforce, and 3 per cent from what the surveyors named the 'leisure class'.[6] Exactly when, and how, the middle class was enticed into film-going is a matter of debate among film historians but this was one of the decisive shifts of the decade, and one which the far-sighted in the film industry assiduously encouraged. As with many forms of working-class recreation in the era, such as dancing and the saloon, nickelodeons attracted the attention of Progressive reformers and morality campaigners. They consistently critiqued their poorly lit, poorly ventilated halls, where 'darkness afforded a cover for familiarity and sometimes even for immorality', in the words of one report in Chicago.[7] (Indeed, such concerns led to the widespread instigation of low-level lighting, rather than screenings in complete darkness.) Reformers worried about the sheer imaginative and ideological power of the cinema, how it was 'literally making the minds of our urban populations today', and functioning as 'a place where people learn how to think, act, and feel'.[8] They praised 'educational' fare, such as the popular 'travel films' of the early decade, but agonised over other aspects of this new entertainment; these included the risks of white slavery to unescorted girls, the moral and socialising impact of films on an audience disproportionately composed of children, and the potential for copycat crime in films glamorising robbery, abduction and violence.

More practically, reformers pointed out the very real risks of fire, especially in an era of flammable nitrate film stock. 'Vulgar' vaudeville shows, foreign (and especially French) films or films with strong working-class political sympathies were also regularly targeted, and this often dovetailed with industry attempts to 'clean up' the movies to attract the 'better classes'. Voluntary self-censorship, as would be the case for much of the life of Hollywood, was seen as the answer to the issue of the moral and political governance of film content, and to this end the National Board of Censorship was instituted in 1909. Increasingly, and tied in with the move to feature-length productions, film-makers drew upon stories with the cultural cachet to attract the middle class; biblical and classical narratives were popular, as were adaptations of classic plays and novels, often featuring big-name stars from the 'legitimate' theatre. This was in contrast to early genres of film, such as chase movies, slapstick and fight films, which borrowed from the more 'morally dubious' styles of vaudeville.[9]

Another factor enticing the middle class to the cinema was the development of converted high-class theatrical venues and purpose-built cinemas. With more seats and luxury than the typical nickelodeon, these began to occupy a larger percentage of the nation's seating capacity in the decade. The nation's film trade press lavished attention on spectacular ventures such as Samuel L. 'Roxy' Rothapfel's Strand Theatre – the first purpose-built cinema on Broadway, which opened to its 3,500 capacity in April 1914 – even though such venues initially served only a fraction of the national film audience. (The average capacity in 1916 was 502 seats.) A sensation, the Strand's decorative opulence attracted forty thousand patrons in its first week, all of whom paid more than five cents (a box seat cost half a dollar). As Rothapfel later commented, he aimed to make his patron feel 'that he is our special guest and that nothing for his comfort and convenience has been overlooked', and that 'a policy of dignity, honesty, and good taste' governed his programming.[10] In May 1918 the weekly programme at the Strand included a live orchestral rendition of Franz Suppe's 'Light Cavalry' Overture, a newsreel, an educational 'scenic' film, four popular songs, the Screen Classics feature *Toys of Fate*, and the First National comedy 'Here Comes the Groom'. Nonetheless, as Richard Koszarski has pointed out, film viewing conditions in such venues were far from what contemporary audiences would expect: films were regularly butchered by exhibitors in these prestigious 'first run' houses to cut them to a length which fitted the overall programme, and projectionists would regularly speed up the projection through dull moments. Marcus Loew, one of the major forces in film exhibition of the era, summed up well the general disregard for the artefact of the film print: 'We sell tickets to theaters, not movies.'[11]

Features and Technique

The shift towards regularly scheduled programmes rather than continuous running, the rise in admission prices and the creation of more opulent and comfortable exhibition venues were inseparable from the move to features as the main attraction in film-going. Among the first of these to achieve widespread success in the United States were Italian-made epics such as *Dante's Inferno* (1911), *Quo Vadis?* (1913) and *Cabiria* (1914), films which used enormous sets and innovative techniques of camera movement to present a new depth and complexity to the sense of cinematic space, as well as providing a new largesse to cinematic spectacle. Giovanni Pastrone's *Cabiria*, a ten-reel epic set in the Punic Wars between Rome and Carthage, was seen by Woodrow Wilson at the White House in an event which indicated the growing respectability of cinema as a middle-class leisure activity. Equally important were the technical aspects of these films, which were eagerly absorbed by early auteurs such as D. W. Griffith, and which informed his spectacular offerings such as *The Birth of a Nation* (1915) and *Intolerance* (1916). The move of the industry towards concentrating on feature production was far from inevitable, and was resisted by many sections of the industry. Nickelodeons, in particular, found the higher charges and the incompatibility of long films with continuous programming hard to bear, and some production companies limited their films to two reels well into the decade (notably Biograph, in a restriction which ultimately forced Griffith to leave). Yet the ability of features for bigger spectacle, as well as greater complexities of narrative, characterisation and improved production values, made them hugely popular and allowed for exhibitors to increase admission prices far beyond a nickel. According to Janet Staiger, by 1916 the multiple-reel feature film had prevailed as the dominant medium – at least in the melodramatic and dramatic genres.[12]

A related development to this increasing complexity of narrative and character typical of the feature was a change in the predominant styles of camera framing, movement and editing. Rather than shooting the cinema space as if it was a theatre – with little movement of the camera into the dramatic space, and shooting the actors from some distance – increasingly, directors began fragmenting that dramatic space and seeking a greater filmic intimacy with their leading actors. As with many developments in the medium, this was not universally welcomed: for example, there were debates in the trade press in the early decade about the merits of closer framing, with one writer in 1911 complaining that 'there is nothing more absurd on the part of the manufacturer, nothing which destroys the art and beauty of the scene more than showing us greatly enlarged faces of the leading actors'.[13] Another critic identified the key element which this closer framing provided, in remarking that 'facial expression – that seems to be the dominating influence . . . The American producers, after they learned the rudiments of their craft, uncovered an entirely new school of pantomime.'[14] An 'American style' of acting developed through closer framings, and tended to dispense with the large pantomimic gestures of earlier film and allow character emotion to be demonstrated through more minimal gesture – predominantly through facial expression. This change was pioneered by D. W. Griffith's early work at Biograph and, before long, had been established as the dominant acting style.

Feature-length films also placed a premium on coherence, whether narrative, spatial or temporal. This period saw the development of a visual language and a system of editing based on these principles which would serve Hollywood for at least forty years. Such principles, as Kristin Thompson has observed, were based on an interlinked system of narrative and compositional technique which established 'the story as the basis of the film, the technique as an "indiscernible thread", the audience as controlled and comprehending, and complete closure as the end of all'.[15] Techniques for ensuring temporal and spatial continuity in what came to be known as the 'continuity system' included, for example, 'eyeline matches' for linking contiguous spaces (where a character looks off-screen, and the next shot cuts to what they see); the use of an 'establishing shot' to locate the action spatially before a 'cut-in' brings the framing closer; a rationalised use of intertitles; and consistency in on-screen movement and screen direction between adjacent shots (for example, a character exiting on the left enters with no temporal disjunction on the right in the next shot). By 1917, such techniques – which had been far from consistent in the previous ten years – had become so widespread in the Hollywood system that they achieved a kind of 'invisibility' for most audiences thereafter. Continuity scripts became standard for directors, and they listed key technical properties of each individual shot and its adjacent shots as a record and a guide for maintaining narrative and spatial coherence. Such developments were also used to present a richer and more complex sense of dramatic space, creating a sense of spectatorial omniscience and deploying techniques to organise viewer attention more closely. Even as continuity became the guiding principle, directors worked to show simultaneous action in different spaces (cross-cutting) or narratively linked episodes occurring at different times and in different places (parallel editing) as a way of broadening their canvas.

The Birth of a Nation (1915)

If there is one film that stands at the centre of the interrelated developments in the economics, audiences, and the technical and narrative structures of film at this time, it is David Wark Griffith's Civil War epic of 1915. Civil War pictures enjoyed a vogue in the 1910s, especially in the key fiftieth-anniversary years of 1911, 1913 and 1915; ninety-eight such films were produced in 1913 alone. Griffith, a Kentuckian and the son of a Confederate veteran, had bought the rights to Thomas Dixon's The Clansman (1905), a successful novel and play which related how the Ku Klux Klan saved the white South from the supposed tyranny of black enfranchisement under radical reconstruction. (In a deal which contemporary novelists would swoon over, Dixon was paid $2,500 up front for the film rights, and received 25 per cent of the profits).[16] Such a sweeping historical project suited Griffith's enormous ambitions for film; he had chafed at the restrictions at Biograph where, between 1907 and 1913, he had built the studio's pre-eminent reputation for quality films with an astonishing and technically innovative body of work. Indeed, Biograph's refusal to release *Judith of Bethulia*, his 1913 epic, partly because he had exceeded their length and budget restrictions without permission, prompted his resignation and signing with Mutual on the agreement that he could make two 'special' films per year. His first was *The Birth of a Nation*. Costing an unprecedented $60,000 to produce, and an almost equal amount in promotion and legal fees, Griffith's twelve-reel film was the most costly, lengthy and expensive to see in cinema history up to that time.[17] It was also by far the most successful: by the end of 1917 it had grossed sixty million dollars.

The film dramatised the fates of two families, one from South Carolina, one from Pennsylvania, in the years surrounding the Civil War. The Southern Cameron family, headed by 'Little Colonel' Ben Cameron (Henry Walthall), are friendly with the northern Stoneman family, headed by Austin Stoneman (Ralph Lewis), the leader of the Republicans in the House of Representatives. Stoneman – modelled on the proponent of radical reconstruction, Thaddeus Stevens – is portrayed as possessing a variety of disastrous personal weaknesses, including vanity (he wears a wig), a fondness for bombast and, most pointedly, a predilection for his mulatto housekeeper, played by Mary Alden. Following the war, and the deaths of sons from both families as well as an elaborately staged reconstruction of Lincoln's assassination at Ford's Theatre, Stoneman pursues a policy (to quote from Woodrow Wilson's history of the period, which was used in many intertitles) designed to 'put the white South under the heel of the black South'. To enforce this he ensures the appointment of Silas Lynch (George Siegmann), his mulatto henchman, as Lieutenant Governor of South Carolina. Meanwhile, Ben Cameron – recuperating in a northern hospital after heroic deeds on the battlefield – has fallen for Elsie Stoneman (Lillian Gish) who is working as a nurse there. The remainder of the film dramatises the threat to white southerners of this political policy, a threat continually dramatised in sexual terms as black men attempt to rape members of both the Stoneman and the Cameron families. The film's climax comes as Cameron devises the idea of the Klan, which is hailed as 'the organization that saved the South from the anarchy of black rule'. Riding to the rescue at the head of a huge posse of Klansmen, in scenes which had white audiences cheering, Cameron saves his sweetheart Elsie from the clutches of Lynch, and his sister from a horde of black militia. The double marriage at the close of the film sees 'the former enemies of North and South . . . united again in common defence of their Aryan birthright'.

Controversy attended this unvarnished white supremacist propaganda from the start. The National Board of Censorship voted fifteen to eight to pass the film, after insisting on cuts (such as a scene depicting the castration of the most malignant black rapist, Gus, and one showing 'Lincoln's solution' of transporting black Americans back to Africa).[18] Riots broke out at screenings in Boston and Philadelphia, and the film was denied a release in several major cities. Moreover, the film was a major prompt to the formation of the second Ku Klux Klan in 1915 by William Simmons, a Methodist minister in Georgia. In the 1920s, the Klan would be a major political force for racism, anti-Semitism, anti-Catholicism and nativism, as its numbers swelled to over four million. Conversely, the film gave a great boost to the national profile of the recently formed National Association for the Advancement of Colored People, which led a vigorous protest against the film aided by many sections of the liberal and Progressive media (Francis Hackett in the fledgling New Republic denounced it as 'aggressively vicious and defamatory'; James Weldon Johnson saw Dixon's attitude as one of 'unreasoning hate').[19] Stung by such criticism, Griffith and Dixon mounted very public defences of the film's historical accuracy and the principles of free speech in films, a publicity which adroitly fuelled the film's notoriety and its box office returns.

One of the things which troubled critics most was the film's astonishing technical virtuosity. 'As a spectacle it is stupendous', Hackett noted glumly, a feature which only added to its persuasiveness and ideological force.[20] Indeed, critics who attempt to separate the film's politics from its technical achievements often overlook the fact that it was precisely these technical achievements that gave those politics both an appeal and a legitimacy to millions of Americans. The war scenes are epic in scale; and the final ride of the Klan, using tracking shots, dramatic high camera angles, and fast-paced cross-cutting between three different locations, was the apogee of a technique which Griffith had perfected at Biograph (where, as Tom Gunning notes, he had frequently utilised the 'archetypal drama of a threatened bourgeois household').[21] Scenes such as the final ball before the Confederate volunteers leave for war – lit strongly from above and behind, to give the characters a glow suggestive of the imminent destruction of a way of life – are beautifully composed; and, as Eileen Bowser notes, the scene of the Little Colonel's homecoming, where the camera withdraws its omniscience at the moment he enters his home and his mother's arms, has an undimmed emotive power. Yet, like the popular fiction of the era such as Tarzan of the Apes, the popularity of The Birth of a Nation must be partly ascribed to its indulgence of fantasies of sexual dominance. Griffith had even swapped Lillian Gish into the lead role of Elsie Stoneman in place of Blanche Sweet because – as Gish recalled – 'I was very blonde and fragile-looking. The contrast with the dark man [a blacked-up George Siegmann] evidently pleased Mr. Griffith, for he said in front of everyone, "Maybe she would be more effective than the mature figure I had in mind."'[22] A turning point in assessments of the aesthetic and economic potential of features, nonetheless the film's ability to represent and market with such wild success such a disturbing and reactionary conjunction of race, gender and sexuality is one of the decade's most disturbing cultural moments.

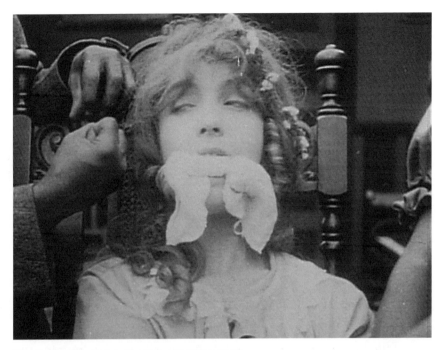

Figure 1.1 Lillian Gish in *The Birth of a Nation*, 1915.

Genres and Stars

The Birth of a Nation was the most viewed film in a style which dominated production in the era: melodrama. It existed in a series of incarnations; at the beginning of the decade westerns were the most popular of these, with stars such as 'Broncho Billy' Anderson, Tom Mix (who broke through in the 1911 *Saved by the Pony Express*) and William S. Hart. Mix was a champion rodeo rider, and filled his films with dramatic roping and riding stunts rather than with subtle characterisations or moral ambiguities (features which endeared him to the child audience that supported the western by the end of the decade). In contrast, Hart had a background in legitimate theatre, and specialised in more world-weary and complex characterisations – especially the 'good-bad man' that would become such a staple of the genre for later stars. Melodramas centring on female stars were also popular; a host of alliterative serials began from about 1913 onwards with titles such as *The Perils of Pauline*, *The Hazards of Helen*, and *The Exploits of Elaine*, and made stars of actors such as Pearl White (heroine of *The Perils of Pauline*). Often these serials tapped into the energies and ideals of first-wave feminism; despite continually being rescued from imminent death by her sweetheart, Pauline is an aspiring author and defers marriage in order to 'live and realize the greatest thrills so that I can describe them in a romance of adventures', as she says in the initial episode. One episode of the Kalem serial *The Hazards of Helen* saw the heroine Helen Holmes leaping aboard a moving train and hand-to-hand fighting two male crooks – all in order to regain her job as a railway telegraph operator.[23] (Helen's job itself was a statement: out of seventy thousand telegraph operators in the United States in 1915, only eight thousand were women).

Balanced against such vibrant assertions of female sexual, physical and workplace agency were the popular vamp films, whose most iconic star was Theda Bara. An anagram for 'Arab Death', Bara (née Theodosia Goodman) gained fame as an alluring and cold-hearted vampire temptress in the film *A Fool There Was* (1915). As Richard Koszarski notes, she was one of the first purely manufactured stars, with Fox studios concocting a fantasy background for her to place with the newly emergent fan magazines (a concoction claiming, for instance, that she had been born in the shadow of the Pyramids and was skilled in black magic). The role of a woman of fatally attractive sexuality, based in a combination of gothic, ethnic and morbid allure, was one she reprised many times in the forty films she made for Fox. Yet, as she later noted, 'The vampire that I play is the vengeance of my sex upon its exploiters. You see, I have the face of a vampire, but the heart of a *féministe*.'[24]

Bara's 'manufacture' as a star is only one example of how important this system had become for differentiating film product, and for marketing those products in ever more intertextual ways to film viewers. Despite the heavy promotion of star performers in sports, theatre and vaudeville, before mid-1909 no American studios exploited the names of their performers for promotional purposes, and it was not industry standard practice to produce screen credits until around 1911. As Richard deCordova has discussed, this was partly due to a general uncertainty about what this relatively new medium involved; it was not until around 1907 that film performers became accepted as 'actors' working within a theatrical model, as 'there was obviously some uncertainty about *what* people did in moving pictures'.[25] Following this time, several productions advertised their use of famous actors from the legitimate theatre, especially the French-made Films D'Art series distributed by Pathé which were first screened in the United States in early 1909. From mid-1909,

American studios began to promote individual actors as a way of publicising films, often without drawing upon notions of previously held theatrical fame. This was tied in with the move towards closer camera framings; as viewers got closer sights of actors on-screen they began to recognise individuals from picture to picture. Much attention in film history has been given to Carl Laemmle's luring of Florence Lawrence from Biograph, where she had been known merely as 'the Biograph Girl'. Laemmle, then the leading force in a group of independent producers challenging the power of the Motion Picture Patents Company (of which more later), hired Lawrence to be the leading player of his IMP production company on the unprecedented salary of $15,000 per year – a far cry from the $5 per day typical for actors in 1907. A series of publicity materials and publicity stunts put her name before a public which had, even before this point, been keen to obtain more information from studios about their favourite actors. Other early stars such as Florence Turner (the Vitagraph Girl) made public appearances at cinemas playing her films; later in the decade 'motion picture balls', where fans could meet the stars, also became popular. The first fan magazines began in 1911 and soon stars, rather than studios, became the key points in film publicity and differentiation.

Richard deCordova observes that, around 1913–14, the system of star production changed. Previously, these figures had been seen as 'picture personalities', whose off-screen lives were given little attention, or were treated as largely continuous with their on-screen roles (and which treated all their identities as an effect of their unique 'personality' which they carried with them from film to film). After this, there was an increased interest in stars' private lives, a change which saw reportage on their off-screen habits as the location of their 'real' selves. Stars' marriages, homes and biographies became the focus of avid fan attention, as did the ways in which they spent their time (and money) outside work. Indeed, they became key figures in the increasing prominence of leisure time and consumption as activities determining social identity. Advertisers were quick to use their images and their roles as 'idols of consumption', in Leo Lowenthal's phrase.[26] In the 1910s, little press attention was given to star scandals; they were feted for their settled, conservative domestic lives, their happy marriages and their loving families, which lent them an air of conservative normalcy. Yet this coexisted with their startlingly abnormal wealth which had often arrived suddenly and while the stars were very young (some of the decade's biggest stars, such as Mary Pickford,

The Immigrant (1917)

Without doubt the most iconic and celebrated star of the silent era was Charles Chaplin, the leading figure of an extraordinary group of comic actors who demonstrated that not all Hollywood's best and most innovative product would be in features. Along with Mack Sennett at Keystone, Fatty Arbuckle, Harold Lloyd and Buster Keaton, he honed a slapstick style which – unlike most other acting of the decade – has retained its power to influence and astonish. His early life quickly became a key part of his star persona: born in Walworth, London, in 1889, Chaplin had a tough working-class upbringing, and his early experiences of poverty and work in music hall would feature strongly in his later films. While touring with the Fred Karno troupe in the United States in 1911 he was seen by Mack Sennett – director, producer and performer at Keystone, then the premier studio for knocka-bout slapstick comedy. Two years later Sennett called him to his studio in California to join his 'fun factory'. Chaplin developed his Tramp character in his work for Keystone and, by 1914, was directing his own material. After a period with Essanay studios, he signed for Mutual in 1916 for $670,000, for which he agreed to produce twelve two-reel comedies over the next year.

This salary was the largest ever given to an entertainer because by this point, Chaplin had not only lifted the appeal of silent film comedy to a new level but had forged one of the most recognisable and iconic images in the world. What contemporary critic Charles J. McGuirk called 'Chaplinitis' had taken off in 1915; by that year, Chaplin's Little Tramp had been used to market a huge range of products; industry imitators of his style abounded (which would prove a future source of litigation); comic strips were devoted to him; and there were up to thirty Chaplin amateur nights in theatres across the country. One of these, in Cleveland, would be won by Leslie T. Hope – the future Bob Hope.[27] By the middle of the next decade Chaplin was also a figure of admiration for many of the leading artists of modernism. Fernand Léger admired his graceful and idiosyncratic pantomime, and paid homage to it in his animation *Ballet Mécanique*. Marc Chagall and e.e. cummings drew him; Hart Crane wrote poetry inspired by him; and a special double issue of *Le Disque Vert*, a Belgian little magazine, was devoted to Chaplin in 1924 with submissions from several prominent surrealist authors. Marshall McLuhan even commented that the Little Tramp was Leopold Bloom's literary twin.[28] Whether it was his everyman status, the extraordinary kinaesthetics of his pantomimic body, his flaunting of bourgeois proprieties or an intimation of the ontological profundity of music-hall clowning that would attract later artists such as Samuel Beckett, modernist intellectuals embraced Chaplin as enthusiastically as did his working-class viewers.

The eleventh of his twelve shorts, *The Immigrant*, has sometimes been taken as his most political film from the Mutual period.[29] It begins with scenes of immigrants, much beleaguered by seasickness, travelling to America on a ship. The Little Tramp befriends Edna Purviance through an act of generosity (Purviance would be Chaplin's leading lady throughout the Mutual period) before they are rudely handled and separated by the immigration authorities at Ellis Island. The second half of the film takes place in a restaurant, where the two meet by accident and the Tramp has to devise a way of paying the bill – in order to avoid the thuggish attentions of the waiter, played by the menacing and enormous 'heavy' Eric Campbell. When a local artist rhapsodises over the Tramp and Edna, and offers to paint them, Chaplin purloins the tip the artist had intended for the waiter to pay for his and Edna's meal. The film ends with him playfully carrying Edna into a Marriage License office.

As revealed in Kevin Brownlow and David Gill's Thames documentary of 1983, *Unknown Chaplin*, the restaurant scene was the original idea motivating Chaplin's work on the film, with the immigrant angle added later. Chaplin would improvise continually on-camera, often going through multiple takes only eventually to discard entire scenes or situations. Here the addition of the immigrant scenes on the boat changed the film from bawdy slapstick to a more romantic, politically engaged piece evincing sympathies that underwrote much of his comedy; as he observed in 1916, 'There may be some in the audience who think it undignified and revolutionary to pull a millionaire's whiskers, but they will be a small minority . . . in their wildest dreams [the audience] never hoped to see a millionaire's whiskers pulled or his hat stepped on. That alone was worth the price of admission.'[30] Deflating 'visible authority' was a stock feature of his comedy from the period, whether it be the boss (as in *The Fireman*), a local gang leader (*Easy Street*), or snooty shop assistants (*The Floorwalker*).[31] In *The Immigrant*, as well as finagling the bullying waiter out of his tip, Chaplin gives an immigration officer a boot in the backside, a scene later produced as evidence of Chaplin's anti-Americanism when he was hounded out of the United States in the 1950s' Red Scare.

Yet *The Immigrant* also tacitly addresses those nativist critics of mass immigration who were particularly vocal in the 1910s, and who charged that America's national 'stock' of intelligence, health and morality was threatened by the influx of people from southern and eastern Europe which had reached such huge proportions in the years surrounding the war. More subtly, it also poked fun at the affectations of artists and intellectuals who perceived immigrants as picturesque or exotic, a trend which – as Angela M. Blake has shown – became a widely deployed strategy of tourist guides and travel literature in the mid-1920s to entice tourists to New York.[32] Yet the indignities, hardships, and trauma of poverty, cultural dislocation, illiteracy and subjection to impersonal authority are present in the film in a way that presents the immigrants as far more complex and sympathetic than much mainstream discourse allowed. Of course, this was alloyed with the sentimentality which typified Chaplin, and often grates with later viewers. But it does indicate Chaplin's global understanding of class, poverty and comedy; as he said in 1916, 'I wasn't paid [$670,000 a year] because I can amuse the American public alone, but because the stuff that makes Americans laugh also makes Chinese laugh, rocking the roof at all sorts of dingy theatres along the Yang Tse; hits the solemn Jap in his risible section, splits the visage of the Turk in Constantinople and gets the money that the Moujik used to spend on vodka.'[33]

Figure 1.2 Charlie Chaplin as the gallant Little Tramp in *The Immigrant*, 1917.

Lillian Gish, Florence Lawrence and Norma Talmadge, had become famous as teenagers). By the mid-decade, studio bosses were offering astronomical sums for the top stars; in 1916, Pickford signed a new contract with Adolph Zukor for $10,000 per week plus 50 per cent of her films' profits (or $500,000 per picture, whichever was greater). Yet even this colossal expense paid off for the studios; by 1918, Zukor at Paramount would use stars such as Pickford, Douglas Fairbanks, Marguerite Clark, Harold Lockwood, William S. Hart, and Wallace Reid to force a system of block booking on exhibitors, which obliged them to take inferior Paramount product in order also to secure the films from these top names.[34]

Film Industry and the Growth of Hollywood

The enormous changes over the course of the decade – to the types of programme typically on offer, to exhibition venues, star salaries and film aesthetics – were completely interlinked with the equally large changes to the industrial organisation of film production in the United States. By the end of the 1910s, a degree of corporate stability had begun to settle in, but this had been preceded by a fluid period where companies flourished, failed, merged and shifted their structures with bewildering speed. The major force in the industry at the outset of the decade was the Motion Picture Patents Company (the MPCC); it had been formed in 1908 to effect a monopoly on film production and distribution. Combining the major production and import companies Vitagraph, Biograph, Edison, Pathé, Kleine Optical, Essanay, Selig, Lubin and Kalem, the MPCC functioned as a holding company for patents connected to film production and projection, and issued licences to producers, distributors and exhibitors. They also signed an agreement with Eastman Kodak for exclusive access to raw film stock. Immediately, however, a small but crucial 'independent' sector reluctant to pay these licences developed, first at the level of exhibition but soon after in production. The MPCC went after this sector with a flurry of litigation based on copyright infringement but, in 1912, it lost an important case against Carl Laemmle's IMP corporation over infringement of the Latham-loop Patent (a key technology preventing the film snapping under the tension of projection), and the same year it became subject to a federal investigation under anti-trust legislation. By the time that case went against the MPCC in 1915, it was already well past its days of dominating the industry; it was those behind the 'independents' who would carry it forward.

That same year, Laemmle opened Universal City, a 230-acre complex in the hills above Hollywood which turned out thirty reels of footage in its first week. If the scale of this production was unprecedented, by this point its location was not. Production companies had been shooting in California since 1908, attracted by its year-round mild climate, the range of its scenery (encompassing desert, mountains, coast and forest within a few miles of one another in southern California), the opportunity to build huge 'back lots' to house elaborate sets, and cheap, largely non-unionised labour. For much of the decade, all California filming was done outside, with a thin muslin screen overhead to diffuse the sunlight. These attractions saw a shift away from New York as the major production centre (although certain forms, such as newsreels and animation, continued to be based there) as well as a decline in alternative winter-production venues such as Florida. As Richard Koszarski notes, by 1915 the West Coast accounted for up to 75 per cent of all American production, and permanent studios, such as Universal City, were starting to replace the temporary facilities which had served solely as winter locations in the previous years. By the end of the decade, indoor stages, sophisticated lighting and streamlined production systems had contributed further to an industrial approach to film creation.[35]

Also by 1915, American producers were starting to profit from the crippling effect of the world war on European film-makers. Although American product had been doing well in some global markets prior to the war, the huge fall in European production allowed them to secure a dominance in most markets (French company Pathé's raw stock factory, for example, had converted to producing munitions at the beginning of the war; its studios were converted to barracks).[36] American producers began opening distribution branches in South America, Australia, the Far East and the European countries which were still accessible; by the end of the war, it had a much more global network of distribution and much less focus on the European market as the primary destination for export. As Thompson and Bordwell note, this gave American cinema an economic advantage it holds to this day: if export sales could be relied upon, films could be made with bigger budgets in the knowledge that production costs could be recouped at home and then profits made from cheap sales overseas. The low cost of importing an American film would also discourage domestic production in competing nations. This led to a situation where American film budgets and production values were (and remain) consistently higher than in any other national cinema; and where buying in an American film was often cheaper than producing one locally.

Principal among the American companies opening these new exchanges were the corporations that would emerge in the 1920s as the American 'majors', companies which, by and large, had chosen to focus on the feature film as their major unit of production. Many of the men heading these companies had begun in nickelodeon ownership; as well as Laemmle at Universal, this was true of Adolph Zukor at Famous Players-Lasky and Paramount, the Warner brothers, Marcus Loew, and William Fox. The economies of scale of global marketing were also evident in the trend towards what is known as 'vertical integration', namely the bringing together of film production, distribution and exhibition under one corporate structure. The most powerful company to pursue this was headed by Adolph Zukor; he had initial success with his company Famous Players in Famous Plays, which specialised in exploiting the star system and utilising the cachet of well-established theatrical performers and material. By 1914 he had merged this company with Jesse Lasky's Lasky Feature

Play Company, and arranged for distribution by the newly organised Paramount Pictures Corporation. By 1917 Paramount was producing 102 features a year and held rights to a huge number of stars; and the strength of this combination allowed them to enforce block booking on theatres to enable them to access the best Paramount content. Angered by this, several exhibitors hit back by organising the First National Exhibitors Circuit, which began to finance production and distribution for theatres unwilling to go along with such strong-arm tactics. Paramount responded by buying up theatre chains, a practice it would continue in the 1920s. From the other direction, Marcus Loew, the owner of a large chain of theatres, bought into the production firm Metro in 1920 (the firm which would later become MGM). In the 1920s, Paramount, MGM and First National formed the 'Big Three' firms of the American industry, heading up an oligopoly which would last until the 1950s when anti-trust legislation finally disbanded their vertical integration.

Not all production was controlled by such a system; maverick film-makers, such as the black director and producer Oscar Micheaux, managed to work outside of it, and even critique it – his *Within Our Gates* of 1920, with its strong condemnation of lynching and white southern discourses of sexuality, was a clear answer to *The Birth of a Nation*. Similarly, innovative animators such as Winsor McCay worked relatively independently, as did a number of small production companies set up by unions or workers' societies, often to combat the distinctly anti-labour tenor of much major studio fare. Nonetheless, the major development of the decade was the studio system of large-scale, vertically integrated production, a concentration of capital and production, distribution and exhibition facilities that continues to be the major player in the global film market.

Vaudeville

Vaudeville shared many features with the culture of the cinema in the 1910s. Like films, it was enormously popular, and had seen a huge expansion in seating capacity over the previous decade; at its peak, over a thousand theatre houses were devoted exclusively to vaudeville nationwide. Like cinema, it saw an increasing centralisation of finance and bureaucratic organisation, which placed decisions about booking and content in the hands of a few people in centres of cultural authority. The presentation of both forms was committed to the principle of mixed programming which, for both, often held comedy as a key ingredient. All this meant that vaudeville and cinema were closely intertwined in terms of material, personnel and conditions of exhibition: they shared actors, celebrities, styles and exhibition space, and magnates such as Marcus Loew were closely involved in the organisation of both. Films were often part of vaudeville bills; indeed, in the early years of cinema, vaudeville houses showing continuous programmes often used films as 'chasers' to encourage recalcitrant audiences to leave. It also served as a seedbed for a generation of Hollywood talent; in the 1910s Fred Astaire, Buster Keaton, Charlie Chaplin, Fanny Brice, Douglas Fairbanks, James Cagney, George Burns and the Marx Brothers all played the vaudeville stage.

Vaudeville was also involved in the forging of a mass culture, one capable of maximising its returns by appealing to all classes and both genders. This was a departure from its roots in entertainments with a predominantly male, working-class audience, such as the dime museum, the minstrel show, the concert saloon and the variety theatre.[37] The raucous and often bawdy humour of these entertainments – and the often rowdy participation they sought to elicit from their spectators – was discouraged by the head of the biggest vaudeville booking circuit of the time, B. F. Keith. Keith's career is instructive of the pattern of change in popular culture from the late nineteenth to the early twentieth centuries; he and his partner Edward Albee began by opening a dime museum in Boston in the 1880s, an institution which based much of its appeal on freak shows (some of his early acts included baby Alice, the midget wonder; the Tatooed Man; the biggest frog in the world; and a farce entitled 'Murphy's fat baby').[38] By 1894, they offered nothing but vaudeville and, by 1910, they owned several theatres and had consolidated a nationwide vaudeville booking circuit. This linked Keith's control over the eastern theatres under the auspices of his United Booking Office (UBO) with the Orpheum Circuit of Martin Beck, based in Chicago, which oversaw the booking of western theatres. As had also happened in 'legitimate' theatre, this established a syndicated lock on the entire big-time vaudeville circuit; as *Variety* put it in 1923, this was the culmination of the 'trustification of vaudeville', as 'it is in the booking office that vaudeville is run, actors are made or broken, theatres nourished or starved'.[39]

Keith's hold over nationwide bookings for big-time vaudeville also extended to a keen attempt to control content, and to promote his ideal that 'the stage show must be free from vulgarisms and coarseness of any kind, so that the house and entertainment would directly appeal to the support of ladies and children – in fact . . . [the] playhouse must be as "homelike" an amusement as . . . possible'.[40] What was true for the act was also true for the audience; famously, Keith told the audience in the cheapest gallery seats on the first night of opening a new theatre in Providence in 1888 that they needed to cut out their noisy demonstrations, as 'others in the audience don't like it, and it does not tend to improve the character of the entertainment'.[41] According to legend, he was treated by a round of applause and perfect compliance.

Such strictures led the Keith circuit to be mocked by its competitors as the 'Sunday school circuit', but this control was a part of the 'bourgeoisification' of working-class cultural forms that underwrote the development of mass culture in the United States during these years. As Lawrence Levine has discussed, an expectation that audiences in many forms of public entertainment would be characterised by 'passive politeness' was consolidated at the turn of the century, part of a broader shift whereby people were newly encouraged to keep a whole range of physical processes and personal feelings which had previously been acceptable to display (or perform) in public firmly within a private sphere. Cultural institutions – including vaudeville – were therefore 'active agents in teaching their audiences to adjust to the new social imperatives, in urging them to separate public behavior from private feelings, in training them to keep a strict rein over their emotional and physical processes'.[42] Moreover, as Keith's language suggests, such 'training' often took on gendered language in seeking to position women as natural censors and arbiters of cultural propriety. He hired female ushers in his own theatres as a way of quelling raucous male patrons, and theatre managers were often encouraged to watch the faces of female patrons to adjudge whether or not acts were morally appropriate.

Yet, as M. Alison Kibler has demonstrated, despite these efforts, vaudeville was not quite as universally sanitised and wholesome as Keith liked to proclaim. The vaudeville theatre was a space of keen contest over the moral, class and sexual dynamics of public behaviour in these years and, despite the enormous influence Keith had in 'cleaning up' vaudeville and selling it to middle-class audiences, raucous galleries, women spectators engaging in rowdy and lascivious behaviour, racy humour, and sexually suggestive performances remained features throughout the period. As Kibler observes, the history of vaudeville 'clearly reveals mass culture's varied approaches to cultural hierarchy: it uplifted low culture and unraveled high culture; it aspired to bourgeois standardization but did not neglect working-class, immigrant pride'.[43]

Keith and Albee's influence was limited primarily to 'big-time' vaudeville, epitomised by his flagship Palace Theatre at 47th Street and Broadway, which opened in 1913 and served as the headquarters of the booking circuit as well as being the nation's pre-eminent vaudeville venue. Big time was characterised by one bill per week, twice-daily shows with up to eight acts, and higher production costs, salaries, and entry prices. Small-time vaudeville, in contrast, developed an alternative to the Keith circuit's more white-collar, higher-price vaudeville; its shorter, cut-price amusements appealed especially to family audiences on tighter budgets. Small-time, 'tab', 'ten-cent' or 'family' vaudeville often played a 'continuous programme' throughout the day, which could involve performers being on as many as six times daily. Often found in working-class or immigrant districts of America's cities, or at least away from its major entertainment districts, it had smaller production costs and lower salaries, and usually six acts at most.[44] Both forms, however, carefully balanced their programmes to have a variety of different kinds of entertainment, and aimed to build audience excitement carefully through the rhythms of the different acts. First on the bill was often a 'dumb act', soundless so that the noise of people entering the theatre would not prove too distracting. Animal acts were popular early acts for the bill, usually involving small or domestic animals that imitated humans: they 'skated, rode bicycles, talked, danced, ate with forks, lit and smoked cigarettes, drank beer, and staggered like drunks'.[45] Usually, at least half the bill would be comedy, interspersed with any combination of playlets, dancing acts, singers, acrobats, magicians, big dance numbers or dramatic readings. As well as films, vaudeville drew on other performance traditions, such as the minstrel show, the circus, legitimate theatre, burlesque and the dime museum. Smaller acts typically got ten minutes; bigger stars, rarely more than thirty minutes. This meant that performers with well-honed acts could build an entire career out of one short piece; as George Burns put it, 'all you needed in vaudeville was seventeen good minutes'.[46]

Vaudeville's Stars

Stars in 'big-time' vaudeville could earn over $3,000 a week for two appearances a day, figures quite comparable to high-end film star salaries.[47] The biggest draws in the decade included Harry Houdini, whose magic shows and thrilling escapology blended performance skills with a flair for publicity and careful manipulation of the 'yellow press'. Indeed, vaudeville promoters paid heavily for newspaper advertising, which indirectly ensured them regular attention (and 'free' publicity) in those same papers for their regular and ingenious promotional stunts. Houdini, for example, had himself thrown into New York Harbour in a fortified box in 1912, in front of 'enough newspaper workers to have got out any New York daily', according to the *New York Times*; another popular Houdini act was freeing himself from a straitjacket while suspended upside-down from a newspaper building or a crane.[48] During the decade, Houdini's most celebrated act was his 'milk can' routine, where he would be locked into a milk can filled with water which was then locked into another case; he was typically out in under a minute. He elaborated this trick with the construction of a 'Chinese Water Torture Cell' which had a glass front, in which he would be fastened upside-down in stocks so that the audience could see his efforts to escape.

Another star of the decade was Eva Tanguay, a performer who drew on the traditions of burlesque for her sexually titillating and suggestive act, sometimes referred to as 'cyclonic vaudeville' for its uninhibited and energetically unbounded physical style. Her songs carried titles such as 'It's All Been Done Before, but Not the Way I Do It', 'I Want Someone to go Wild with Me', and her signature tune, 'I Don't Care'. Tanguay, too, was a skilful manipulator of publicity; at a press conference to promote a new costume for her Salomé dance (a Salomé craze gripped the country early in the decade), she walked in fully clothed – only to reveal she was holding her entire costume in her clenched fist.[49] Frequently flaunting Keith's rules on propriety, she nonetheless continued to headline at his theatres because of her immense popularity.

The biggest vaudeville star of the decade, however, was Al Jolson. Like so many stars and entrepreneurs in show business at the time – including vaudeville, legitimate theatre, Tin Pan Alley, and cinema – he was Jewish, indeed, the son of a Jewish cantor (a story he would return to in 1927's *The Jazz Singer*). Jolson was born Asa Yoelson and, by the 1910s, was a firm star in musical comedy and vaudeville; he was so successful that he was able to negotiate the highly unusual arrangement of securing a percentage deal on the profits of his shows. He headlined musicals at the Winter Gardens for many years, the showpiece theatre of another of New York's showbusiness impresarios, the Shubert Brothers. Famous for his energetic delivery of songs

– he later claimed he had to be physically restrained when recording them into a microphone because he instinctively wanted to bound around while performing them – he was also the twentieth century's most important performer in blackface.

Vaudeville and fictions of identity

That vaudeville's biggest star performed under a racial mask indicates the importance which impersonation and masking held in the performance culture of the decade. Vaudevillians frequently built their acts around lampooning other cultures; skits ridiculing German Americans, Irish Americans, Chinese Americans, Jewish Americans and African Americans, particularly in immigrant vaudeville, gave audiences a way of mediating their fears, hopes and uncertainties over their own identity in a multi-ethnic urban environment. It provided what Irving Howe memorably called 'a sort of abrasive welcoming committee for the immigrants', a cultural sphere for audiences to formulate and express their apprehensions and ambitions on the subject of Americanisation and assimilation, as well as the inter-ethnic competition for space, jobs and political influence in the highly dynamic cityscapes of the early century.[50] This was highly codified, as performers put on skits based not in their own ethnicity but in a portrayal of ethnic 'type': Jewish skits played in 'stage Yiddish'; Dutch and German impersonators wore peaked caps and clogs; and 'greenhorn' acts, about new arrivals to the city, were particularly popular. As David Nasaw remarks, 'each "type" spoke its own language, dressed in readily identifiable costumes, and had its own routines.'[51] These ethnic masks allowed the freedom of licence – to say and perform things more difficult if one was 'playing it straight' – as well as providing a mechanism for both ridiculing and borrowing from other cultural traditions.

As well as racial and ethnic impersonation, female impersonators were some of the biggest stars of the vaudeville stage; Julian Eltinge built his whole career on female impersonation, to such success that he headlined big-time vaudeville bills and had a 42nd Street theatre named after him in 1912. Critics enthused about Eltinge's perfect impersonations and costuming, his grace, poise and beauty; morality campaigners complained that his act was degenerate. In order to manage such criticism, Eltinge regularly invited newspapermen 'behind the scenes' to see how his artifice was created; and he cultivated a public image which emphasised his rugged off-stage masculinity, including his love of boxing and horse riding. Key to Eltinge's popularity was the increasing concern – and fascination – with the figure of the 'fairy', especially during a period characterised by the forging of a highly visible male gay subculture in America's urban centres. As George Chauncey has discussed, the 'fairy' – a cross-dressing or flamboyant homosexual – was 'the dominant pejorative category in opposition to which male sexual "normality" was defined', and therefore 'influenced the culture and self-understanding of all sexually active men.'[52] Eltinge's cultivation of an aggressively masculine and heterosexual off-stage persona helped him negotiate the forces of moral censure, while this spectacular and ambiguous gendered and sexual positioning (one critic referred to him as 'ambi-sextrous', and he received large quantities of amorous fan mail from women) ensured his continuing popularity.[53] All these traditions based in the performative transgression of ethnic, racial, gendered and sexual boundaries expressed something particular about American cities, which had been built so rapidly and from so many disparate ethnic and cultural elements: they were places where a combination of available anonymity and extraordinary dynamism allowed people to become someone, or something, else with unprecedented ease.

The dominant tradition of impersonation in the decade, however, remained blackface. By this point, many other ethnic minorities had enough political and consumer power to protest effectively and to curtail ethnic and racial slurs in on-stage representations. Black patrons, however, were regularly refused admittance to high-class theatres and routinely segregated into the worst seats elsewhere, even in northern cities where this was technically illegal. In consequence, they could exert little consumer influence on the mainstream entertainment industry. Yet, despite being physically absent from most American vaudeville audiences, black representations were central in these years. As David Nasaw remarks,

> It is impossible to overstate the popularity of . . . black misrepresentations in the 1890s and early 1900s. African-American caricatures were a staple of the vaudeville bill, black musicals were playing on Broadway and touring the first-class theatres of the country, and 'coon' songs were the hottest-selling item in sheet music.[54]

Moreover, as critics like Michael Rogin have noted, recent immigrant groups were particularly attracted to blackface. Jewish comedians, such as Eddie Cantor, George Burns, George Jessel and Jolson, gave blackface 'a new lease of life' in the decade and, indeed, used it as a cultural form capable of accelerating Jewish Americanisation and cultural assimilation. That assimilation, however, was at the expense of black Americans; this 'sinister paradox' involved an 'assimilation . . . achieved through the mask of the most segregated; the blackface that [offered] Jews mobility keeps the blacks fixed in place'.[55] The mask of blackness, which performed and reproduced both its own cultural centrality and the social exclusion of the racial group it purported to designate, was therefore a complex mechanism. It included and excluded African Americans from America's largest entertainment institutions; it provided a cultural form for America's ethnic minorities to use in positioning their own racial and national identities; and it presented a kind of plantation nostalgia while being intimately involved in the modernisation of America's entertainment industry. Nowhere was this complexity more evident than in the career of Bert Williams.

Bert Williams

Bert Williams was born in 1874, in Antigua in the West Indies; his family moved to California in 1885. By the 1910s he had long been the most celebrated black comedian in American show business, having built a career with his blackface act in musical comedy and vaudeville. For much of the 1900s this was with his on-stage partner, George Walker, who played the graceful, showy and well-dressed dandy to Williams's bumbling and lanky sidekick; in the 1890s they had billed themselves the 'two real coons' to differentiate themselves from white performers in blackface. Their greatest success had been starring in the 1902 play, *In Dahomey*, a show based partially on their experiences pretending to be Dahomeyans in an ethnological exhibit at the San Francisco Midwinter Fair in 1893 (the real Dahomeyans had been delayed: Williams, Walker and the other 'sham native Dahomeyans' were dismissed when they arrived).[56] The show saw their first appearance on Broadway, a command performance at Buckingham Palace and a subsequent nationwide tour; it also featured as a British showcase for the cakewalk dance which Walker and his wife, Ava Overton, had helped make famous. By 1910, however, Walker was terminally ill, and Williams turned his back on assembling another African American company in favour of working the white vaudeville and revue circuit. During the decade he earned $2,000 per week in vaudeville, a greater salary than was afforded to the president of the United States.[57]

His major work came with Florenz Ziegfeld's Follies, which he began in 1910 in a move which 'integrated Broadway'.[58] For his performances in the Follies, Williams insisted that he should not be on-stage at the same time as any white female actors or chorus girls; Ziegfeld also agreed that the Follies would not tour below the Mason–Dixon line. Several of Ziegfeld's other performers protested at him hiring a black man, but he reputedly told them 'Go if you want to. I can replace every one of you, except the man you want me to fire.'[59] Williams's act – performed in a woolly wig, white gloves and burnt cork – was a mixture of song and comedy; his trademark song was 'Nobody', a lament about isolation and perpetual bad luck, which he first performed in 1905. One verse runs as follows:

> When winter comes with snow and sleet,
> And me with hunger and cold feet,
> Who says, 'Here's twenty-five cents, go ahead and get something to eat'?
> Nobody!

> I ain't never done nothin' to nobody,
> I ain't never got nothin' from nobody, no time,
> Until I get somethin' from somebody, sometime,
> I'll never do nothin' for nobody, no time.[60]

So clamorous were audiences for this song over so many years that Williams later remarked 'I could have wished that both the author of the words and the assembler of the tune had been strangled or drowned or talked to death.'[61] His comedy was marked by exquisite timing and a portrayal of the long-suffering, hapless 'Jonah Man' figure; as he described it, this was 'the man who, even if it rained soup, would be found with a fork in his hand and no spoon in sight'.[62] Yet he also insisted that this attempt to 'portray the darkey, the shiftless darkey', was a constant effort at crafting a persona; the on-stage 'darkey' had nothing to do with his own character or personality. As he remarked in an analogy clearly very deliberately chosen, 'It's in a monkey to make people "feel funny" because he's born that way, but it's not in me. To make people laugh I have to work it out carefully.'[63]

Such comments, matched against Williams's success within a minstrel tradition so linked to portrayals of African Americans as lazy, deceitful, uneducated and ruled by physical appetite, has divided critics. In his obituary in 1922 in the black magazine, *The Messenger*, it charged he had 'rendered a disservice to black people' for playing Jim Crow theatres that segregated or barred African Americans and for presenting a character who represented 'the lowest form of intellection'. Others criticised him for 'defecting' to the white theatre and thus setting back the possibility of an independent black theatre.[64] Subsequent critics, and even novelists, have been more inclined to regard him as a tragic figure, trapped into the only role available to him in a thoroughly racist theatrical business; such views regard him as a wasted talent institutionally prevented from employing his true comic subtlety and range, and emotionally devastated by these suffocating prescriptions.[65] This was an image Williams himself cultivated; as he said in 1916, 'If I were free to do as I like, I would give both sides of the shiftless darky, the pathos as well as the fun. But the public knows me for certain things.'[66] Most recently, a wave of scholarship on the ways minstrelsy can trouble and question subjectivities and identifications, rather than simply reinforce racist stereotype, has seen Williams as an interesting figure. As Susan Gubar suggests, 'white appropriation of African or slave cultural forms could be re-manufactured by the black performer in ways paradoxically both demeaning and empowering'.[67] Louis Chude-Sokei has been particularly interested in the dynamic of a black West Indian man impersonating a white man impersonating an ignorant black man from the American South; not only was this masquerade one which 'ultimately mocked and erased that primary caricature', but this 'cross-cultural, intra-racial masquerade constituted a form of dialogue at a time when tensions between the multiple and distinct black groups in New York City were often seething despite various attempts at pan-African solidarity'.[68] Despite such attempts at critical recuperation, by the end of the decade, Williams was undoubtedly going against the emerging trend in African American culture towards developing fresh and empowering cultural forms. The need to craft representations of African Americans in America's mass culture which were not based in minstrelsy – a pressing need in films and in vaudeville – marked many of the efforts of small-scale independent black theatrical and film production in the 1920s. As the Harlem Renaissance theatre historian David Krasner notes, these efforts contributed to a developing aesthetic of black modernity, one which sought to 'transform the image of black culture from minstrelsy to sophisticated urbanity'.[69] Yet Williams is perhaps best considered as one of a handful of African American performers in the twentieth century who have utilised clownish or demeaning racial personas in ways more complex and subversive than might initially be obvious. Comics like Williams engaged the spectacularisation of race that is such a feature of American mass culture, but were well aware of the psychological, social and economic investment his audiences had in the 'darky' figure; and Williams's act perpetually carried an edge of menace, a suggestion that this investment might not be as secure as his audience might like. As Ann Douglas observes, 'His was the art of patience protracted despite abuse and misfortune, but his act also reminded viewers that all patience wears out sometime; that's always the end of the story, whether depicted or not.'[70]

Conclusion

That the decade's most popular film and a good proportion of its most popular vaudeville stars relied on blackface testify not just to a persistent and objectionable form of racism, but to the demands of a nationalising imperative which characterised vaudeville and films of the time – namely the need to develop a singular product capable of being distributed or toured across national exhibition circuits. That blackface and a related 'southernisation' of national attitudes to race facilitated the forging of a national entertainment market should hardly be surprising: in part this reflected the anxieties around white identity in the period, but it also demonstrated a particular balance between novelty and continuity in the huge upheavals in popular entertainment in the decade. It introduced an old form of comedy (in existence since the 1830s) into new media in a way that was socially reassuring to white audiences – the 'plantation darky' was a figure who suggested that some Americans would always remain comfortingly static and reliable rather than mobile and challenging. Blackface, however, was simultaneously given an aesthetic newness – as anyone watching Bert Williams in the Follies, his short film 'A Natural Born Gambler', or the dramatic final rescue scenes of *The Birth of a Nation*, could testify.

This balance of conservatism and novelty, moral rectitude and technological exhilaration, the reactionary pull of sentimentality or stereotype and the exciting potentialities of a new medium, was key in developing the audience for cinema in the decade. Yet the conservative elements of this formula should not obscure the fact that what Hollywood did in the 1910s was establish a form and an industry which simply had not existed before, and which, as Walter Benjamin observed, amounted to 'a revolutionary criticism of traditional concepts of art'.[71] As Benjamin and many others have recognised, this altered the very nature of what culture was, what it could do, and whom it could speak to (and for). Vaudeville and theatre had to react to this change, but so did every other medium – as the following chapters will explore.

Chapter 2

Visual Art and Photography

In 1913, former president Theodore Roosevelt pointedly skipped Woodrow Wilson's inauguration to attend the International Exhibition of Modern Art which was taking place at the Armory of the 69th National Guard Regiment in New York. In his review, he praised the Armory Show – as everyone called it – for addressing 'the need of showing to our people in this manner the art forces which of late have been at work in Europe, forces which can not be ignored'. Yet he spent much of the review pouring scorn on what he called the 'lunatic fringe' of painterly 'extremists', artists whom he surmised 'represent in the painters the astute appreciation of the power to make folly lucrative which the late P. T. Barnum showed with his faked mermaid'.[1] Always well attuned to the popular sentiment, Roosevelt's double-edged review illustrated the contrasting reactions which much of the United States displayed towards this sensational exhibition. On the one hand, it demonstrated an exhilarated awareness that recent developments in European art had altered the medium in fundamental ways. On the other, it expressed a concern which easily morphed into ridicule, a worry that the rapid process of experiment and innovation which would later be called modernism had turned to strategies of defamiliarisation and abstraction which amounted to a disregard for the general public and a rejection of long-held notions of beauty, morality and technique. These were developments which either threatened or liberated the whole function of art, depending on one's perspective.

Roosevelt's views were echoed in many of the thousands of newspaper column inches that attended the show, and in the popular reaction to it. Students at the Art Institute of Chicago planned to burn Matisse in effigy on the day the exhibition closed in the city; the *New York Times* pronounced elements of the show revolting.

Such strong feelings were partly a product of the show's colossal scale and ambition. Altogether 250,000 people filed past the 1,300 works (about one-third of them European) exhibited in New York, and then in subsequent hangings in Chicago and Boston. Publicity had included fifty thousand postcards sent out to the nation's arbiters of taste, lapel buttons, posters all over New York, and the ubiquitous display of a pine tree against a white background, an emblem borrowed from flags carried by Massachusetts regiments in the War of American Independence. The iconography of revolution suited the mood of the show; 'it cannot help but prove an earthquake to the sleeping villages', said the painter Marsden Hartley, then scornfully immersed in the heady art world of Paris; and the Armory Show's mixture of sensation and revelation would, indeed, leave a long legacy in the culture of the visual arts in the United States.[2] It prompted the first purchase of a Paul Cézanne painting by a major American museum (for $6,700, by the Metropolitan Museum of Art), the beginnings of several private modern art collections which later founded the holdings of major public modern art galleries, and a change in the United States tariff laws which made it cheaper to import art from overseas. It demonstrated New York's rapidly growing appetite for modern art in the decade, and its dominance of the national art scene; in 1907 there were five modern art shows in the city; in 1917 there were sixty-three.[3] Moreover, for thousands of American visitors, the chronological hanging of the European galleries sketched a narrative of artistic development which was new and exciting. Beginning with old masters such as Ingres, Goya and Delacroix, the show then exhibited the Impressionists, such as Edgar Degas, Claude Monet, and Pierre-Auguste Renoir, followed by post-Impressionists such as Paul Cézanne, Paul Gaugin and Vincent van Gogh. The exhibit finished with rooms devoted to fauvist and cubist art.[4]

The event also provided a showcase for the American moderns, and demonstrated the sharp divergence between contemporary American and European styles – a fact not lost on the show's many reviewers. (That divergence extended to price as well; right through the 1930s the work of American modernists was considerably cheaper than that of their European counterparts.) Americans exhibited included James Whistler, Mary Cassat, Albert Pinkham Ryder, photographer Alfred Stieglitz, Marsden Hartley, John Marin, Edward Hopper, Joseph Stella, Margeurite and William Zorach and Stuart Davis. Many American modern artists not featured – such as

Arthur Dove, Georgia O'Keeffe, Man Ray and John Covert – would nonetheless draw inspiration from the exhibit.

Also featured was the school of urban realists whose exhibition at the Macbeth Galleries show, just five years earlier, had also been an iconoclastic sensation. In particular, it had been 'the eight's' depictions of the urban poor (which led to five members later being derisively labelled the 'ashcan school', a term John Sloan detested) which helped break the grip of the more genteel National Academy of Design on the exhibition of the visual arts. The most prominent of this 'aschcan school' at the Armory Show were Robert Henri, Arthur Davies and John Sloan, as well as two prize pupils of Henri's who had not been a part of the anti-academy exhibition at the Macbeth Galleries in 1908: George Bellows and Edward Hopper (the latter's sole picture in the Armory Show, 'Sailing', went for $250, and was the first he ever sold). Throughout the 1910s, in painting, graphic illustration and print-making, the 'ashcan school' made images of America's urban life which evoked the eye for satire and squalor of earlier urban portraitists such as Hogarth or Daumier. The public spaces of the street, the 'stag' boxing party, the dance hall, the bath house, the saloon and the prison occupied their attention, in scenes presenting a frequently exhausting crowd of detail and people. In those crowd scenes, a grotesque smirk here, a glance of inquiry or desire there, give a jumble of interpersonal anecdote strikingly at odds with the rational, geometric and often depopulated vision of the city which modernists such as Joseph Stella, Max Weber and John Marin would develop in the decade. Typically, the bodies in these ashcan images are non-idealised, often starkly white and bulbous, and naked rather than nude; a dark palette casts corners and doorways into deep shadow, suggesting the suffering and bleakness hovering at the edges of public urban space. Moreover, this rejection of a rational or geometric view of the urban scene, and their frank treatments of sex and poverty, were closely connected to the politics of the artists. Sloan became art editor for the radical Socialist magazine *The Masses* and, together with Bellows and Stuart Davis, contributed satirical drawings in support of campaigns against the Comstockian suppression of birth control, the Preparedness movement and plutocratic excess. Their less pointed works, however, caused fellow staff cartoonist, Art Young, to question whether 'pictures of ash cans and girls hitching up their skirts in Horatio Street' really furthered the publication's political campaigns.[5]

Figure 2.1 The urban vision of the Ashcan School: George Bellows, 'The Street', 1917. Courtesy of the Library of Congress, LC-USZ72-165.

American Modern and Dada

By 1913, and hung next to the formal radicalism of the latest work from Europe, this brand of iconoclasm began to look limited and provincial. The art of the ashcan school exhibited Henri's belief that '"significant form", to use the term then in vogue – did not suffice by itself; the form

of the work of art . . . had to serve as a vehicle for some profound human-
istic content transmitted through the artist's personal experience', a
view which seemed dated when contrasted to the assaults on humanism
and 'artistic personality' being made by the avant-gardists of European
modernism.[6] Arch-modern Alfred Stieglitz branded their work passé,
and Henri had signalled his distaste for the avant-garde by describing the post-Impressionists as 'strange freaks'.[7] Most freakish of all in
1913 was cubism, and the Armory Show's place in popular memory
rests largely on its exhibition of work by Picasso, Francis Picabia,
Constantin Brancusi and Jacques Redon. It was Marcel Duchamp's
'Nude Descending a Staircase', however, that became the *succès de scan-
dale* of the exhibit. In characteristically cubist subdued tones of brown,
black and yellow, but deploying the impression of movement then
being developed by the Italian Futurists, it fractured perhaps the most
hallowed art subject of the western tradition – the female nude – into a
swirling mass of intersecting two-dimensional planes. It replaced the
smooth, curved, organic female body inviting a male erotic gaze with a
series of hard, flat fragments, assembled in the geometry of the mechanical; and, rather than inviting an erotic gaze, it challenged its viewers to
order and assemble it into representational meaning. Memorably dubbed
'an explosion in a shingle factory' and satirised by Sloan in a cartoon
showing New Yorkers entering the subway, 'The Rude Descending the
Stairs', Duchamp's painting sold for $324 (the average salary in 1915
was $687). One of the last canvasses he would ever produce, the paint-
ing both epitomised the 'Shock of the New' for the 1913 viewers, but
also prefigured the irreverent and provocative energy he would bring to
New York two years later as the figurehead of Dada.[8]

The staple place the Armory Show has in most accounts of modern
art in America is partly a testament to a fondness in art history to dwell
on moments when modernist experimentation had the affect of shock;
but it is also the key event consolidating the hegemony of modernist
style in painting and sculpture in the United States. That process of consolidation informed the objective of many American artists in the 1910s
and 1920s to develop a visual cultural nationalism – a search for what
Georgia O'Keeffe memorably called the 'Great American Thing'.[9] As
Wanda Corn attests, this first generation of American modernists
sought to discard 'older definitions that linked America to nature, wilderness, democracy, and a "new Adam"', and instead sought to render
'Americanness in an abstract, formal language drawn from . . . modern
inventions [such as skyscrapers, billboards, brand-name products,
factories and plumbing fixtures] to give their art a distinctive but not

necessarily literal American identity'.[10] Such a modernist Americanism would encompass the precisionist fascination with American industrial architecture, O'Keeffe's turn to the landscape of the Southwest, or Stuart Davis's 'tobacco pictures' of the early 1920s, which were based on the advertising and packaging of tobacco. Moreover, in time, claims for a quintessential American visual style would also embrace the commercial illustration of the 1910s – dismissed as 'kitsch' by Clement Greenberg in his influential 1939 essay 'Avant-Garde and Kitsch', which took a particular swipe at Norman Rockwell's cover art for the *Saturday Evening Post*. The first of those covers, 'Boy with a Baby Carriage', appeared in 1916 within the highly particular visual culture of the 'slick' family magazine which, along with films, were the most important *national* media of the time (the *Post* sold two million copies a week nationwide). As Carolyn Kitch observes, these magazines favoured illustration over photographs for their covers because, for middle-class readers in the 1910s, 'illustrations implied ideals, whereas photographs connoted realism'.[11] Rockwell's folksy celebrations of the white, middle-class American family, the idealisation of the 'American Girl' by Howard Chandler Christy and Harrison Fisher, and J. C. Leyendecker's handsome and stylish young businessmen and college athletes formed an influential 'aesthetic of imitation', in the words of Miles Orvell – a highly distinctive visual lexicon which crystallised national aspirations of culture, leisure and consumption.[12]

The seemingly exceptionalist imperative of modernists to develop an American style, however, (an imperative which took a much greater hold in the 1920s) was born out of a unique and complex moment of international dialogue and cultural exchange. It was shaped not just by the exhibition of European artists in America, but by the enthusiasm of prominent European artists for American vernacular and mass culture in this decade, and their rapid incorporation of its formal properties into their products and performances. As Duchamp declared to Tristan Tzara, Dada was impossible in New York because 'all New York is dada, and will not tolerate a rival'.[13] Duchamp had arrived from a war-torn Europe in 1915, pre-empted slightly by his friend Francis Picabia. Taken under the wing of Walter and Louise Arensberg, hosts of one of the decade's most prominent art salons, they developed the New York incarnation of the international Dada movement that had originated in Zurich and which would blossom in Berlin and Paris. Committed to irreverence, the anarchic and the subversive (which could, and often did, veer into the nonsensical) and the humorous, Duchamp and Picabia initiated a number of influential innovations into the global art

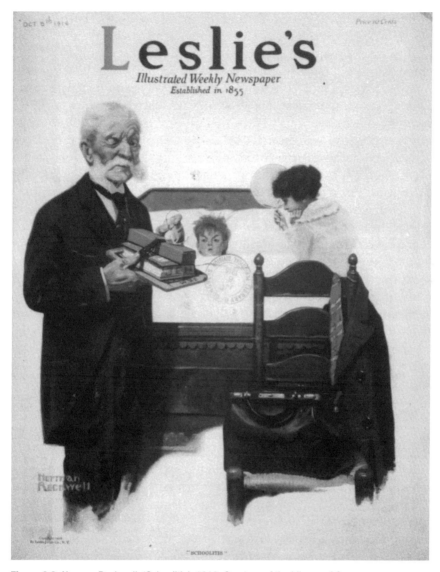

Figure 2.2 Norman Rockwell, 'Schoolitis', 1916. Courtesy of the Library of Congress, LC-USZC4-698.

scene during their time in America. Duchamp's ready-mades – which included bicycle wheels, bottle racks, shovels, a urinal and, most ambitiously, the Woolworth building – asked questions about the relation of mass production and functional design to categories of 'art', the significance of institutional context for an object's artistic valence, and the aesthetic value of excess and disruption, questions which continue

to resonate today. (Indeed, in 2004, in an adjunct to the Turner Prize
– Britain's premier annual contest for modern art – Duchamp's urinal
ready-made 'Fountain', produced in the United States in 1917, was
voted the single most important modern artwork by a panel of five
hundred art experts.)[14] He, Picabia and the Mexican artist, Marius de
Zayas, frequently mixed typeface with graphic art, often drawing upon
styles of industrial design or advertising copy. This places them at the
centre of a tradition which Yve-Alain Bois and Rosalind Krauss have
claimed as the distinctive contribution of modern art – namely what
Michael North has called 'the mutual interference of the linguistic and
the optical'.[15] (This would inspire modernist poets as well, particularly William Carlos Williams.) Their playful attitude towards gender
identity was often manifest; Duchamp would cross-dress and be photographed by Man Ray as his female alter ego 'Rrose Selavy' (a pun on
'eros – c'est la vie', which translates as 'love – that's life'), and Picabia
would entitle his industrial design drawing of a spark-plug 'portrait
d'une jeune fille Américaine dans l'état de nudité.' As Alex Goody
suggests, they must 'be seen as part of a *collective*, crucially constituted
in large part by women, who recognized and explored the productive
tensions arising from the disintegration of traditional gender norms
and identities and the explosion of cultural forms and forums'.[16]
Moreover, Picabia's use of a spark-plug to represent an American girl
was no throwaway gesture; in an interview in the *New York Tribune* in
1915 he noted that 'The machine has become more than a mere adjunct
of life. It is really a part of human life, perhaps the very soul.'[17] His
own work, as well as that of Man Ray, Duchamp, Morton Schamberg
and Baroness Elsa Freytag von Loringhoven, attempted to ascribe gendered associations to portrayals of 'the machine'. Yet this went beyond
a derogatory association between mass culture and ideas of female
identity which critics such as Andreas Huyssen have persuasively seen
as underwriting a misogynist cast to certain strands of modernism.
Instead, their investigations informed an ongoing fascination within
both the visual and the verbal avant-garde with how increasingly
mechanised modes of production, transportation and leisure would
transform the very nature of gender and sexuality.

This was just one part of the fascination with 'the machine' as
formal example, thematic concern and exhibited object which became
a preoccupation of the visual art of the 1910s. Although this was
fuelled by the French artists of New York Dada, it was taken on and
developed by an American who became a central figure in the transatlantic visual avant-garde of Dada and later surrealism, Man Ray.

Man Ray

Born in Philadelphia in 1890 as Emmanuel Radnitzki to Russian Jewish parents, by the early 1910s Man Ray was thoroughly immersed in the New York art scene. He had been greatly impressed by the Rodin sketches on display at Alfred Stieglitz's '291' gallery in 1908, by the Cézanne watercolours exhibited there in 1911, and by the Armory Show. He was also a quick learner; stylistically, his own canvasses moved from the fairly conventional techniques of the 'ashcan school' in his 'Portrait' of 1909, through his quasi-cubist portrait of Alfred Stieglitz in 1913, and on to his remarkable developments in the late 1910s. In 1915, while living in the suburban retreat of Ridgefield, New Jersey, he met Duchamp and Picabia, and became a regular visitor to the salon at the Arensberg home which became the epicentre of New York Dada. In that year he moved back to New York, to an apartment opposite Grand Central Station (which had been completed two years earlier). Work was continuing on the Lexington Avenue subway and, as he noted in his autobiography, 'the racket of concrete mixers and steam drills was constant'. Yet 'It was music to me and even a source of inspiration – I who had been thinking of turning away from nature to man-made productions.'[18]

In pursuit of this objective, and as Duchamp had done, Man Ray resolved to move away from hand-painted canvasses. Taking heed of Duchamp's notion that 'painting should not be exclusively visual or retinal, it should have to do with the grey matter, with our urge for understanding', Man Ray developed a series of collages, assemblages and airbrush paintings which posed complex questions about the institutional nature of art, and how much art could be 'cerebral' rather than concerned with craft or beauty.[19] As Andreas Huyssen has noted, the most daring challenge of the Dada avant-garde was that 'bourgeois ideology had lived off the separation of cultural from economic and industrial reality, which of course was the primary sphere of technology'. Critics of the time, such as Van Wyck Brooks, were bemoaning this very separation but – locked into notions of the essentially moral definitions of art laid down by Matthew Arnold – proffered few aesthetic solutions with much applicability to contemporary conditions. In contrast, as Huyssen notes, by reintegrating technology and the mechanical with the sphere of culture in such shamelessly amoral and iconoclastic fashion, Dadaists both 'liberated technology from its instrumental aspects and thus undermined both bourgeois notions of technology as progress and art as "natural", "autonomous", and "organic"'.[20] This challenge was mounted in a series of artworks: Man Ray produced many collages in this period, as well as assemblages and 'found objects', the last of which included photographs of an eggbeater (entitled 'L'Homme',1918), and his presentation of a clamp holding a series of wooden strips at a 45-degree angle ('New York' 1917). Perhaps most striking, however, was his self-portrait of 1916.

The 'portrait' was an assemblage consisting of a painted panel vaguely resembling a face; it featured a doorbell button in the location where a mouth would normally be, connected to two bells which serve as eyes. Man Ray's own handprint in paint serves as the only signature to the piece. As Man Ray recollected, 'everyone who pushed the button was disappointed it did not ring . . . I was called a humorist, but it was far from my intention to be funny. I simply wished the spectator to take an active part in the creation.'[21] The piece provoked many questions: why were the spectators disappointed? Was it because the machine had failed to fulfil its functional promise? And what is a functionless machine good for? How did the invitation to interaction complicate the notion of an artwork's status as self-contained, original, precious, and inviolable (a status Benjamin would famously call 'aura') – a notion which 'institution art', to use Peter Burger's term, had as one of its central tenets of the time? And how did an artwork which failed to announce the presence of a spectator function as a self-portrait? Such questions arise from a fundamental shift which Man Ray was closely involved with in what was considered art – as Joseph Kouth put it in 1969, such pieces 'changed the nature of art from a question of morphology to a question of function. This change – one from "appearance" to "conception" – was the beginning of "modern" art and the beginning of "conceptual" art.'[22]

Man Ray's triangulation of the vernacular/technological, the conceptual, and an art which was moving away from the tactility of the brush stroke, was also manifest in his development of what he came term 'aerography'. He had encountered airbrushes in his work in commercial design, where its use was commonplace; but, taking it home one day in 1917, he found it a liberating technique to use in his own art. He described it as a 'revelation', as it was 'wonderful to be able to paint a picture without touching the canvas; this was a pure cerebral activity'.[23] Not only was it cerebral rather than tactile, it embraced the mass culture and the quotidian which 'institution art' had often defined itself against. He used everyday objects, such as keys or wrenches, as stencils for some paintings, which prefigured his similar use of small everyday items in his later rayograph photography. Moreover, as well as his use of commercial and mass cultural techniques of composition such as airbrush painting, he sought out indigenous forms of popular culture to use as subject matter. 'The Rope Dancer Accompanies Herself with Her Shadows' is a highly figurative airbrush painting of a rope dancer Man Ray had seen at a vaudeville show; 'Jazz' (1919) echoed the forms of brass instruments and musical notation; and 'Admiration of the Orchestrelle for the Cinematograph' praised with a simple elegance the mechanical organs which provided the soundtrack to the films. An exile to Paris in 1921 (where he would remain for nineteen years), Man Ray absorbed more than any other American in the 1910s the transatlantic spirit of iconoclasm that was transforming almost every aspect of artistic production, display and circulation, as well as indicating key vernacular resources for the artistic search for the 'Great American Thing' that was soon to become so widespread.

Figure 2.3 Man Ray, 'Self-Portrait, Assemblage', 1916. Gelatin silver print. The J. Paul Getty Museum, Los Angeles. © Man Ray Trust/ADAGP, Paris and DACS, London 2009.

The Stieglitz Circle

That preoccupation with the American technological vernacular was not shared by everyone in the 1910s, however. On the issue of the place of 'the machine' in cultural work, artists such as Man Ray, Duchamp, Picabia, De Zayas, Charles Sheeler and Katherine Dreier were notably at odds with the other main circle of modernist and avant-garde artists in the decade, a group which coalesced around the figure of Alfred Stieglitz. Of German heritage (although born in Hoboken) and famous since the 1890s as a brilliant photographer, Stieglitz had organised some of the pioneering institutions of visual modernism in the United States: the Photo-Secession group, the journal *Camera Work*, and the '291' gallery which showcased many of America's modernist firsts. (These included pioneering exhibitions of the work of Matisse, Cézanne, Picasso, Toulouse Lautrec and Rodin's sketches – all well before the Armory Show.) Even at the time, '291' had a privileged place in modern art's self-mythology; housed in a small brownstone building just off Fifth Avenue, it was celebrated variously as a shrine, a refuge, a laboratory and what Harold Clurman called a 'place of contact', facilitating the attempts of an unapologetically metropolitan, avant-garde and elite coterie towards innovation and a quasi-spiritual pursuit of the aesthetically authentic in the visual arts.[24]

The 1910s was a decade which saw many influential art salons, a necessity for mutual exchange and support at a time when public art institutions encouraging the avant-garde were non-existent. Walter and Louise Arensberg, the Stettheimer sisters (Carrie, Florine and Ettie) and Mabel Dodge all hosted important meetings, but '291' was the only one to combine effectively the notion of a group spirit with an exhibition space. An exception to this trend was the Whitney Studio Club; founded in 1918, and later to become the Whitney Museum, it played a similar role to the '291' gallery, but for less avant-garde work. As Wanda Corn has noted, Stieglitz's circle changed dramatically through the 1910s; at the outset, he had an eclectic and international focus, supporting the work of the continental artists already mentioned, as well as that of De Zayas, Picabia, and Constantin Brancusi, together with American artists who had drawn extensively on European styles of cubism and expressionism, such as Max Weber, Abraham Walkowitz, Oscar Bluemner and Alfred Maurer (many of whom painted vivid and exhilarated cityscapes in these new formal modes, especially of New York). During the war years, Stieglitz refocused his circle to a group he named 'six + x', with the six constantly as

Arthur Dove, John Marin, Marsden Hartley, Georgia O'Keeffe, and himself and Paul Strand as photographers, and one variable member – 'x' – who might interest him at any one time. Unashamedly nativist and nationalist in rhetoric, the group 'posited the artist as outside, not inside, his own culture and envisioned art as a rarified and enlightened activity that would serve as antidote to, and therapy for, a money-driven and bourgeois society'.[25] Stressing the linked values of org-anicism, vitalism, spirit and soil in promoting an American aesthetic that could counter the degrading effects of industrial capitalism, this second circle disdained the celebration of the 'machine' and American mass culture that had so enchanted the Dadaists.

Probably the two most important painters of the Stieglitz circle were John Marin and Georgia O'Keeffe. Especially known for his work in watercolour, Marin's most significant paintings of the 1910s drew on cubist styles, and especially the work of the French artist Robert Delaunay, to present a series of watercolours of New York architecture. This was one of the privileged themes of 1910s artwork; Joseph Stella, much engaged with the Italian Futurists, would paint Brooklyn Bridge and Coney Island in the decade, and Abraham Walkowitz and Max Weber would also draw on cubist styles in particular to represent the New York skyline and the metropolitan experience. Marin presented pictures of the Brooklyn Bridge, street scenes on Fifth Avenue, the Woolworth Building and the Municipal Building in his early paintings. Yet, unlike much of the Dada response to the city – which saw it as heterogeneous, inorganic and incompat-ible with spiritual or humanist systems of understanding the world – Marin instead saw the city as a place of balance and organic harmo-nies. As he noted in an exhibition catalogue in 1913, and introducing his cityscapes:

> In life all things come under the magnetic influence of other things; the bigger assert themselves strongly, the smaller not so much, but they still assert themselves . . .While these powers are at work pushing, pulling, sideways, downwards, upwards, I can hear the sound of their strife and there is great music being played. And so I try to express graphically what a great city is doing.[26]

He also stressed the importance of an emotional art – especially in how art would be seen and received – rather than an intellectual art; as he would remark at the end of his career, abstract art tended to say 'nothing . . . at all' as 'there are *no* relationships'.[27]

Marin's stress on spiritual and emotional affect, organic harmony, and his participation in what the critic Marcia Brennan has recently called an aesthetic of 'embodied formalism', were also all apparent in the early work of Georgia O'Keeffe. Her early work, including her extraordinary charcoals of 1915, involved a clear and simple use of semi-abstract organic and geometric form, often with a bold palette when working in oil or watercolour and with a commitment to both organic and musical definitions of harmony. Yet her representations of the natural forms of flowers, shells and plants became, from the very outset of her career, an aesthetic linked to female eroticism and sexuality; it encoded her place in the Stieglitz circle wherein her abstract paintings were presented and celebrated as 'veritable gestalts of her femininity'.[28] Especially in an era which had taken a much-diluted and popularised version of Freudianism into its cultural criticism, her work was often presented by Stieglitz, and read by critics, in highly sexualised and gendered ways – ways which were not applied to the work of male painters. O'Keeffe later adamantly rejected such readings, and critics have seen her recourse from the mid-1920s onwards to subject matter such as the austere landscapes of the American Southwest and New York architecture as partially motivated by a rejection of this masculine framing of her early work. What was obvious from the 1910s, however, was her incredibly original style, her personal situation as a pioneer in abstract art for women in the United States, and her bold challenge, both in terms of form and subject matter, to a culture which still often saw art for women as a genteel and conservative occupation.

Photography in the 1910s

Of course, Alfred Stieglitz was not just an exhibitor, curator, fixer, publisher, polemicist, and all-round trumpet for the cause of modernism in the visual arts. He was also a photographer, and probably the most important figure in America for establishing photography as a fine art. This was no easy task: it was a common assumption in the era that the photograph was purely mimetic, essentially a chemical process of perfect reproduction. As the conservative critic Thomas Craven remarked in *The Nation* in 1924, photographers were deluded if they believed that photography – 'largely a matter of chemistry and mechanics' – was as 'intense and exciting as the canvases of imaginative painters whose forms are not the result of simple impressions but the product of knowledge, reflection, and a genius for construction'.[29]

This perception was widespread even in the artistic avant-garde; consequently, photographs were often believed to be exempt from the creative powers of subjective genius that produced brilliance in other more established visual media.

Not only that, but the boundaries of 'art' photography jostled for space alongside photography's growing use in other contexts. These included political and social reportage, as best exemplified in the work of Lewis Hine; advertising and commercial photography; photo-engraving in new technologies of printing; in newspapers and magazines; in medicine; and in aerial reconnaissance in the war. Good-quality half-tone reproductions of photographs had been available in printed media since the 1890s, a technology which allowed photographs and print to appear on the same page. Photographs had been pioneered in the American daily press by William Randolph Hearst's papers in the 1900s; they increased in prevalence throughout the 1910s. Advertising was slower to catch up; in the early 1920s fewer than 15 per cent of illustrated advertisements utilised photographs, but by 1930 that figure was close to 80 per cent.[30] Camera ownership and private photography increased throughout the decade, boosted by the continuing popularity of advertising figures such as the 'Kodak girl', resplendent in a stripy dress and ready with a box Brownie. Such figures testified to the increasing stress by big manufacturers such as Kodak on the importance of photographs for consolidating a sense of domestic memory – and therefore conditioning the modern experience of memory itself. As they warned in a famous slogan of the era, 'the snapshot you want tomorrow you must take today.' That sentiment struck a chord with American women, and the snapshot became an ever more important product in the fashioning of family narratives. Of course, photography is always a technology of absence, used to recall people distanced by time, space or both; and one poignant fact about the decade's camera sales was their boom during the war years.[31]

This wide array of photographic utility (and aesthetics) presented a problem for figures like Stieglitz, keen as they were to provide a workable definition of the art photograph. He had began in the decade by organising the International Exhibition of Pictorial Photography in Buffalo's Albright Gallery in 1910, a major retrospective which was by that point the largest, best reviewed and most widely seen exhibition of art photography in the United States. Featuring photographs by some of the leading American practitioners of the style known as pictorialism, including Clarence White, Gertrude Käsebier, and

Edward Steichen, the exhibition led to the first major art gallery in
the United States acquiring a substantial quantity of photography
for its permanent collection. This exhibition also marked the end
of Stieglitz's association with pictorialism, however, and with the
Photo-Secession group which had done much to define American
photography in the previous decade. Instead, as the 1910s progressed
Stieglitz and his immediate followers in what became known as
American formalism would come to favour a 'straight' photography,
an always rather vague aesthetic which seemed clearest when placed
against what it was not. Principally, what it was not was either a
painting or an advertisement. Stieglitz – like many of his friends such
as Sherwood Anderson, Paul Strand and Paul Rosenfeld – struck the
posture of the artist as heroically aloof from commercialism, mass
society and industrialism. As Paul Rosenfeld eulogised in one of
the first important estimations of Stieglitz's work, 'The machine has
turned men mechanical. It has forced them to forego experiment and
the search for finer products for the sake of repeating incessantly the
few gestures demanded of them by the arms of steel,' and Stieglitz's
great contribution was that 'He has made his machine a portion of
the living, changing, growing body; and the act of photography an
experience.'[32] The best photography (as exemplified by Stieglitz's
work), argued Rosenfeld, was organic, unconnected with the aesthetics of mass reproduction, and heroically individual. Moreover, it was
faithful to its own medium; pictorial photographers, he felt, were
'betraying the machine'.[33]

    Stieglitz's refutation of pictorialism, the aesthetic he had champi-
oned a decade earlier, was in essence a move away from trying to make
photographs resemble sentimental Victorian paintings. He urged a
rejection of the soft-focus, diffused lighting, sentimental content,
soft-paper printing, and silver or golden toning that had dominated
pictorial art photography in America in the previous decade, and
decried working on the negative with retouching pencils or etching
knife. Instead, he increasingly emphasised the importance of what
was formally unique in photography – its ability for a level of detail,
focus, gradation of tone and immediacy that painting could never
accomplish – as a way of establishing photography's artistic legitimacy. Although these qualities would be very evident in Stieglitz's
own work from the late 1910s onward, its most powerful early incarnation was in Paul Strand's work of 1916 and 1917.

Paul Strand's *Camera Work* Photographs

Strand had come to photography through the Ethical Culture School in 1907, under the tutelage of Lewis Hine. After visiting Stieglitz's '291' gallery with Hine in 1907, he became engrossed with Stieglitz's approach to photography, and their close association began in late 1914 to early 1915. In 1916 Strand showed Stieglitz a collection of prints which so impressed the older photographer that he provided Strand with a one-man show at his '291' gallery, and printed six of his photographs in the October 1916 issue of his magazine *Camera Work*. The final edition of the magazine, in June 1917, carried eleven Strand photographs. From the beginning, these images were heralded as a new direction in straight photography; Stieglitz chose not to reproduce them on the Japan tissue customary for photographs in *Camera Work*, as a way of emphasising their 'brutal directness'.[34] Strand pushed home the point by advancing the formalist argument for photography in 1917, asserting that photography possessed an 'absolute unqualified objectivity' capable of rendering a 'range of almost infinite tonal values which lies beyond the skill of human hand', an objectivity which was at once 'the very essence of photography, its contribution and at the same time its limitation'.[35]

Although Strand's work in 1916 and 1917 did not always follow through rigorously on these precepts, nonetheless it demonstrated a formal and thematic originality which befitted the final issues of Stieglitz's influential magazine. With some exceptions, the photographs fell into three groupings.[36] The first were street scenes of Manhattan taken from raised angles, gained by way of viaducts, overpasses in Central Park, gallery rooms overlooking Fifth Avenue and, most strikingly, the steps of the Federal Hall looking down on to the Morgan Guaranty Trust Building on Wall Street. The second was a series of abstract photographs, taken at a holiday cottage in Twin Lakes, Connecticut, of domestic objects such as chairs, crockery and fruit, and also of the shadows on the porch of the cottage. The final group was a series of portraits of New Yorkers in poor districts of the city, taken using a fake lens which allowed Strand to get very close to his subjects without them knowing they were being photographed.

Of the first group (the style of which often recollected that of the pictorialist Alvin Langdon Coburn, then also making innovative raised-angle photographs of New York), the most striking was Strand's photograph of Wall Street. Using massive blocks of tone to present the foreboding building in the background, and a low shutter speed slightly to blur the human figures in the foreground as they walk into the low, flat early-morning light of the rush hour, Strand presented a powerful statement about the fragile and ephemeral status of the individual in a modern America dominated by the megalithic institutions of international capital. Such a photograph resonated with the project of the 'Young American' critics and artists, which included Stieglitz, to critique what they saw as the growing erasure of individualism and 'spirit' in a world of mass production, corporate employment and crass materialism. Yet, if the bold slabs of tone and reductions of human figures to little more than blurry automatons pushed this photograph away from the purely representational, that move was established much more completely in his work at Twin Lakes. Often credited as the first abstract photographs, Strand utilised rotated camera angles, close framing and radical cropping to defamiliarise the most commonplace of domestic objects. In doing so, he began investigations into how to present a photographic art that balanced spaces, volumes and tonal relationships into a formal coherence without concern over representational fidelity to the objects depicted. Such an art was heavily influenced by Strand's interest in painters such as Pablo Picasso, Georges Braque, Henri Matisse and Fernand Léger, whose paintings had done much to disrupt the renderings of space, depth and point of view away from notions of classical perspective. As Strand himself remarked, these photographic 'experiments' gave him an understanding of 'what the principle was behind Picasso and all the others in their organization of the picture space, of the unity of what that organisation contained, and the problem of making a two-dimensional area have a three-dimensional character'.[37]

His final group of photographs revisited the terrain of perhaps the most celebrated of New York social photographers, the area of Five Points which had been made (in)famous by Jacob Riis in the 1880s. Strand adapted his camera to have a fake lens on the side, which he pretended was the real lens – with the intention of photographing people at right angles to him without their knowledge. Strand's photos captured the ethnic diversity of the Lower East Side, which had long been the focus of reformist Progressives as well as nativists keen to impose immigration restrictions. Yet, rather than the aesthetic which had so often been used to represent the immigrant working class in social photography – the tendency to see individuals as 'types' who embodied broader categories of identity, a tendency that transformed people into a visual index of social problems – Strand's photographs had more of a fidelity to the uniqueness of personal experience. Without abandoning the social engagement he had learnt from Lewis Hine, his 'candid' photographs portrayed New York's poor at moments of emotional intensity, suffering and powerful interiority in ways that had rarely been achieved before. This ability to present subjects as both firmly located in their social identity and yet possessed of a rich interior life would inspire a later generation of social photographers; Walker Evans would later recall finding Strand's 'Blind' 'strong and real . . . And a little bit shocking – brutal . . . I thought to photograph [in the manner of 'Blind'] was the thing to do.'[38]

This element of Strand's photography was clearly indebted to the work in social photography of his early mentor, Lewis Hine, who (as discussed in the Introduction) was involved throughout the 1910s with compiling a powerful series of photographs for the National Child Labor Committee to support its campaign for reform of the

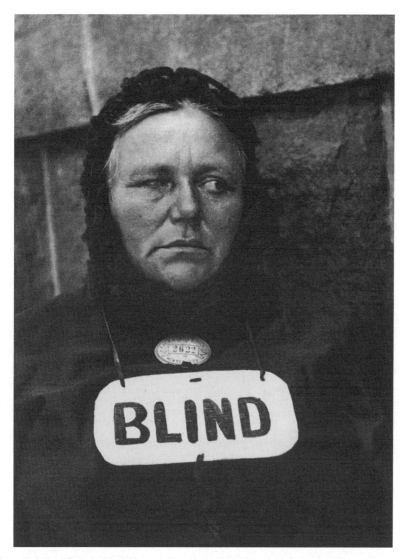

Figure 2.4 Paul Strand: 'Blind Woman', New York, 1916. Copyright © Aperture Foundation, Inc., Paul Strand Archive. Photograph courtesy of Science and Society Picture Library.

child labour laws. Moreover, the tension in Strand's work between the explicit sociopolitical engagement of his Five Points photographs and the more politically remote work of his abstract compositions suggested the dichotomy that would orient much of the next thirty years of American photography, and it is Hine and Stieglitz that sit at the opposite ends of this polarity. Stieglitz's uninterest in politics was both legendary and provocative; in the late 1910s, Edward Steichen

would characterise his brand of modernism as little more than narcissistic self-absorption, a navel gazing carried on while the Great War,
a 'psychological element of universal consequence' that had served
to 'grip humanity at its very entrails', was engulfing the attention
of more socially concerned artists. This prefigured similar criticism
of Stieglitz during the Great Depression by younger photographers
who were keener than he to record and interpret the economic hardships of the 1930s.[39] Moreover, Stieglitz's singular importance in the
world of exhibiting photography and establishing its institutional
parameters in the world of fine art meant that, in the words of Alan
Trachtenberg, his role in establishing 'an institutionalized community
capable of conferring prestige on photographers' served to cordon off
a more socially engaged photography into the rather limiting category
of 'documentary' photography. As Trachtenberg observes, Stieglitz's
'success' by the early 1930s was to have established 'a hegemony in the
photographic community of a division between "art" and "documentary" photography, and the validation of museum exhibition as the
supreme mode of conferring value (marketplace as well as aesthetic)
on photographs'.[40] Hine's critical neglect until the 1930s was one
repercussion of this; but so, of course, was the increasing tendency for
photographs to be seen as 'high' art.

    That tendency would be bolstered in the 1910s not just by the pio-
neering work of Strand and Stieglitz but by another of what Stieglitz
dubbed the 'trinity of photography' in 1918, the others being Morton
Schamberg and Charles Sheeler. Sheeler was one of the few painters of
the era equally proficient in photography, and accounts of his career
often note how his photographic aesthetic of sharp focus, full-frontal
framing, penchant for regular, geometric shapes, and exquisite detail
would also inform his participation in the art movement known as
precisionism. He had exhibited his paintings at the Armory Show,
but his first major photographic work was produced between 1915
and 1917. This was a series of photographs of farm buildings in Bucks
County, Philadelphia, and also the eighteenth-century farmhouse in
Doylestown which he rented with his friend Schamberg. Steichen
would remark that Sheeler 'was objective before the rest of us were',
and the exteriors (of barns in particular) of his Bucks County photography often demonstrated a sharpness and a flat perspective which
represented the functional purity of the rural Pennsylvania architecture with a simplicity and directness unrivalled at the time (and which
drew on Sheeler's earlier work in commercial architectural photography).[41] As he remarked, 'I would arrive at the picture . . . through

form that is architectural, whether the subject was buildings or flowers.'[42] Such flatly rendered celebrations of American vernacular architecture would be picked up and expanded in the 1930s by several of the photographers working for the Farm Security Administration, and Sheeler himself went on to produce other series of photographs of architecture, similarly notable for their sharp detail and exquisite rendering of formal and functional purity – the most striking of which was, arguably, his 1927 collection of photographs of the Ford plant at River Rouge. This visual economy stood in contrast to the penchant for symbolism in some of Strand's work of the time, and Sheeler himself later characterised his own work as completely disinterested in symbolism. Like Strand, however, he was engaged by the developments of cubism in painting, and his interiors of the Doylestown farmhouse series, with their sharp contrasts of large forms of tone, disorienting rendition of familiar domestic scenes, and chiaroscuro artificial lighting, went to show – in the words of Marius de Zayas – that 'cubism exists in nature and . . . photography can record it'.[43]

Photography beyond the Museum

Sheeler had cut his teeth on these styles for representing architectural exteriors in his photographic work for architectural magazines in the early 1910s, and such labour was not unusual for modernist American photographers. Indeed, of all those who would later form the canon of American modernism, it was only Stieglitz, independently wealthy through both birth and marriage, who had the ability to detach himself completely from the business of commercial photography. During the 1910s, several of the most influential photographers of the era did commercial work: a young Edward Weston was producing pictorialist-style portraits in his studios in Tropico, California; Strand produced hand-tinted photographs of universities for sale to students; and Karl Struss produced advertising photographs. Important in this sphere of photographic activity was Clarence H. White, himself a pictorialist photographer of note who had been a member of the Photo-Secession with Stieglitz, and who opened his own school of photography in 1914. White's success over the next decades in teaching the craft of photography can be seen in the roll call of his students: pupils included such luminaries as Paul Outerbridge, Margaret Bourke-White, Dorothea Lange, Karl Struss, and Doris Ulmann; and Max Weber led classes at the school to emphasise what he called 'the first authentic, geometric approach to the basic construction of photographs as art'.[44] White's class exercises in encouraging innovative approaches to composition and the photography of everyday and mundane objects became legendary, and undergirded much of the strikingly original views of commonplace domestic commodities that characterised the advertising photography boom of the 1920s. Catholic in its stylistic approach, White's school was the opposite of Stieglitz's high-handed and prescriptive approach to his apprentices, and consequently was a very diverse and successful force in training the next generation of American photographers.

The decade also saw the beginnings in commercial photography of one of America's best-loved studio photographers, James VanDerZee. An African American from the small town of Lenox, Massachusetts, VanDerZee opened his first studio in Harlem in 1917 as the selective service draft increased demand for studio photographs of departing loved ones, or shots of family and sweethearts at home. At this point in American history, images of black Americans in visual culture tended to gross caricature and distortion. The iconography of the minstrel stage, or Social Darwinistic hierarchies which saw some races as more advanced than others, still dominated the portrayal of African Americans in film, advertising, illustration and news photography. Against this background, VanDerZee produced studio portraits that showed his clients as elegant, beautiful, sophisticated and, above all, modern inhabitants of the Harlem community which Alain Locke would later call the 'Mecca of the New Negro'. VanDerZee was alive to the new poses to be found in fashion magazines and promotional film posters; he had a wardrobe of fashionable clothes at his studio; and he would carefully retouch his negatives to 'take out the unbeautiful ness' in the faces of his sitters.[45] His would come to be a visual art that perfectly exemplified the spirit of optimism, enthusiastic modernisation and upward social mobility that attended the early years of the Great Migration of African Americans from rural South to urban North.

The other major archive of ethnic minority photographs with a stake in the 1910s, and one which moved well beyond the hallowed circle of New York which circumscribed much of the decade's visual production and ambition, had a very different set of politics in attendance. Six volumes of Edward S. Curtis's encyclopedia, *The North American Indian*, appeared in the 1910s; his project would eventually encompass twenty volumes (produced between 1907 and 1930) and include 2,200 photogravures of indigenous tribes from across the North American continent. Curtis, a white ethnographer and photographer from Wisconsin, took as his major life's work the attempt to record as much about North American Native tribal customs, history, religion and social organisation as possible. He saw this work as invested with an especial urgency given the increasing pressure on Native American traditions from local white populations, and in the light of a government policy which, between the 1880s and 1930s, attempted to assimilate Native Americans to Euro-American patterns of land ownership, family structure and cultural practice. His work involved the taking of approximately forty thousand negatives, 125 cross-country trips, studies of eighty tribes and seventy-five languages and dialects, the recording of more than ten thousand native songs, a team of up to seventeen assistants at any one time, and a cost in excess of half a million dollars. His images were exquisitely executed in pictorialist style, and printed on the finest available papers; they move from frame-filling shots of the faces of tribal elders to full-length pictures of traditional tribal dress, or depictions of religious customs.

Curtis's dedication to his task, and anger at the ravages which Euro-American expansion and culture had enacted on indigenous peoples, is palpable throughout the project. Yet his willingness to erase signs of cultural contact – touching out mass-manufactured objects from photos, or photographing dances staged purely for his benefit, for example – has led to critiques of him seeking to preserve Native American culture as a romanticised, ossified relic rather than as a dynamic entity.[46] Moreover, $400,000 of his funding came from the House of Morgan, a company whose railway expansion in the nineteenth century had done much to decimate the lives of the plains tribes. His work is perhaps the most engrossing, politically multifaceted, and complex engagement of a white artist-ethnographer with Native Americans in the first part of the century, inspiring questions about the relation of art to documentation, the play of power and interpretation between sitter and subject that the medium of photography involves, especially across barriers of race, and the implications of pursuing an ethnographic 'salvage' of cultures perceived to be dying out. These questions are epitomised in one of his most (in) famous photographs, 'The Vanishing Race' (1907), which showed a pictorially rendered single file of Navajos riding towards a dimming sunset and the looming black mass of a mountain; Curtis explained that 'the thought which this picture is meant to convey is that the Indians as a race, already shorn of their tribal strength and stripped of their primitive dress, are passing into the darkness of an unknown future'.[47] Such an approach helped reinforce the problematic notion of

Native American life as an exquisite (and static) aesthetic object under threat of imminent demise, a demise which art and ethnography could in some ways prevent through their own privileged forms of capture.

The reputations of VanDerZee and Curtis did not really become established until the 1970s, in the moment when interest in photography and its artistic significance underwent a great revaluation (Curtis's seventy-six word obituary in the *New York Times* in 1952 closed with the statement – almost as an afterthought – that Curtis, an 'Internationally known authority on the history of the North American Indian', was 'also widely known as a photographer'.)[48] VanDerZee was evicted at the age of eighty-two from his home in Harlem the day after the 'Harlem on my Mind' exhibition at the Metropolitan Museum closed in 1969, the event which initiated the rise in his critical fortunes. That it took so long to accord them a place in the annals of American photography is partially a testament to the success of Stieglitz's project to distinguish between the artistic and the utilitarian and/or commercial in defining photography.

Stieglitz himself had not undertaken much photographic work of his own in the early 1910s, too preoccupied with the editorship of *Camera Work* and the role of exhibitor at '291'. Yet, with the end of both *Camera Work* and the '291' gallery at the time of United States's entry into World War I, Stieglitz took up the camera again for what would be an inspired decade and a half of producing images that would figure largely in canons of modernist photography. In particular, Stieglitz pursued the lead Sheeler had established in creating a photographic series; of note in the 1920s and 1930s were his sequences 'Equivalents' (originally titled 'Songs of the Sky') – a series of photographs of clouds – and photographs of the New York skyline taken from his window at the Shelton Hotel. But his longest-running and most compelling series was the portrait sequence he undertook of his fellow artist, lover and later his wife, Georgia O'Keeffe.

Alfred Stieglitz's Portrait Sequence of Georgia O'Keeffe

Stieglitz and O'Keeffe first met in 1908, but it was not until 1916 that their relationship really began. On New Year's Day Stieglitz had seen a set of O'Keeffe's charcoal drawings, brought in to '291' by her friend, Ann Politzer; Politzer later recollected (and romanticised) his ecstatic reaction as the exclamation: 'finally, a woman on paper!'[49] Stieglitz's effusive response attests to O'Keeffe's discovery of her own distinctive style in 1915, a strikingly original combination of interlocking organic form, a bold and often reduced palette and simple and semi-abstract figuration. Moreover, it also attests to his positioning of her art as the embodiment of the female – and the sexual – principle in his coterie of artists which developed after World War I. Her charcoals evinced a tendency towards semi-abstraction and boldly rendered organic shapes which produced a spare visual language of eroticism, violence and fecundity – all features which would figure large in her style and reception in subsequent years (a reception she would often bitterly contest). On seeing these works, Stieglitz – with his customary imperiousness – took the liberty of exhibiting them without her permission. In 1917 hers was the last exhibition ever to appear at '291', an event which was also her first one-woman show. She herself missed it, but he re-hung the pictures just for her on her return to New York, and it was then that he took his first photographs of her. As he would do with many of his male compatriots, Stieglitz saw the taking of a portrait as a way of forging a personal and artistic bond – but no other bond in his life, photographic or otherwise, compared to this.

The photographic project continued, in fits and starts, for another twenty years, until the ageing Stieglitz (he was fifty-two in 1916, compared to the twenty-eight-year-old O'Keeffe) could no longer hold steady his camera. In that time, he made five hundred prints of her, of which two hundred dated from their first two years together. In the words of their biographer, Benita Eisler, these photographs made between 1917 and 1919 'document the most intense, passionate, and complex transaction between a man and a woman ever recorded by a camera'.[50] The photographs are both a testament to, and an integral part of, Stieglitz and O'Keeffe's developing relationship as lovers, artists and collaborators; they document, instigate and investigate. They include every aspect of O'Keeffe's body, some so explicit that they have never been exhibited. They abstract with a visual aesthetic of the fetish – cropping hands, feet, torso and genitalia so that the part is charged with an erotic energy through substituting for the whole. They range from the most intimate of photographs, some with the lens so close that the pores of O'Keeffe's skin form the tactile tonalities of the surface, to O'Keeffe seeming distanced, aloof, and encased in heavy black overcoats and hats. They feature her in front of her own work, framed as if her body has blended with the dark, swirling and evocative forms of her painting. They demonstrate a strikingly new and complex choreography of the pose, with O'Keeffe positioning herself in the bodily articulations of abjection, power, control, anguish, desire, submission and, above all, ambiguity. Moreover, they are a record of self-reflection; O'Keeffe would remark later that the portrait was Stieglitz 'always photographing himself'.[51] The range of photographs and the totality of the project engage with the most complex of sexual politics: is this a record of domination, selfish pleasure and objectification – or mutual fantasy, collaboration and exploration? Moreover, it asked questions about the boundaries and pluralities of selfhood, questions at the centre of new notions of Freudian psychoanalysis and of much modernist thinking about subjectivity.

Many photos from the so-called 'composite portrait' were exhibited in 1921, when it caused a sensation. The portrait was divided into six categories – twenty-seven images entitled 'A Woman', eight images of 'Hands', three entitled 'Feet', three images of 'Hands and Breasts', three of 'Torsos', and two images entitled 'Interpretations'.[52] Reviewers were keen to see Stieglitz in the manner which he desired – as a seer of the American *genius loci*, an heroic figure 'whose hope beats against the slagheap of an age of steel and fear and exploitation', in the words of early reviewer (and Stieglitz acolyte) Herbert J. Seligmann. Such reactions were marshalled by Stieglitz's own terse autobiographical statement in the catalogue: 'I was born in Hoboken. I am an American. Photography is my passion. The search for truth my obsession.'[53] Yet even these early reactions held an awareness of the misogyny which resided among the aesthetic radicalism on display, and its powerful expression of love and passion. If the show was full of 'the fear which human beings have of themselves lest those selves be made known to others', this was inextricable from a fear of femininity – for, as Seligmann remarked, 'Do not Americans fear women as they fear the plague?'[54]

Such comments prefigure much of the recent interest in modernist politics of gender and sexuality. Critics such as Roberta McGrath and Susan Sontag see the modernist portrait photography of figures like Stieglitz and Edward Weston as fundamentally about masking the conditions of its own production; both criticise these figures for representing their photographs as the heroic labour of a singular individual and suppressing connections to contemporary ideological and material contexts.[55] McGrath goes further in seeing the photographic portraiture of women in American modernism as embedded in the visual strategies of voyeurism and fetishism – strategies designed to control the threatening potential (to men at least) of the female body and female sexuality. Other critics have seen the portrait as the clearest possible example of the way Stieglitz attempted to set an interpretative context for O'Keeffe's work which focused almost exclusively on her sexuality. In contrast, critics such as Susan Fillin-Yeh have celebrated Stieglitz's portraits of O'Keeffe, seeing them as 'more than simply portraits; they are agents in the construction of new artistic, cultural and sexual meanings, even of personal narrative'. Describing the photos of O'Keeffe dressed in masculine clothing as exemplary of her assumption of the pose of the dandy, a 'modernist icon/pose/mode', Fillin-Yeh celebrates her embrace of androgynous dandyism as a part of her own artistic self-creation and sexual liberation, a process facilitated, rather than constrained, by Stieglitz's camera work.[56] Critics are therefore divided on the politics of the portrait, and more broadly on the implications of what Sontag calls an ideology of the 'heroism of vision' that the American formalist photographers often subscribed to, and which Stieglitz did so much to shape. Yet few would argue that the portrait's new articulation of intimacy, not to mention its ambition, scope and technical audacity (especially its use of the crop), would be greatly influential for subsequent photographic portraiture.[57]

Figure 2.5 Alfred Stieglitz, Portrait of Georgia O'Keeffe, 1918. Gelatin silver print. Alfred Stieglitz Collection, 1949.742, The Art Institute of Chicago. Photography © The Art Institute of Chicago. © ARS, NY and DACS, London 2009.

Conclusion

The 1910s, therefore, was a decade which saw European modernism decisively setting the patterns of future development in American visual culture, even if, by the end of the decade, a new spirit of isola-tionism was informing influential practitioners. It was an art indelibly linked to social contexts in its various responses to a growing mecha-nisation of production, and especially to the increasingly distinctive forms of American urban architecture. Moreover, avant-garde artists were not sealed off from mass consumption of images; most artists and photographers also worked commercially as well as producing pieces for small-scale exhibition and elite consumption. Photography entered its phase of modernist experimentation, and abstraction entered the lexicon of visual art in several media. An extraordinarily diverse decade, by its close the United States had lost much of its parochialism in art matters, and had invented most of the visual styles which would dominate the next fifteen years.

Chapter 3

Fiction and Poetry

The prose fiction of the 1910s is often overlooked in accounts of American literary history, a myopia somewhat unfair to texts whose frequent awkwardness is often the mark of a moment of representational transition. It was a decade which saw older modes such as local colour, realism and naturalism extended, modified and critiqued, while newer styles of linguistic and formal experimentation developed to suggest innovative perceptions of ontology and interior experience. Preoccupied above all with the incredible rate of social change in the previous forty years – in ways as diverse as the rapid growth of urban centres and urban technology, the speed and the incline of social mobility, enormous changes in cultures of print and media, the rise of a new bureaucratic tier of employment in corporate America, mass immigration, the quantity and power of capital agglomeration and new social conditions for women – authors struggled to generate forms capable of dealing with this capital, temporal and demographic expanse. As Theodore Dreiser complained, in a manner which demonstrates the strains such a topic could put on a sentence (and a novel):

> The tremendous and complicated development of our material civilization, the multiplicity and variety of our social forms, the depth, subtlety and sophistry of our mental cogitations, gathered, remultiplied and phantasmagorically disseminated as they are by these other agencies – the railroad, the express and post-office, the telegraph, telephone, the newspaper and, in short, the whole art of printing and distributing – have so combined as to produce what may be termed a kaleidoscopic glitter, a dazzling and confusing showpiece which is more apt to weary and undo than to enlighten and strengthen the inquiring mind.[1]

Naturalist Fiction

Believing that 'we live in an age in which the impact of materialized forces is well-nigh irresistible', Dreiser was the leading proponent of naturalist fiction in the decade, a mode which proposed that these new material conditions of modernity were all but overwhelming.[2] His first novel of the decade, *Jennie Gerhardt* (1911), returned to *Sister Carrie*'s (1901) fictionalisation of the life of one of his sisters, and again referenced the popular genre of the 'working girl' novel: yet, unlike them, it touched on cross-class sexual liaison not as a mechanism for upward social mobility and ultimate respectability but as a way of exploring taboo subjects such as pre-marital sex, non-marital childbirth and contraception. His new publisher, Harper and Brothers, eventually insisted on cuts of 16,000 words, excising the most provocative moments of Dreiser's sexual candour and critiques of religion; he ran into trouble again later in the decade as the New York Society for the Suppression of Vice sought to suppress his novel *The Genius*.

Jennie Gerhardt was followed by his 'trilogy of desire', three novels dealing with the business oligarch Frank Cowperwood: *The Financier* (1912), *The Titan* (1914) and *The Stoic* (1947). Based on the career of Charles T. Yerkes who, after business failure in Philadelphia, went on to hold a controlling interest in Chicago's streetcar and 'L' operations, the novels exemplify the decade's literary fascination with social mobility. Indeed, Mencken, Dreiser's great supporter in the decade, had identified this class precariousness as the characteristic feature of American life; as he noted, the American was 'never absolutely safe and never absolutely contented. Such a thing as a secure position is practically unknown among us.'[3] The figure of the socially ascendant businessman-as-hero (or anti-hero) populated several novels in the decade, often counterbalanced by the downward mobility of characters clinging to outmoded forms of social status: such novels include Sherwood Anderson's *Windy McPherson's Son* (1916, featuring an arms trade executive); Booth Tarkington's *The Magnificent Ambersons* (1918, featuring a car manufacturer); Abraham Cahan's *The Rise of David Levinsky* (1917, featuring a cloak manufacturer); Ellen Glasgow's *Virginia* (1913, featuring a cigarette manufacturer); W. E. B. Du Bois's *The Quest of the Silver Fleece* (1911, featuring a cotton trust) and Edith Wharton's *The Custom of the Country* (1913, featuring a Wall Street financier). So formulaic was this story that Sinclair Lewis's early effort, *Our Mr Wrenn* (1914), toys throughout with the narrative expectation of upward social mobility but triumphantly leaves his middlebrow, middle-managerial, boarding-house-dwelling hero resolutely on $29.50 a week at the novel's close.

Dreiser's ambivalence over Cowperwood is fairly typical of these many portrayals. He is both magnetic and terrifying, a ruthless robber baron who, by dint of his skill and audacity, is able to amass unprecedented quantities of power and capital – a man who mesmerises the general public as 'an astounding figure: his wealth fabulous, his heart iron, his intentions sinister – the acme of cruel, plotting deviltry'.[4] His characterisation expresses Dreiser's unashamed admiration for a ruthless competitor far outside the bourgeois moral codes which had underpinned much realist fiction of the previous century. (Much of his criticism of Cowperwood came far later in *The Stoic*, a period when his politics had shifted decisively to the left.) Moreover, that moral radicalism had formal as well as philosophical implications. Dreiser has long been derided for his clumsy style; Mencken called him the 'Hindenberg of the novel'.[5] Yet subsequent reassessments of naturalism have seen this clumsiness rather as a rejection of realist conventions, conventions including assigning intention to characters, a faith in moral responsibility, and a belief in the agency of an autonomous subject. According to this interpretation, rejecting the moral purview of realism produces the formal characteristics of naturalist determinism that Dreiser established most influentially on the American scene: a mix of formula and description characterised by melodramatic scenarios, prolix interruptions of the narrative for social reportage, and attraction to the so-called 'plot of decline'.[6]

It was Dreiser's grasp of social scope and the dense interconnection of economic, infrastructural and psychological systems that was recognised as his major achievement from the outset; as a contemporary critic remarked, his prose felt like a composite of 'cameras, kodaks, Baedeckers, and historians'.[7] This composite was especially vivid in Dreiser's depiction of urban environments. Informed by the social theories of Charles Darwin and Thorstein Veblen, he presented a sprawling urban canvas of sexual and financial competition frequently conducted through the mechanisms of conspicuous consumption. Indeed, Dreiser's scorn for notions of self-knowledge or individual agency, and his materialist conception of social life, mean that his most rapturous moments of prose are devoted to the material fabric of American cities rather than to its inhabitants. *The Titan*, for example, is not an eponym for Cowperwood, but for Chicago; he effuses over this 'Florence of the West', 'This singing flame of a city, this all America, this poet in chaps and buckskin, this rude, raw

Titan, this Burns of a city!'[8] This exhilaration about the urban scene was typical of the decade, particularly from those writers dealing with Chicago (which had doubled in size to two million inhabitants in just twenty years). A tone of awe, horror, excitement, pride and shock coloured writing about the 'Stormy, husky, brawling / City of the Big Shoulders', in Carl Sandburg's words, a tone intensified by the fact that many of the novelists and poets who wrote about the city had migrated there from its hinterlands in the Midwest – Sherwood Anderson, Dreiser, Floyd Dell, Edgar Lee Masters, Carl Sandburg, and Margaret Anderson among them.[9] As Margaret Anderson put it, 'I came to love Chicago as one only loves chosen – or lost – cities' and, in the middle part of the decade, it was regarded as the leading city for the literary avant-garde, the home of America's most exciting native poets and of its two most important magazines, the *Little Review* and *Poetry*.[10] As Henry May remarks, 'neither the sleepy backwaters nor the great metropolis alone provided the crucial experience [for this movement], but the shock of moving from one to the other.'[11]

Novels about the city were often structured around a series of bifurcations, including the lonely individual and the crowd, culture and commerce, proletarian and bourgeois, consumption and production, hinterland and metropolis, the home and the marketplace. Underlying many of these – as was famously opined by both George Santayana and Van Wyck Brooks – was a gendered division, one which feminised the sphere of bourgeois culture even as it dissociated that sphere from the masculine world of business. If Dreiser's women frequently accept that situation with relative passivity, this was not the case with the characters of Edith Wharton, whose *The Custom of The Country* (1913) was the decade's most arresting business novel narrated from a female perspective. It centres on Undine Spragg, a beautiful but selfish and headstrong social arriviste and serial divorcee with fierce but ill-defined ambitions for social station and pleasure. Midway through the novel, and following her marriage to a member of New York's old social elite, we are told that the domestic turmoil Undine is causing her young son and husband is the result of the marital 'custom of the country' whereby business and domestic lives are so separated that 'money and motors and clothes are simply the big bribe [women are] paid for keeping out of some man's way'.[12] Undine's immense capacity for consumption is 'a monstrously perfect result of the system: the complete proof of its triumph', and is presented as one of the few aspects of life in which she can express choice and agency – as well as in choosing (and re-choosing) her husbands.[13]

Indeed, a dual logic of consumption attends Undine: she is both the arch consumer and arch consumed, the desired object and desiring subject. This duality plays out in a complex dynamic of looking, as Undine spends much of the book looking at commodities, spectacular entertainments, and men – and as her prospective suitors gaze at her in a view we as readers are rarely permitted to share. Shunning all aspects of production – whether it be domestic labour or childbirth – Wharton suggests Undine exhibits that 'the logic of consumption and disposal being urged in contemporary advertising extends most insidiously into the home, where familial relations that transmit identity, continuity and tradition [were]. . .at risk of being "unmade"'.[14]

The novel never quite heaps the censure on divorce that frequently accompanied the rising divorce rate in the decade, however – a rate particularly high among the super-rich class of Americans that Undine has joined by the end of the book. (As Michael McGerr notes, in 1920 fewer than 1 per cent of Americans had been divorced, yet 20 per cent of the younger generation of Americans worth $20 million or more had done so).[15] Wharton had herself recently divorced, a move which provided freedom from an unhappy and untenable marriage, and had allowed her to move permanently to France. Perhaps in consequence, Wharton shows little sympathy with an old tier of New York 'society' which disdains both divorce and the rapacious methods of contemporary American business. By the novel's close, divorce has done more than anything to indicate that society's obsolescence and fragility; in the triumph of what Wharton often referred to as the 'invaders' over the 'aboriginals', Undine marries a man of 'epic effrontery' remarkably similar to Frank Cowperwood.[16] As well as striving to imitate certain customs of gender identity and marriage, then, Undine also effects their dissolution, as what Wharton calls 'the exclusive and the dowdy' make way for the 'future [that] belonged to the showy and the promiscuous' – a narrative arc she would revisit with considerably more nostalgia in *The Age of Innocence* (1920).[17]

Rural Fiction

The flip side of cities becoming the inevitable scene for narratives of social mobility and opportunity was the changing perception of rural America. As cities grew, so rural areas rapidly depopulated throughout the period; by 1910, an estimated one-third of urban inhabitants were of rural American origin. With that demographic shift came an increasing tendency to view rural areas as sites of stagnation and

backwardness: as Brian Lee and Robert Reinders note, by the 1880s, a
literature of rural degeneracy had begun to emerge which would have
been inconceivable before the Civil War, and, in the 1910s, a series of
novels emerged which presented a newly acerbic vision of rural life.[18]
Edith Wharton's rural Massachusetts novels *Ethan Frome* (1911)
and *Summer* (1917), the plays of Susan Glaspell, and also the writing
of Ellen Glasgow, particularly *Virginia* (1913), all move away from
the twin tendencies towards condescension and nostalgia that had
informed the earlier tradition of local colour, which thrived on selling
quaint stories of rural life to urban readers. Moreover, unlike the
upper middle class's careful removal of women from a world of economic productivity as outlined in *Jennie Gerhardt* and *The Custom
of the Country*, these fictions show the absolute indispensability of
female domestic labour for the rural economy – and the rigours that
labour involves. In Glasgow's *Virginia*, the eponymous heroine is a
quintessential southern belle from a small Virginia town who marries
in a haze of inflated romantic expectations, and is contented to devote
her life to her husband's and children's happiness. As we are told, at
the moment of marriage 'she thought of the daily excitement of marketing, of the perpetual romance of mending his clothes, of the glori-
fied monotony of pouring his coffee, as an adventurer on sunrise seas
might dream of the rosy islands of hidden treasure'.[19] Yet, by the close
of the novel, she has witnessed her husband desert her for a Broadway
actress, her children become involved in college educations and sexual
moralities she does not understand, and the sacrifice of her earlier
beauty in decades of domestic toil.

Unlike local colour – which frequently abstracted rural labour,
parochial mores and lack of education into a version of the picturesque – *Virginia*, *Ethan Frome* and *Summer* examined the devastating
consequences of borderline poverty, lack of opportunity and the frequently imprisoning institution of marriage on rural lives, especially
those of women. *Virginia* tackles the specifically southern dimension
of this, namely how the so-called 'myth of southern womanhood'
– an ideology much deployed at this time to cement a series of rigid
gender, racial and class hierarchies in the formerly Confederate states
– could easily lead to the emotional and intellectual starvation of the
very women it nominally sought to idolise and protect. Moreover,
all these novels contain representatives of a more modern perspective
who look on with a mixture of superciliousness, incredulity and affection towards these rural women whose lives seem so removed from an
international, urban society poised for global political and economic

dominance. Yet the fact that over 50 per cent of America's population lived in communities of less than eight thousand inhabitants until
around 1914 suggests how many lives still faced the types of problems
which Glasgow and Wharton sought to investigate. This was corrobo-
rated in a survey sent out to 55,000 rural women by the Department
of Agriculture in 1915 asking for evaluations of the quality of life
for women on farms. As the *New York Times* soberly reported, the
majority of the 2,241 respondents found life hard – with 'loneliness,
isolation, and lack of social and educational opportunities . . . dwelt on
by many writers, representing every section of the United States'.[20]

These themes also preoccupied the major novelist to emerge in
the decade, Willa Cather, whose work is seen by Judith Fetterley and
Marjorie Pryse as the culmination of a female tradition of 'regionalist'
writing – a genealogy Cather tacitly acknowledged by dedicating *O
Pioneers!* to the New England regionalist, Sarah Orne Jewett. Moving
on from a successful career in journalism and short fiction, in the
1910s Cather produced *Alexander's Bridge* (1912) followed by the
'Prairie Trilogy' of *O Pioneers!* (1913), *The Song of the Lark* (1915)
and, most lauded of all, *My Ántonia* (1918). *O Pioneers!* and *My
Ántonia* are set in Nebraska, the state Cather had moved to at the age
of nine, and celebrate in frequently epic terms the lives of immigrant
women in the first generation of European settlers who struggled to
cultivate and domesticate what she called the 'vast hardness' of the
prairie, a land typified by 'its own fierce strength, its peculiar, savage
kind of beauty, its uninterrupted mournfulness'.[21] Her work has often
been read as a celebration of American exceptionalism, a figuration
of Manifest Destiny, rugged individualism, and the winning of the
West. Certainly her fiction supports such readings, carrying a powerful sense of teleology as it celebrates the process of prairies being
turned into cornfields, wheatfields and orchards in a prose distinctive for its sensuous style, subtle characterisation and richly textured
imagery. Frequently it lingers over the traces of human endeavour on
the land, a figurative textuality which brings the wilderness into the
realms of human understanding and order. Her novels' focus on different ethnic groups in the Midwest – Swedes, Austrians, Norwegians
and Bohemians – has also been lauded as a tribute to the enduring
exceptionalist narrative of America as a land of multi-ethnic opportunity, melting ambitious immigrants from Europe into a new and
prosperous people.

For many recent critics, however, the power of Cather's writing lies
in how it explores the complexity and the ideological work of these

ideas in ways that exist in fascinating tension with the often sonorous
and nostalgic appeal of her style. She has lately been discussed as a
writer thoroughly engaged with Progressive politics, with America's
tortured national policy on immigration and foreign relations in the
decade, with transnational views of America in the world, and with
an exploration of lesbian sexuality.[22] Such complexity and contrari-
ness certainly reside in *My Ántonia*, which Cather claimed showed
'the other side of the rug, the pattern that is not supposed to count in a
story. In it there is no love affair, no courtship, no marriage, no broken
heart, no struggle for success.'[23] This applied to national as much as to
personal narratives; just as conventional marriage endings are notably
played down, so any straightforward celebration of national progress
is disturbed by the novel's structure. It is framed as the nostalgic
memoir of Jim Burden, a boy raised on the prairie in a farm next to the
Bohemian Shimerda family. His lifelong friendship with, and uncon-
summated love for, their eldest daughter Ántonia is lyrically related
in his memoir, which mixes numerous sections of oral narration from
their neighbours and relatives with a self-conscious attempt to emulate
Virgil's Georgics, and 'be the first, if I live, to bring the Muse into
my country'.[24] Yet Jim now works as a salaried lawyer in New York,
investing capital in entrepreneurial schemes in the West. This was
exactly the kind of bureaucratic and corporate work that was replacing
small businesses nationwide, including family farms, as well as dissolv-
ing traditional cultural forms such as oral storytelling. Jim's actions,
therefore, are eroding the very representational, agrarian and economic
forms he rhapsodises over so nostalgically – an erosion Cather would
return to ever more frequently in her fiction of the 1920s. Moreover,
feminist critics have long been disturbed by Jim's narration of Ántonia,
noting his admission of both possession and partiality in the pronoun
'my'. What women can own, and what women can own to, is a theme
that links *O Pioneers!* and *My Ántonia*, and has been much explored
by critics seeking to place Cather in a tradition of lesbian writers – who
'have contended that Jim is an autobiographical mask for the confusing
attractions Cather felt toward the pioneer women of her own Nebraska
youth, or that both characters are homosexuals whose friendship is
built out of their mutual experience of sexual deviance'.[25]

Popular Novels

Tellingly, Jim Burden is reading a 'life of Jesse James' as he takes the
train, aged ten, to begin his new life in Nebraska; and he remembers

it as 'one of the most satisfactory books I have ever read'.[26] Jim's love of dime novels – which in the 1880s regularly covered the activities of notorious criminals in the West – illustrates Cather's keen awareness that the West would forever now be encountered primarily as a literary conceit. By the 1910s, fifty years after the first dime novels had appeared, it was a conceit with well-established and highly formulaic narrative structures centring on nostalgia, masculine formation and boyhood, regenerative violence, captivity-and-rescue plotlines and battles between savagery and civilisation. Moreover, it was a notably American genre among the decade's best-selling fiction, much of which continued to come from Britain (long-forgotten British romance novelists such as Florence Barclay, Jeffrey Farnol, Ethel Dell – as well as the more familiar H. G. Wells and May Sinclair – enjoyed huge American sales).

The western's place as a key part of America's cultural industry was reinforced in these years, as the genre became a staple of Hollywood fare; this was also the time when pulp magazines began to replace dime novels as the most popular format for mass-market fiction. Partly, this was because dime novel publishers found it ever harder to convince the Postmaster General that these novels qualified as magazines, and thus were eligible for second-class postage. Yet it was also due to the success of pulp magazines that began to specialise according to genre. The leading publisher of dime novels in the era, Street and Smith, diversified into *Detective Story* in 1915, the first detective pulp magazine; their hugely popular *Western Story*, which ran for 1,285 issues, began in 1919. As well as format – pulps often contained readers' letters, quizzes or news items – pulps differed from dime novels in their greater reliance on advertising revenue. Accordingly, they began to do more market research; one survey showed that their typical reader was 'a young, married man in a manual job who had limited resources and lived in an industrial town'.[27]

Some of the most important writers of western fiction rose to prominence in the decade, and demonstrated the growing importance in both financial and cultural terms of multimedia tie-ins and the transference of intellectual property rights. Zane Grey, who would become one of the first Americans to earn over a million dollars for his writing, had his first novel, *Heritage of the Desert*, accepted for serialisation by *Popular Magazine* and novel publication in 1910. From 1915 to 1924, one of his books was in the top-ten best-sellers list every year except one. After a decade including some of his most famous novels, such as *Riders of the Purple Sage* (1912), *The Rainbow*

Trail (1915) and *The Desert of Wheat* (1919), Grey formed Zane Grey Productions in California to produce films of his novels, but soon sold the company. Eventually Hollywood would make forty-six films of his novels. Yet even Grey's prolific output was dwarfed by other popular writers of the time; for example, Frederick Faust, who wrote under twenty pseudonyms (including Max Brand for most of his westerns) published 196 novels, 226 novelettes, 162 stories, and fourty-four poems. His personal best was twenty thousand words of fiction written in a day.

Faust also worked in Hollywood later in his career but, like Grey, he faced constant anxiety about the cultural value of his output – detesting the formulaic nature of his own writing so much that he kept none of his books in his house, and lied to his children about his occupation.[28] Such anxiety and such a prolific, formulaic output suggest the significance of the 'great divide' in the period between mass and high culture which, as Andreas Huyssen has demonstrated, played a vital part in the self-articulation of both. Other critics, however, have been interested in the 'cultural work' which such fictions accomplished, and why exactly these novels were so popular. Grey's best-selling work, *Riders of the Purple Sage*, offers some clues: it has a characteristically complex, fantastical and often bewildering plot; it has many moments of sensational violence, and hints at sexual slavery; it appeals shamelessly to fantasies of male dominance – over nature, over other men, and the sexual conquest of women. It also features a scene wherein two of the leading characters discover a 'surprise valley', an Edenic idyll of natural bounty abandoned by long-dead cliff-dwelling Native American tribes, and which is totally isolated and unknown to any of the white settlers. Ultimately, three of Grey's characters choose to remain there, in an act which seals them off from a Utah of religious conflict, theft, sexual abuse and murder. This establishes a fantasy of reversion to a state of nature quite distinct from the social life of urban, industrial, corporate America to which most of the novel's readers belonged, a fantasy which speaks directly to the widespread feelings of personal alienation and dislocation attending the speed and complexity of social, technological and demographic change in urban American life. Such fantasies of 'reversion' were common in western fiction of the time, and had been successfully exploited by Jack London in particular in the previous decade. The most enduring example, however, and the most widely disseminated through the popular culture of the next three decades, took place not in the West but in the jungle.

Edgar Rice Burroughs, *Tarzan of the Apes* (1914)

In 1914 *The Nation* sniffed that 'Only persons who like a story in which a maximum of preposterous incident is served up with a minimum of compunction can enjoy these casual pages.'[29] Yet, as it turned out, this applied to millions. First appearing as a serial in the pulp *All Story* in 1912, and as *Tarzan of the Apes* two years later, Tarzan became a minor industry over the course of the next thirty years. Burroughs's creation accounts for between thirty and sixty million book sales of this and the twenty-three sequels; there were nine silent films, the first appearing in 1918, and many subsequent ones with sound – including six Johnny Weissmuller-Maureen O'Sullivan outings in the 1930s and 1940s, and the Disney treatment in 1999. Tarzan licences were sold for comic strips, radio shows and a huge range of merchandise, including bubble gum and sweatshirts.[30] Burroughs even bought a 540-acre ranch named Tarzana in 1919 with his proceeds, which formed the basis for today's Tarzana – home to 30,000 people. A global icon, and one who taps into numerous long-standing national myths and legends of feral children and noble savages, Tarzan nonetheless mediates a host of commercial, sexual and racial issues informing the 1910s.

As Burroughs suggested, 'perhaps the fact that I lived in Chicago and yet hated cities and crowds of people made me write my first Tarzan story.'[31] He was also a failed businessman, having watched a series of small ventures collapse; he had been denied a place in Theodore Roosevelt's famous Rough Riders regiment in the Spanish–American War; and, after a childhood in middle-class comfort, he had experienced the sharp end of American social mobility. As Gail Bederman notes, 'he was, in short, precisely the sort of middle-class man who had most reason to crave potent new ways to remake ideologies of powerful manhood.'[32] He did so by yoking together a series of contradictions: a hero who is both primal and civilised, capable of murderous and wanton violence yet also capable of chivalrous restraint, the acme of racial perfection who reveals the degeneration of that very same racial stock, and a paper-thin fantasy of white male dominance whose popularity revealed the prevalent feelings of disempowerment among its many male readers.

The story begins as John Clayton, Lord Greystoke, and his wife Alice are on a diplomatic mission to West Africa. Greystoke is presented as the epitome of Anglo-Saxon racial supremacy, 'the type of Englishman that one likes best to associate with the noblest monuments of historic achievement upon a thousand victorious battlefields – a strong, virile man – mentally, morally, and physically'.[33] Abandoned in Africa by their ship's mutinous crew, they fall foul of a race of anthropoid apes, but their young son is adopted by a female ape who has just lost her own child. This ape, Kala, raises Tarzan (which means 'white skin' in the ape language) as her own. As he grows, his intelligence and skill with a knife he found at his father's cabin gives him a supremacy over the tribe of apes and the other beasts of the jungle; he also teaches himself to read from primers left in the cabin. He terrorises the nearby village of black cannibalistic Africans, and frequently kills their men by hanging them with a noose made of vines – a method replete with the overtones of lynching which the text does little to dispel. When Tarzan is twenty, the beautiful Baltimorean Jane Porter, her father, and Tarzan's cousin, Cecil Clayton, are similarly cast adrift. This sets in motion a plot which covers Tarzan's rescue of Jane from a rapacious ape, their developing love for each other, Tarzan's learning of his ancestral heritage, his travel to France and the United States and Jane's eventual marriage to Cecil.

Tarzan's plot twists through some unlikely avenues, but it invariably engages a discussion of the problems and potential of American 'civilization'. Tarzan is presented as effortlessly superior to Cecil in his ability to navigate the jungle and defend the castaways from its dangers, and his physique is lingered over in exactly the sort of ambivalent homoerotic terms which characterised the Popular Culture movement of the time, with its lavish photographic magazines of semi-naked men in bodybuilding poses. Such a representation mediates the common contemporary fear that American men were becoming 'over civilised' and effeminate, disconnected from what Theodore Roosevelt had earlier defined as the 'strenuous life' of toil, ennobling hardship and willingness to engage in righteous violence. Yet, Tarzan cannot be *too* uncivilised and still retain his heroic status. When he encounters the moral choices that undergird modern Western culture, Tarzan instinctively behaves 'correctly': he avoids eating the flesh of the black men he has killed, and he chooses not to rape Jane when he has the opportunity, in both cases because 'heredity spoke louder than training'.[34] At the close of the novel, Tarzan arrives in Wisconsin, driving a car and having learned to speak French, to save Jane from a forest fire: yet she decides to marry his cousin instead, because, as Tarzan is now an urbane Frenchman, he no longer appeals to 'the primal woman in her, as had the stalwart forest god'.[35] Once he is civilised, he loses his sexual appeal; if he remained uncivilised, a life in America would be impossible. *Tarzan* ultimately founders on how contemporary American life could effectively reintegrate this version of masculinity – a masculinity of violent self-assertion which was frequently so longed for.

This irresolution, however, was not what the public wanted. Tarzan's early readers hated the ending which saw Jane and Tarzan fail to be married, and complained loudly enough that, within months, Burroughs was plotting a sequel in which they are reunited in Africa.[36] Like other important texts of popular culture in the decade – *The Birth of a Nation*, in particular – the book is an articulation of Anglo-Saxon and male supremacy, a supremacy which Burroughs represents as justifiably global and imperial in its character and methods. In suggesting that 're-masculinization' might be difficult at home but is possible in adventures abroad, Tarzan thus plays a part in a broader cultural turn of normalising and legitimating American imperialism; it is worth noting that the United States invaded the sovereign nation of Haiti just a year after Tarzan was published, and remained there until 1934; and that, in the 1910s, US troops were still engaged in hostilities with 'rebels' in the Philippines, which had been transferred to American control in 1902.

Ethnic Minority Fiction

The nativist and Anglo-Saxon supremacist sentiments of *Tarzan* were widely shared in a decade that saw increasing agitation against America's 'open door' policy of mass immigration. Yet writers from ethnic backgrounds regularly targeted by nativists gained an increasingly palpable fictional voice in these years, mediating both the criticisms levelled at their ethnic groups in the ongoing debate over immigration and the often painful and ambivalent process of assimilating into American customs. Writers such as Abraham Cahan, Anzia Yezierska and Mary Antin wrote of the experiences of Jewish Americans, and frequently balanced an admiration for the religious, political and economic freedoms and opportunities offered by the United States with nostalgia for eastern European Jewish community life and religious piety. Cahan's *The Rise of David Levinsky*, for example, closes with his protagonist reflecting on his successful establishment of a multimillion dollar clothing business, but also his aching, unmarried loneliness and sense of spiritual vacuity. As he laments, 'my past and present do not comport well. David, the poor lad swinging over a Talmud volume at the preacher's synagogue, seems to have more in common with my inner identity than David Levinsky, the well-known cloak manufacturer.'[37] Levinsky also ends the narrative childless, just one example of the issue of generation in this group of texts – how a second generation of immigrants would, or could, relate to their parents, and the divisiveness that a younger generation's cultural assimilation into American ways could cause within the family. As one of the sons laments in Yezierska's most famous story, 'The Fat of the Land', 'the trouble with us is that the ghetto of the Middle Ages and the children of the twentieth century have to live under one roof'.[38] At the same time, such texts celebrated this assimilation, and often emphasised the economic and cultural role such second-generation immigrants were playing in the national life – rebuking nativist claims that recent migrants threatened national cohesion, or a national future frequently envisioned in eugenicist terms.

Similar themes were prevalent in the work of Sui Sin Far, acknowledged as the first writer of Asian American fiction in English. Daughter of a white Englishman and a Chinese mother, she lived in England and Canada before moving to the United States, and many of the stories in her *Mrs Spring Fragrance* (1912) are set in the Chinatowns of Seattle and San Francisco. The stories in *Mrs Spring Fragrance* refuse a consistent didactic line on assimilation; in some, marriages based on love rather than prearrangement are celebrated, as is American potential for social mobility. In others, an anxiety to adapt to American ways leads to disastrous results, and American institutional hostility to Asian immigrants comes in for sharp criticism. Sui Sin Far also based much of her fiction on women's lives, presenting the stress that immigration placed on the domestic environment in a style rooted alternately in light comedy and the melodramatic. Engaging with the prevalence of sinophobic stereotype, she was the first to sketch out in fiction situations of cultural, familial and national tension involved in the process of Chinese immigration which would be picked up by later writers such as Maxine Hong Kingston and Amy Tan.

This was also the decade in which the first stirrings of the Harlem Renaissance were felt, the efflorescence of African American writing and artistic productivity which gave much to the cultural tenor of the 1920s. This was most palpable in the 'New Negro' movement of socialist and nationalist radicalism which emerged in the ferocious political and social struggles of 1919 – a year of widespread race riots which saw the firebrand poetry of the Jamaican writer Claude McKay emerge as the most powerful voice of a new black sentiment. His bold reconfiguration of the sonnet transformed it into a vehicle for black social protest, and also expressed the psychological anguish of what Du Bois had formulated as 'double consciousness' – as McKay said in his later poem 'America' (1921), 'Although she feeds me bread of bitterness / And sinks into my throat her tiger's tooth / Stealing my breath of life, I will confess / I love this cultured hell that tests my youth!'[39] Harlem was just becoming a black enclave in Manhattan in these years, and two of the crucial arbiters of the Renaissance – James Weldon Johnson and W. E. B. Du Bois – produced work in the decade which would influence its modes and preoccupations.

Du Bois's novel, *The Quest of the Silver Fleece* (1911), which he called an 'economic study', outlined the linked necessities of educational and agricultural reform in the South and presented a faith in Progressive narratives of feminism and professional expertise. He also edited *The Crisis*, the magazine of the newly formed NAACP, which over the next twenty years formed a vital outlet for publishing the work of a new generation of black authors. Of particular interest to recent critics has been James Weldon Johnson's *The Autobiography of an Ex-Colored Man* (1912), one of the central works in the African American tradition of 'passing' narratives.

Johnson's novel tells of an African American man, light enough in appearance to 'pass', who faces the agonising choice between a life of black self-identification, on the one hand, and racial masquerade as white on the other. This choice develops into one between a life of cultural richness and connection to the memory of his mother but also one fraught with the risk of terrible and arbitrary violence – his decision to 'pass' is precipitated by viewing a lynching – and a life of bland conformity, marriage to a white woman and moderate success in the white world. In the end the narrative becomes one of self-erasure – the narrator famously closes his account with the lament that 'I have sold my birthright for a mess of pottage.' It also critiques the one-drop rule which undergirded what Werner Sollors has called a 'hypodescent' society, where a partial aspect of ancestry becomes all-defining.[40] The book caused controversy; Johnson's name was left off the original edition, leading many reviewers to mistake it for a real autobiography (he didn't claim it as his until 1927). Reading this as truth rather than fiction was so aggravating to white supremacists that, in legal defences of the right to screen Griffith's racist epic film *The Birth of a Nation* in northern cities, the text was produced as an exhibit to demonstrate the risks Anglo-Saxon purity and hegemony were under from the light-skinned African American population.

Modernist Prose and Poetry

Most of the work discussed so far adhered to formal conventions well established for some time: linear plots, definite closure, clear distinctions between interior and exterior modes of narration, a stress on continuity rather than disruption, and a tendency to play down the constructedness of fictional form. Later in the decade this was increasingly being challenged by modernist views of language and representation, and a move to subjective explanations of reality – an experimentalism brought forward by a new generation of New York publishers keen to support new American writing, which included Alfred Knopf, Albert Boni and Horace Liveright, Ben Huebsch, Alfred Harcourt and Donald Brace. One of the most important early authors of this movement – who began with Huebsch but switched to Liveright in the 1920s – was Sherwood Anderson.

Sherwood Anderson, *Winesburg, Ohio* (1919)

Anderson's collection of short stories marked a new direction in American prose when it appeared in 1919. Individual stories had already appeared in little magazines: the Socialist periodical *The Masses*, the modernist *Little Review*, and *The Seven Arts*, a journal committed to a 'Romantic Radicalism' of cultural and economic transformation of the United States. Anderson's Winesburg stories – modernist and indigenous in style, committed to a searching critique of capitalist standardisation and division of labour, and convinced of the value of art and imagination as ways of challenging the increasing atomisation of American social life – fitted well with all of them.

All but one of the collection's twenty-five stories are based in the fictional village of Winesburg, Ohio, in the 1890s – and draw heavily on Anderson's boyhood experiences in Clyde, Ohio. The individual tales relate the frequently unhappy, frustrated, and lonely lives of Winesburg's residents: Wing Biddlebaum, a man run off from his job as a teacher in his home town in Pennsylvania because of accusations of paedophilia; Alice Hindman, a woman who has spent her whole adult life waiting for a lover who promised to return to her; Seth Richmond and Elmer Cowley, both young men struggling with the loneliness, self-doubt and inarticulateness of adolescence. The stories function as a cycle, loosely linked together by their shared geography and also by the character of George Willard, a young reporter for the local paper. George's growing ability as a writer, and his imaginative sympathy with Winesburg's residents, provide a connective structure to the disparate stories as well as a source of catharsis for characters with stories they desperately seek to tell. Moreover, George's growth to sexual maturity demonstrates Anderson's awareness that sexuality often functioned for Americans as a rare promise of communication and intimacy in a social scene where few other opportunities for this existed; yet it also demonstrates that sexuality in practice was beleaguered by misunderstanding and disappointment. The issue of sex figured large in its reception from the outset and, despite his protests to the contrary, Anderson's book was taken as the foremost example of the new Freudian approach to sexuality wherein repressed desires became manifest in physically and emotionally crippling symptoms. Later critics took Anderson to task for his creation of women who can express agency only in sexual terms; and certainly he shared the sentiment of many male modernists that the most vital expressions of artistic creativity could be produced only by men.

The other issue that preoccupied critics was form. H. L. Mencken observed that the work 'lifts the short story, for long a form hardened by trickery and virtuosity, to a higher and more spacious level'; Anderson himself had proclaimed that one of his objectives was to get away from the practice of 'Our writers, our storytellers, [who] in wrapping life up into neat little packages were only betraying life.'[41] Instead of the formulaic 'slick' magazine story, which focused on plot conventions of surprise, reversal and marital conclusions – a style worked to great commercial success by

O. Henry in the previous decade – Anderson crafted stories based more in character psychology, oral styles of narration and ambiguous or indefinite endings. Few critics, however, linked this with Anderson's preoccupation in his two novels of the 1910s – *Marching Men* (1917) and *Windy McPherson's Son* (1916) – with the struggles of labour. For many years an advertising copywriter, he had an abhorrence of growing standardisation in American markets and American culture, and saw the formulaic short magazine story as an example of all that he hated – a symptom of a broader erosion of craft and creative labour within the American economy. As T. J. Jackson Lears has noted, there was a strong strain of anti-modernism in many modernist writers who sought an aesthetic of authenticity that they felt was disappearing in the new markets and products of mass culture. For Lears, Anderson was

> embarrassingly, almost self-parodically obsessed with authentic experi-
> ence and expression; and he revealed that obsession in flagrantly sexual
> language. Yet his quest for authenticity. . .echoed Anglo-American traditions
> of social critique and spiritual longing, traditions that encouraged more sig-
> nificant critiques of mass culture than a masculine cry of pain.[42]

These issues are foregrounded in *Winesburg, Ohio*, which is at once a critique of the small town and a nostalgic evocation of it. On the one hand, it slams its aesthetic, emotional and moral limitations, its petty obsessions, its intolerance of all but a narrow range of social, sexual and racial identities – so much so that it was seen as the quintessential example of what Carl Van Doren labelled the 'revolt from the village' school. Yet, on the other hand, it sees in 1890s Winesburg a moment before standardised national markets in newspapers and commodities had completely penetrated rural America, before 'the farmer by the stove [was] brother to the men of the cities . . . talking as glibly and as senselessly as the best city man of us all'. What had been lost, as well as an 'old brutal ignorance', was a 'kind of beautiful childlike innocence'.[43] It is a collection about America in transition, and struggling with the dualities that so many writers of the decade recurred to – between men and women, young generation and old, public and private, the individual and the collective, the voice and the written word. Yet, ultimately, as well as his formal innovations, Anderson's most obvious gift to the emergence of modernism in prose in the United States was his celebration of an aspect of life which seemed to him to negate such 'senselessness', namely what he loosely termed 'adventure'. This was the thrill of direct, unmediated, uninhibited experience, the force of desire, and the capacity for vital intensity; and, as has often been remarked, it is open to charges of patriarchal republicanism, anti-modernist nostalgia or political quietism. But for Anderson – as for many others in the early generation of modernists in the United States – it was 'the thing that makes the mature life of men and women in the modern world possible'.[44]

While the modernist temper would not emerge fully in prose until the next decade, it flourished in the extraordinary range and achievement of the American poetry of the 1910s. Setting down precepts for an innovative and radical break with much of the American poetic tradition and the anglophone canon, the poets who emerged in this decade did much to shape the direction of verse in English in the twentieth century. They were also the foremost American participants in the new international cultures of modernism, closely engaged with centres of intellectual activity in London and Paris in particular. The little magazines that emerged in the decade, most prominently for poetry Margaret Anderson and Jane Heap's *Little Review* and Harriet Monroe's *Poetry*, plus the body of poetry, prose and criticism that emerged from Ezra Pound, T. S. Eliot, Robert Frost, Wallace Stevens, William Carlos Williams, Amy Lowell, H. D., Mina Loy and Gertrude Stein, asserted as only James had done before that aesthetic leadership in anglophone literature was possible from America.

As Douglas Mao notes, literary criticism at the time was becoming 'what seemed a last refuge of the total view – of an attempt to survey modern life in terms of broad ends and local means', and the brilliance of several of the decade's key poets was their ability to fuse literary criticism and practice in ways which were conducted in such influential and totalising terms.[45] Foremost among these poets was Ezra Pound, who gave direction and intellectual energy to many of the key poetic movements and institutions of the 1910s – so much so that one distinguished scholar of modernism has typified the cultural landscape of the first half of the twentieth century as the 'Pound Era'. During the decade (which he spent most of in London) he shaped and assisted imagism, vorticism, T. S. Eliot's renovation of French symbolism, literary cultures in New York, London and Chicago, the modernist interest in poetic interdisciplinarity and non-western cultures, and little magazines including the British *The New Age* and *Egoist*, and the American *Little Review* and *Poetry*. Particularly significant for subsequent poetry was imagism, and Pound's contribution to its development perhaps best exemplified his energy, *modus operandi* and overweening self-belief. Imagism had originated first in the British poet T. E. Hulme's theory of the image, which he shared with Pound in a poet's club in London in 1909. But it was Pound who brought together a group of poets from England and the United States under this branded banner, who pushed its uptake in *Poetry* magazine, who organised its initial anthology and who produced its most memorable theorisations and manifestos. Imagism demonstrated Pound's view that a modern poetry must be one steeped in the precision of craft. He argued that this poetry must be stripped of sentiment, verbiage and strict adherence to metronomic metre; allied to an effect of visual instantaneity; and based in ideational compression, which presented 'an intellectual and emotional complex in an instant of time.'[46] This movement helped launch the career of H. D., whose *Sea Garden* poems (1916) (along with Pound's own, especially in *Cathay*) are perhaps the finest examples of this aesthetic; and it was deeply influential to the next generation, particularly on poets such as William Carlos Williams and T. S. Eliot.

This interest in poetic energy, economy and concision also informed Pound's growing interest in eastern poetic forms, particularly the Chinese ideograph and the Japanese Noh theatre, an interest he shared with his close friend and some time mentor, W. B. Yeats. As the literary executor of the oriental art scholar, Ernest Fenollosa, he completed his work on a series of translations from Chinese (*Cathay*, 1915) and published 'The Chinese Ideograph as a model for Poetry' which became an influential piece in modernism's complex and fruitful examination of the relationship between verbal and visual art. In his thoughtful disquisition on American culture in 1913, 'Patria Mia', he was encouraged by the possibility of a new American Renaissance but so frustrated by elements of the contemporary scene that he concluded 'if you have any vital interest in the arts, and happen to like talking about them, you sooner or later leave the country'.[47] This all demonstrated two central features of modernism: firstly its constitution of culture as fundamentally international, its interest in looking beyond the anglophone cultural heritage for aesthetic and philosophical models – a trait very evident in T. S. Eliot's poetry as well. Perhaps the major figure for them both was Dante, and this was evident in Pound's publication in 1917 of 'Three Cantos'. These were the so-called 'Ur-cantos' which formed the template for the epic project which occupied him from 1915 to 1969. Secondly, it indicated how certain modernists would define their project in opposition to elements of contemporary Western society: mass consumer culture, capitalist democracy, and middle-class hegemony. Pound was a fierce critic of these things: in 1920 he warned that a 'tawdry cheapness / Shall outlast our days', a cheapness caused by a society which had 'the press for wafer / The franchise for circumcision'.[48] These two factors fused in the aesthetic and political project which made Pound infamous: his growing interest in economics and C. H. Douglas's ideas of social credit, and from there his support of Mussolini's Fascist regime in Italy which, in 1943, led him to be indicted as a traitor to the United States.[49]

Pound's importance to American literature in the decade was also as an editor. Much of the important innovative fictional and poetic work at the time appeared in the little magazines whose circulations ran (at most) in the low thousands. They published work largely free from the constraints on content demanded by the bigger circulation magazines, which had advertising revenue to consider; they sold to a small readership of practitioners and supporters. Traditionally thought of as elite and hermetic – what Richard Poirier has called a 'snob's game' – recent work has instead assessed little magazines as engaged in an attempt to rejuvenate the public sphere, and keen to utilise the techniques of mass publicity and advertising in order to do so.[50] Moreover, they were read and discussed in the book review sections of large newspapers and popular magazines nationwide; in such a way, even highly experimental work, such as Gertrude Stein's, was widely known and discussed (even if that discussion was frequently based in ridicule).[51] The most adventurous in the United States at the time was Margaret Anderson and Jane Heap's *Little Review*, founded in Chicago in 1914, which carried the masthead 'making no compromise with the public taste'. Pound served as foreign editor to the *Little Review* between 1917 and 1919, during which time he secured funds for the magazine from the influential American patron, John Quinn; he also secured the coup for which the magazine is best remembered in serially publishing Joyce's *Ulysses*. Pound also served as foreign editor to *Poetry* magazine, a tempestuous relationship that saw him frequently lock horns with its editor Harriet Monroe – who was much more committed to more traditional modes of verse, and fond in a way Pound could never be of homespun writers of the Chicago Renaissance such as Vachel Lindsay, Edgar Lee Masters, and Carl Sandburg. Perhaps his most important fight with her was over the inclusion of T. S. Eliot's first published verse since his undergraduate days, his 'The Love Song of J. Alfred Prufrock'. Monroe disliked it for its overbearing sense of futility, but Pound persuaded her to print it in June 1915, praising Prufrock to Monroe as 'the best poem I have yet seen or had from an American'.[52]

With its startling imagery that wholly rejects Romantic apprehensions of nature (the poem begins with the lines 'Let us go then, you and I / When the evening is spread out against the sky / Like a patient etherized upon a table'), the prevalence of its allusions to other literary texts, its discontinuities and parataxis, and the way the dramatic monologue form is modulated so as never to allow a fixed or stable speaking identity to emerge, Prufrock was a crucial harbinger of central tenets of modernist poetic practice in general and Eliot's own aesthetic in particular.[53] In 1919 he published his second major production of the decade, his essay 'Tradition and the Individual Talent', the first of a series of highly influential critical interventions that would under-pin the New Critical theoretical perspective which dominated the American literary academy in the 1940s and 1950s. Arguing against the cult of poetic personality that had characterised the previous century, Eliot insisted instead on an escape from personality and into tradition, whereby the great poet would function through holding in his or her mind what he called the 'simultaneous order' of 'the whole of the literature of Europe from Homer and within it the whole of the literature of his own country'. Once that consciousness is achieved, 'we shall often find that not only the best, but the most individual parts of [a poet's] work may be those in which the dead poets, his ancestors, assert their immortality most vigorously'.[54] In this view the poet was catalyst rather than a supreme individual; rather than the primacy of imagination and a personal response to the phenomenal world, the poet must be a self-effacing technician steeped in learning and highly respectful of the ever changing (but also somehow never changing) 'ideal order' of the literary canon. Taken together, these two texts exemplify the mixture of aesthetic radicalism and politi-cal reactionism in Eliot's work, his faith in new and difficult poetic language capable of responding to social complexity, and simultane-ously his attraction to authoritarian systems of order arbitrated by enlightened elites. He has been much critisised for his attraction to the aristocratic and culturally homogeneous 'organic society' he saw in the Renaissance, and his disdain for the capitalist liberal democracy that had overseen a nineteenth century he generally felt to have been a cultural and political disaster.[55] This critique sits alongside frequent accusations of his anti-Semitism, misogyny, and distaste for democ-racy; consequently, Eliot has often been a (drastically oversimplified) lightning rod for discussions of the imbrication of politics and aesthet-ics in high modernism.

The paralysis Prufrock experiences in the face of a roomful of women was indicative of a broader hostility to women and what was felt to be cultures of femininity held by many members of the mod-ernist movement. Pound pondered over producing a magazine with only male contributors, because 'active America is getting fed up on gynocracy'; James Joyce famously hailed Eliot's 'The Waste Land' (1922) as the poem that would end 'the idea of poetry for ladies'.[56] Frequently, as several critics of modernism have noted, femininity was associated with nineteenth-century cultures of sentimentalism – the 'Genteel Tradition' lambasted by George Santayana in his essay of 1911 – or with the consumerist energies of mass culture. Male modernists in particular frequently spoke of their ambitions for difficulty, for authenticity, and for a cultural sphere disconnected from consumer exchange in explicitly gendered terms. Ann Douglas has characterised their project as 'matricidal', devoted to 'the demolition of that block to modernity, or so she seemed, the powerful white middle-class matriarch of the recent Victorian past'.[57]

Until recently, this tended to marginalise important poetic innovators such as Marianne Moore, H. D., Amy Lowell, Edna St Vincent Millay and Mina Loy from cultural narratives of the decade. Their intellectual engagements were wide and diverse – with European modernisms such as futurism and cubism; with revisiting classical myth; with Chinese translation; and with botany and biology, to name but a few. Their poetry ranged in form: Millay's feminist rehabilitation of the traditional love sonnet in *Renascence and Other Poems* (1917) and *A Few Figs from Thistles* (1920) brought her a wide and often mildly scandalised readership, and her high reputation at the time was capped by winning the newly established Pulitzer Prize for poetry in 1923. Lowell and H. D.'s contributions to imagism were crucial: H. D. was often praised as the 'perfect imagist' for her ability to craft crystalline short lyrics whereby 'the image becomes not merely a vehicle for transcribing a sensation but presents the sensation itself', in the words of Peter Jones.[58] Lowell demonstrated formidable editorial skills in wrestling control of imagism from Pound and assembling three imagist anthologies, as well as demonstrating her own poetic ability in developing what became known as 'polyphonic prose'. Frequently, the work of these poets sought to reconfigure notions of female embodiment and sexuality in a fashion much more daring than mainstream feminism; Janet Lyon remarks that Mina Loy's scandalous 'Love Songs' of 1915 'baldly challenged the gendered hierarchy of sexuality that would leave to women the passive role of coital helpmeet', and in doing so 'found an audience in nascent American cosmopolitan communities that were forming around dialogic explorations of the physical and psychological dimensions of sexuality'.[59] Perhaps the most important of these innovators was Gertrude Stein, whose syntactic and generic experiment, close engagement with visual forms of perception and representation, and articulation of female sexualities and experiences into a language of play, repetition, and startling contrast continue to play a significant role in contemporary poetic practice.

Gertrude Stein, *Tender Buttons* (1914)

Stein's first commercially published work, poetic portraits of her close friends Pablo Picasso and Henri Matisse, appeared in Alfred Stieglitz's magazine *Camera Work* in 1912. By this point she was a keen collector of modernist art, and was closely involved with modernist intellectual circles in Europe. She was also living with her lifelong partner, Alice B. Toklas, and had recently seen her brother, Leo Stein, move out of their house at 27 rue de Fleurus in Paris after nearly forty years of living together. *Tender Buttons* marked a bold change in her writing, moving away from the narrative or biographical basis of her earlier work to present a much more abstract consideration of the relation of language and grammar to the object. It was published in a small run of one thousand, but gained a fame (and notoriety) across the mainstream press; it was quoted (and derided) in major newspapers in Chicago, Baltimore and St Louis.[60] Stein's breakthrough text, it was committed to a rejection of denotation, and delighted in referential instability. It is a collection which defamiliarises language both to amplify its sensuousness and to present surprising and often challenging new combinations – combinations which explore the limits of both literary and social convention.

This was recognised by her early supporters. Sherwood Anderson praised her as a 'restorer of "the word"', someone who was 'laying word against word, relating sound to sound, feeling for the taste, the smell, the rhythm of the individual word'; Mina Loy called her 'Curie / of the laboratory / of vocabulary'.[61] Her poem 'Apple' in the collection gives an indication of this:

> Apple plum, carpet steak, seed clam, colored wine, calm seen, cold cream, best shake, potato, potato and no no gold work with pet, a green seen is called bake and change sweet is bready, a little piece a little piece please.

> A little piece please. Cane again to the presupposed and ready eucalyptus tree, count out sherry and ripe plates and little corners of a kind of ham. This is use.[62]

The textual and sensual experience of eating an apple crumble – as well as asking for it and sharing it – are evoked here as much by rhythm, anagram, rhyme, consonance and assonance, as by the denotative 'apple', 'plum' and 'sweet.' Stein saw *Tender Buttons* as above all an attempt to break 'the simple form of the noun the simple noun poetry' which had formed the anglophone literary tradition up until that point; her work instead was concerned with new ways of 'using losing refusing and pleasing and betraying and caressing nouns'.[63] This refraction of the object by approaching it from multiple and simultaneous perspectives recalled the visual project of cubism she admired in Picasso and Braque's work, but her collection was also linked to specifically linguistic concerns. Her recalibration of the place of the noun in poetry sought to re-engage the love of naming which she saw as the bedrock of all poetry, but which had been degraded in the contemporary as people 'go on using the name until perhaps they do not know what the name is'. Her attempt in *Tender Buttons* was to discover a way 'of naming things that would not invent names, but mean names without naming them'.[64]

Stein's language of caressing the noun, and definition of all poetry as love poetry, indicate the erotics of the work, as well as a materialism which is resolutely domestic. *Tender Buttons* (in itself a French slang term for nipples) is split into three sections – objects, food, and rooms – and is immersed in both the domestic quotidian which interested cubist paint-ers, as well as a lesbian sexuality which flourished within, and was deeply interwoven with, private and domestic life. This proposed a different mod-ernism to that of Eliot and Pound, who developed a poetry based in what Peter Nicholls has called 'an attempt to dissociate desire from any form of identification, and on the appeal to the visual and objective which affirms distance and difference'.[65] In contrast, Stein's text 'collapsed the autono-mous, negative modernist form with exactly that which it sought to resist and negate: the feminine realm of consumerism, romantic affection, and quotidian, material life – and worse, a homoerotic vision of that realm'.[66] Critics have attempted to unlock a 'lesbian code' in the text, but some of Stein's erotic playfulness is fairly obvious; the second of four poems on 'Chicken' reads 'Alas a dirty word, alas a dirty third alas a dirty third, alas a dirty bird.'[67] One of Stein's favoured techniques of 'losing refusing' the noun was homophones, and 'alas' for 'Alice' is just one of several ('aches' for 'eggs', 'to let' for 'toilet', and 'flower' and 'flour' are others). Repeated use of the colours of flesh and sexual organs – red and pink – and Stein's fondness for sexually loaded verbs in the continuous present (spreading, reddening, mounting, jerking) interweaves the sensuousness of lesbian sexuality with the sensuality of food and cooking. In doing so the poem presents a challenge to what Stein later called 'patriarchal poetry', a poetry based in hierarchy and temporal sequentiality.

Yet any attempt to read Stein purely as 'code', a text which can be inter-preted and transcribed into one that is comprehensible and continuous, does an injustice to the sheer plurality of the text, its inability to be reduced into anything other than its own sometimes overwhelming sequence of non-sequiturs, bewildering juxtapositions, and aural and visual pleasure. ('A canoe is orderly. A period is solemn. A cow is accepted.')[68] Some critics, such as Marianne DeKoven, have gone to the other pole of critical possibility and seen the content of Stein's work as essentially irrelevant to its larger function; 'I do not think it matters that the work contains these particular words in this particular order', she remarked, seeing that 'form alone raises a challenge to patriarchal language'.[69] Yet as Stein said, 'I took individual words and thought about them until I got their weight and volume complete and put them next to another word, and at this same time I found out very soon that there is no such thing as putting them together without sense.'[70] What occurs instead of nonsense is what Stein describes as the 'bent way' in *Tender Buttons*; 'a bent way that is a way to declare that the best is all together, a bent way shows no result, it shows a slight restraint, it shows a necessity for retraction'.[71] Having the best all together encourages readers to pick their own moments of humour, double meaning, revitalised perception and sensual relish in language; it forces readers to retract and restrain any ambitions for a totalising inter-pretation. Of course, the poem can read as a frustrating private game, referring only to things within itself or inside the walls of 27 rue de Fleurus; it often hints at the existence of an undivulged intimate code, and there is no shame or apology for its self-indulgence. Yet to see it as so aggressively hermetic misses several of its important connections. It must be read in the context of the decade's various and ambitious programmes to reconfigure the potentialities of female identity in political, social, sexual and cultural terms. It must be read in the context of how women artists and writers sought to coexist with, and often to challenge, an emerging masculinist avant-garde which was explicitly self-defined in contrast to cultural, bodily and linguistic figurations of women. And it must also be seen as one of the most influential examples of how an increase in transatlantic cultural flow was producing a new self-reflexivity about the American language. As she said, she liked living in Paris because she enjoyed 'being alone with English and myself'.[72]

Figure 3.1 Gertrude Stein at 27 rue de Fleurus in Paris, 1923. Courtesy of the Art Archive/Culver Pictures.

The Homemade World

This use of transatlantic experience to theorise national and aesthetic identity was a feature of the decade. For example, in the *Little Review*'s tribute number to Henry James, who had died in 1916, Pound praised James's 'great labor, [the] labor of translation, of making America intelligible, of making it possible for individuals to meet across national borders'.[73] This praise for a cosmopolitanism which Pound was clearly also celebrating in himself went hand in hand with his frequent hostility to what he called the 'post-Whitmanians', those poets who chose not to engage in the international exchanges and stylistic experimentations of modernism but produced instead modern versions of Whitman's expansive, nationalist free verse and his republican, working-class, prophetic, and self-aggrandising persona.[74] These included the poets of 'Porkopolis', such as Carl Sandburg, Vachel Lindsay, and Edgar Lee Masters, who together produced many of the key texts of the Chicago Renaissance of the 1910s. Although much of this poetry now seems somewhat prolix, parochial and naive, its stress on sexual and imaginative liberation, its fierce opposition to bureaucratic capital, its vernacular cultural nationalism, and its imaginative sympathies with the working class set much of the tone for the cultural left of the decade. The canonisation of modernism as the period's dominant style has not been kind to these poets, and has seen a sharp reassessment of their high critical reputation at the time. Nonetheless, Sandburg's republican, vernacular and multicultural urbanism would influence poets such as Langston Hughes and Allan Ginsberg, even as it often recoiled in bewilderment about the place of art in facing the harsh enormity of the American cityscape in the way Dreiser did in prose: 'Try with your pencils for these crooked faces / That pig-sticker in one corner – his mouth – / That overall factory girl – her loose cheeks. Find for your pencils / A way to mark your memory. . .'[75]

Other poets who emerged in the decade and chose eventually to detach themselves from Pound, Stein and Eliot's projects of transatlantic modernism included three of the century's most important poetic voices in Wallace Stevens, William Carlos Williams and Robert Frost. Stevens and Williams did not publish their first major collections until the 1920, but, like Williams's close friend Marianne Moore, they all printed significant early work in the little magazines of the decade. With poems such as 'Sunday Morning' (1915) 'Peter Quince at the Clavier' (1915) and 'Thirteen Ways of Looking at a Blackbird'

(1917), Stevens set out many of the themes which preoccupied his career: the poetic investigation of perception and phenomenology; the experience of beauty in a godless world; a Platonic interest in idealism and art's ability to suggest it. In contrast to much of the decade's interest in the image, his was a poetry predominantly of music and sonority, interested in music's multiple techniques for concordance, pattern and affect. His deeply philosophical and symbolic poetry contrasted with Williams's stress on the absolute primacy of material life, his interest in representing what he later called 'a world detached from the necessity of recording it, sufficient to itself, removed from [the poet] . . . with which he has bitter and delicious relations and from which he is independent'.[76] Committed to what he later called the 'American grain', Williams would come to promote an American poetic localism which especially detested Eliot and Pound's allusive and expatriate poetry, seeing them as 'too quick to find a culture (the English continental) ready made for their assertions. They ran from something else, something cruder but, at the same time, newer, more dangerous but heavy with rewards for the sensibility that could reap them.'[77] Williams's collection of 1917, *Al Que Quiere* ('To Him Who Wants It') was originally to be subtitled 'The pleasures of democracy', and this interest in the democratic and quotidian (as well as in an expressly visual understanding of these things) would be central to his more mature work.

Robert Frost, too, would mine the local cultures of New England for his best writing, although he shunned the paratactic and free-verse experimental approach of modernism for the deceptively 'plain' speech of Yankee good sense. Like Williams, he held to nativist values in his staunch anti-academicism, his rejection of Anglophilic attitudes to literary tradition, and with his later stated objective that 'a poet should not include in his writing anything that the average reader will not easily understand'.[78] Despite this stress on locality, Frost's transatlantic connection was also vital in launching his career. The small London firm David Nutt brought out *A Boy's Will* in 1913, and the stronger collection *North of Boston* in 1914, both of which were lauded by the influential friends Frost had made in London – Pound, Edward Thomas, Ford Madox Ford and Richard Aldington. The work drew on Frost's experience of farming in New Hampshire, and featured some of his best-known poems: 'Mowing', 'The Death of the Hired Man', 'Home Burial', 'Mending Wall' and 'After Apple-Picking'; his *Mountain Interval* of 1916 included 'The Road Not Taken', An Old Man's Winter Night', 'Out, Out—' and 'Birches'.

In some later remarks on Emerson – a writer with whom he was often compared – Frost opined that 'a melancholy dualism is the only soundness', and the poems in these early volumes often function through this structure. As Richard Gray points out, they commonly hover 'between the daylight world of commonsense reality and the dream world of possibility, the voices of sense and of song, the visions of the pragmatist and the prophet, the compulsions of the road and the seductions of the woods'.[79] What Frost called the 'sound of sense' is at play in these poems, the way meaning is generated through the pace and rhythm of speech rather than the 'sense' of content: as he memorably put it, 'the best place to get the abstract sound of sense is from voices behind a door that cuts off the words . . . It is the abstract vitality of our speech.'[80] The blank-verse dramatic monologues or dialogues of *North of Boston* dramatise that vitality, often exploring the melancholy and harsh exigencies of rural life. Yet this is balanced against the comforts of ritual and the natural world, particularly the natural world as ordered through the interlinked labours of farming and poetry. This tension has led Frank Lentricchia to describe Frost's poetry as 'guilty pastoral', guilty through its awareness of the severe limitations of 'conventions of sentiment concerning the supposed simplicities and therapies of the pastoral life', and yet unable wholly to resist deploying them.[81] It was partly because of that sentiment that Frost rose to fame as a people's poet, a staple provider of the high school aphoristic lyric; he won four Pulitzer Prizes and received over forty honorary degrees, and delivered the oration at John F. Kennedy's inaugural. Frequently, however, on close inspection he shows himself to be a 'terrifying poet', as Lionel Trilling observed – a poet attuned to the metaphysical darkness of grief, isolation and obliteration.[82] His moments of didactic wisdom often suggest the reassurance of platitude without actually delivering, maintaining a disturbing balance between menace and pastoral serenity, and offering the possibility of both a sentimental and a cynical reading within the same piece.

Conclusion

Pound had called Frost 'VURRY Amur'k'n', and his work echoes other evocations of rural life in the decade in its cautious awareness of the pleasures and pitfalls of sentiment in representing rural communities – communities rendered backwaters by the rising dominance of metropolitan life. His poetry also demonstrates the nativist search for what Frost called 'a language absolutely unliterary', and perhaps it was in the different models of how to craft a literary language for America, and a public role for the author, that the biggest aesthetic divisions emerged in the decade.[83] The poetic debates laid down in these years – between native and cosmopolitan, plain speech and literary allusion, poet as bard or poet as catalyst, quotidian as structure or myth as structure, modernism and something different – would do much to underwrite the literary history of the next thirty years. The classic era of American poetry, to a sizeable extent it shaped the contemporary canon around these divisions.

Chapter 4

Performance and Music

Although it was the cinema which led the golden age of public, commercial entertainment of the 1910s, other forms also generated a new appeal to the youth of the middle class. The dance craze of the 1910s saw that demographic drawn into commercial dance venues for the first time; as F. Scott Fitzgerald noted, the Castle Walk 'gave the modern dance a social position and brought the nice girl into the café, thus beginning a profound revolution in American life'.[1] These dances and the music that accompanied them were often adapted from African American forms in a mixture of racial fascination, perturbation, and denial which had much to do with changing attitudes to the public performance of sexuality. As Lewis Erenberg observes, the growth of cafés, cabarets and revues in the decade accompanied and augmented a shift in middle-class social norms, as 'after 1910 both men and women included elements of passion, expressiveness, and a wider conception of self into their formerly formal culture', a conception of self possible as 'publicly expressed intimacy and informality [no longer] undercut class status'.[2] The sex farce, the chorus girl revue, the dance craze, and the birth of jazz all reflected this shifting attitude towards public expressiveness, and all benefited from the expanding class basis of commercial entertainment. At the same time, modernists brought a new experimentalism to theatre and dance which sought to break from the conventions of Broadway and social dancing, often articulating a quasi-spiritual and communitarian ethos of performance which celebrated their distance from mainstream commercial formulas.

Social Dance

In June 1913, the waspish and unconventional journalist (and future modernist icon) Djuna Barnes published the vignette 'You can Tango

– a Little – at Arcadia Dance Hall'. It follows the foppish and upper-class Reginald Delancey as he decides to dispel his ennui one evening by indulging his curiosity (and unacknowledged interest in class and ethnic slumming) by following up an advertisement in the paper and visiting the Arcadia dance hall. A new facility, owned and run in a working-class district by the 'Social Centers Corporation', it is committed – as he is informed by the conspicuously Jewish secretary, Sydney S. Cohen – to 'elevat[ing] the tone of dancing and to plac[ing] the dance-hall business on a clean and wholesome basis'.[3] Once there, Reginald is surprised to see dance censors, helping to enforce an atmosphere where dancing a 'modified' tango is permitted. Eager to dance, he inveigles his father's Irish office boy into providing an introduction to Delia O'Connor, shopgirl at the perfume counter of the Paris department store on Broadway. 'Everyone had a glorious time,' and when the dancing is over, Delia reflects on her way home about the 'real frangipani sort of guy' she met earlier – while Reggie resolves to become a patron of the Paris.[4]

Barnes's article suggests a good deal about social dance in the 1910s, especially the tone of innocent fun that accompanies much of the writing about it. It was truly a craze; by the 1910s over five hundred public dance halls were open each evening in the Greater New York area, and the decade saw the construction of several of the dance palaces which became such a feature of 1920s dance – New York's Grand Central and Roseland Ballroom among them.[5] Many young women in particular became obsessed with dance; a New York entertainment survey of 1911 showed that 96 per cent of girls enjoyed dancing, and Barnes's Delia enthuses that dancing has the movies 'beaten to a thirty-nine-cent bargain sale on a rainy Monday'.[6] Moreover, Barnes also hints at some of the sociopolitical forces attending this relatively new form of public leisure. The dance craze was deeply enmeshed with the progressive discourse of moral hygiene which had an especial concern for unescorted young women; but it also evidenced the progressive faith that vice and public health problems in America's big cities could be solved through systems of physical culture and exercise. Reggie's Arcadian adventure also suggests how new cultures of commercial entertainment were encouraged by – but also sustained – new forms of advertising, new magazines, and dancing celebrities who became 'idols of consumption' in much the same way as did early film stars. And it suggests how the language and the barriers of class, race, gender and ethnicity were both inescapable in the dance and music of the 1910s, but also open to often titillating and exhilarating redefinition and flexibility.

As was true of films and vaudeville in the 1910s, the class profile of those who attended social dances in commercial entertainments underwent significant change in the decade, a change which led to a big increase in overall participation. Like vaudeville and films, social dancing was a well-established feature of working-class recreation by the 1910s; and the language of respectability was similarly crucial in enticing the middle class to get involved. This applied to both styles and venues. 'Tough dancing', or barnyard dancing, had emerged from African American dance styles and the Barbary Coast vice district of San Francisco in the 1900s, and encouraged close proximity between dance partners as well as jerky physical movement supposedly copying the movements of animals (the turkey trot, for example, involved flapping the arms; the grizzly bear involved close hugging). Middle-class reformers were horrified at the sexual suggestiveness of these dances, which were described as 'not dancing at all, but a series of indecent antics' of 'disreputable origins', and they were widely banned at prominent middle-class dance venues and hotels.[7] (Woodrow Wilson even cancelled the ball planned for his inauguration in 1913, fearing the scandal that might ensue if preventing these dances proved impossible).[8] Dance censors, dance manuals and a new set of dance magazines all focused on adapting and 'refining' these dances through a discourse of respectability in dancing, one which defined dance's benefit as healthy exercise and the cultivation of 'grace' rather than focusing on its romantic or sexual potentialities. It was even discussed in the terms of racial–national improvement so common in physical culture; in the words of one booster, regular dances in public schools, properly instructed and chaperoned, would 'do more good to the race than . . . discussing eugenics or . . . indulging in a flippant study of social economics'.[9]

Commercial venues also emerged to cater for a middle-class clientele emerging from a tradition whereby dancing took place primarily in private homes and at society balls. As Lewis Erenberg discusses, the rise of the cabaret as a middle-class venue in the decade broke down barriers between performers and audience that had structured theatrical and concert hall stages in earlier entertainment cultures; cabarets became a 'new public environment for the exploration of alternatives to the private character of the nineteenth century'.[10] Cabarets expanded the spaces they had for exhibition dancers to cater for public dancing; elegant hotels began to hold 'tea dances' for afternoon dancing; and there was a boom in dance instruction classes.[11] Attempts to regulate this expansion were also extensive;

Erenberg observes that middle-class cabaret tables were organised to discourage contacts between unacquainted men and women and, as Kathy Peiss notes, 'the "couple on a date" became an increasingly important cultural construct for the middle class, since it provided a way to structure potentially promiscuous heterosocial relations at the new resorts'.[12] Campaigning Progressives in cities across the country helped pass licensing ordinances regulating dance halls and dancing academies. Committees even opened and ran dance halls in some working-class areas, although 'tough dancing' – as well as greater freedom in heterosocial contact – persisted in working-class dance culture in the decade, often in defiance of the standards of the more recent uptake of public dance by the middle class. Peiss's seminal work in particular has explored how young working women generally enjoyed greater freedoms in how they danced and with whom they danced than did middle-class women of the time, and how they forged a distinctive culture of personal style, qualified sexual freedom and female friendship in public dance. Such a culture is important for understanding that the nature of the 'new woman', one of the decade's most enduring archetypes, did not emerge purely through a 'trickle down' model of cultural transmission. Although critics still tend to define that new woman as primarily a middle-class figure, the cultures of working-class dance demonstrate that working women were also instrumental in redefining the limits and nature of female agency, style and independence in the period.[13]

Despite this, the decade's dancing icons were those who presented dancing to the middle class not just as wholesome, unthreatening, elegant and fun but as articulated to a whole new mode of fashion and social aspiration. A swathe of celebrity dancing instructors emerged, such as Maurice Mouvet and Florence Walton, and Joan Sawyer and Wallace McCutcheon. By far the most influential and successful couple, however, were Vernon and Irene Castle.

Vernon and Irene Castle

Like many other stars of the decade, Vernon Castle had his start in light musical comedy and, like Charlie Chaplin, he had migrated to the United States from England. He married the star-struck and ambitious Irene Foote in 1911, and together they travelled to Paris to star in a comedy sketch Vernon had performed with Lew Fields in New York. When that scheme failed, they contracted to exhibition dance at the Café de Paris. Never having danced together before, and improvising as they went along, they performed the 'tough' dances then current in New York. They were a sensation, and the clamour in France led to a demand for them to return to America – where they began a lucrative career as the decade's pre-eminent dance celebrities.[14]

The Castles' success rested on three elements. The first was their ability to present simple, easy-to-learn dances designed to be danced to ragtime music. The easiest and most popular were the walk steps, including the one-step and the castle walk, which involved simply walking in a classic closed hold in time to the music. As well as simplicity, this step's popularity relied on the rhythmic power of syncopated ragtime; as Vernon Castle said, 'when a good orchestra plays a "rag" one has simply *got* to move'.[15] To this end the Castles hired the African American bandleader James Reese Europe to provide their ragtime orchestration; he became a crucial part of their success, and also introduced them to the slower-tempo W. C. Handy's 'Memphis Blues' – which formed the musical accompaniment to the Castles' later popularisation of the foxtrot.[16] The second element of their success was their ability to retain the sense of energy and fun emerging from the 'tough dances' of the working-class halls, but to make these steps 'respectable' for a nervous but intrigued middle-class audience. The Castles were quite candid about their role as adaptive conduits; Irene Castle later praised Europe for being 'the first to take jazz out of the saloons and make it respectable', and talked about how they got their new 'nigger dances' from the Barbary Coast but had to have them 'considerably toned down before they can be used in the drawing room'.[17] Instead, they offered a vision of dance as refined, healthy, asexual and – their key term – 'graceful', a concept which was simultaneously moral and aesthetic; as Vernon Castle suggested, 'grace of manner and grace of mind must be forerunners of all kinds of grace, and most certainly must lie back of the grace of dancing'.[18] This respectability was carefully cultivated through a public image of aristocratic associations and high-profile mixing with New York's social elite. Vernon had changed his name from William Vernon Blythe to Vernon Castle, and the press frequently reported that Vernon had noble antecedents.[19] Rich patrons paid up to $100 an hour for private dance instruction, and the Castles regularly entertained at soirées in homes on Long Island and 5th Avenue.[20]

The final element of their success was their ability to master a discourse of fashionability across a range of marketing and commercial opportunities. They were alive to the power of branding: ventures included the exclusive dancing school, Castle House, the sophisticated (and horribly overpriced) Sans Souci Restaurant, and other clubs such as Castles by the Sea at Luna Park in Coney Island and the rooftop café Castles in the Air.[21] They appeared in dance instruction films and in the pages of the new dance magazines. They starred in musical comedies, vaudeville and touring shows which travelled the country; at one point, Irene was reputed to have earned $1,500 for a fifteen-minute turn at the Hippodrome. They popularised the foxtrot in Irving Berlin's first musical comedy, *Watch Your*

Step. The dances themselves were faddish; as one journalist put it, it was a discovery of the age that 'dances could be made up like cocktails and gin fizzes'.[22] Their own dancing manual, *Modern Dancing*, detailed new dances such as the hesitation waltz, innovation waltz, maxixe, and the lame duck (a dipping, limping step described as 'the *dernier cri* in Waltz steps').[23]

Irene also became an icon of women's fashion; Cecil Beaton later remarked that she 'was as important an embodiment of the "modern" in the social and fashion sense as [Igor] Stravinsky and [Pablo] Picasso were in the world of art'.[24] As their biographer Eve Golden discusses, the early 1910s was an era of revolutionary fashion changes when the look of fashionable women in 'acres of petticoats, loosely piled mounds of hair, [and] elaborate hats' shifted rapidly to leaner lines, less restrictive corsets, hair worn closer to the head and smaller hats – and Irene Castle became a leader in effecting that change.[25] Moreover, the allure of lending their name to many fashion products was enhanced by the way the Castles became positioned as 'idols of consumption', in Leo Lowenthal's phrase. Their own leisure choices and habits of (extravagant) consumption became features of admiration and aspiration for their fans, fans cultivated by the new magazines such as *Modern Dance Magazine* and *Dance Lovers Magazine* which relied heavily on advertising revenue from the cosmetics and clothing industries.[26] As one reviewer noted, 'one reason everyone in New York is keen about the Castles is that they are the living exhibits of a get-rich-quick romance'.[27]

That romance acquired the seal of permanence during the war. Vernon Castle volunteered for the Royal Flying Corps, and flew in many missions over the Western Front; he recorded two kills, was promoted to captain, and was decorated for his heroism. Irene began a career in films, and appeared in the preparedness serial *Patria* – financed by one of her favourite dancing pupils, William Randolph Hearst. When Vernon was killed in a training accident in Texas in February 1918 he was buried with full military honours in New York. An affectionate homage to the couple was given in Fred Astaire's and Ginger Rogers's *The Story of Vernon and Irene Castle* in 1939, which replicated much of the couple's choreography and fashion (although Rogers refused to bob her hair). What it skirted over was what had arguably cemented the Castles' success: their unique ability to present public dancing in a way that balanced the huge appeal of new cultures of leisure and consumption with the very real concerns over what the breakdown of traditional courting rituals and heterosexual socialisation would mean for the middle class.[28] It was this that connected them to the tensions in the decade between progressive social planning and the often unruly energies of new forms of consumption and leisure – and also what separated them from the more unbridled cultures of social dance in the 1920s.

Figure 4.1 Vernon and Irene Castle, 1913. Courtesy of the Library of Congress, LC-USZ62-120307.

Modern Dance

The social dance craze was not the only form of dance struggling for legitimacy, or struggling to define itself as quintessentially modern. Modern dance – alternatively called barefoot dance, interpretive dance, free dance or art dance – was becoming institutionalised in these years as a new form of high culture following on from the groundbreaking choreography of figures such as Maud Allan, Isadora Duncan and Ruth St Denis in the 1900s. As with social dance, transatlantic cultural capital was important in building this legitimacy. Duncan and St Denis were initially lauded in Europe, and returned to America to build on this success. Duncan began to institutionalise the opera house dance concert, and performed at the Metropolitan Opera House in the decade; and St Denis spent much of it touring the nation on the vaudeville circuit and building an audience for modern dance.[29] She also founded the influential modern dance school, Denishawn, with her husband Ted Shawn – which educated future stars such as Martha Graham and Doris Humphrey.

Both Duncan and St Denis had rejected the enervated and uninspiring forms of American ballet in the late nineteenth century, as well as decrying the predominant style of dance in American theatres, with its focus on chorus-led risqué entertainment. As Ann Daly has put it, Duncan aimed to '[elevate] dance from low to high, from sensual to spiritual, from black to white, from profane to sacred, from woman to goddess, from entertainment to "Art"'.[30] This was not the easiest of missions; sniggering at the pretensions of figures like Duncan and St Denis was a regular feature of press coverage. The *New York Times* in 1916, for example, chortled at the army of 'bare-limbed dancers [who] have run the risk of splinters and pneumonia while bringing out the hidden meanings of the compositions of the masters', and it was only in the late 1920s that it would appoint a permanent dance critic.[31]

Both Duncan and St Denis drew on ancient and mythological sources for their interpretive dances. Duncan was renowned for her appropriation of Greek myth and choreography (she would often claim to have rediscovered a form that had been dormant for two thousand years) and produced interpretations of Orpheus, Oedipus Rex, and Iphigenia in the 1910s. She favoured simple, flowing robes, and elemental staging. Although she typically performed alone, in dances of around two hours, she claimed she had never danced a solo – which Daly interprets as her belief that solos were 'enactments of agency, the self in the process of engagement with the external world, whether that meant love or fate, oppression or death'.[32] She was infamous for her sexual morality – she was a firm advocate of voluntary motherhood and women's right to sexual love, and had a child outside marriage. She had political engagements with suffrage, was a fierce supporter of France during the war (her dance to 'The Marseillaise' in New York in 1914 was probably her most famous performance of the decade) and later fell foul of the Red Scare owing to her enthusiasm for the new Soviet republic. Her dances were not improvised, as was often thought, but carefully choreographed to the music of classical figures such as Christoph Gluck, Beethoven, Chopin, Wagner, Tchaikovsky and Brahms – often to the horror of music purists.[33] She was a beloved symbol of artistic and personal liberation for many modernists and village bohemians, even as her egotism and airy idealism were critiqued by more pragmatic thinkers like Walter Lippmann, who saw her as an 'archaic moralist . . . who tells men to be good, be true, be beautiful, and forgets to say how'.[34] Nonetheless, her own feelings about modernism and the modern world were more vexed; in her famous 1927 essay 'I See America Dancing' she found it 'monstrous for anyone to believe that the Jazz rhythm expresses America'; for her it expressed 'the sensual convulsion of the South African Negro'.[35] Committed to an aesthetics of wholeness rather than fragmentation, seriousness rather than irreverence, classicism rather than the popular or avant-garde, and the appeal of the Romantic artist–prophet, she held a distance from both the leading curve of modernism and from popular dancing icons like Irene Castle.

If Duncan was associated with Hellenism, Ruth St Denis built her career on eastern exoticism – particularly dances modelled on the myths and costumes of Egypt and India. Far more in the mainstream of American stage production than Duncan, St Denis had toured extensively with theatrical impresario David Belasco in the early 1900s and worked the vaudeville circuit for much of her career; her appreciation of the populist elements of American stagecraft informed her lavishly costumed and staged performances. Even the story of her moment of inspiration to invent a new form of dance is one embedded in the cultures of the commercial, particularly the sexualising, appropriative and commodifying apprehension of eastern cultures that Edward Said later called orientalism; she was inspired to create her breakthrough dance 'Radha' after seeing a poster for Egyptian Deities cigarettes. 'Radha' was based on Indian choreographies and costumes, but she began the 1910s with a lavish touring production entitled 'Egypta', a full-length drama which ended with a boat arriving to carry the soul of Egypt to the afterlife.[36] Subsequent eastern productions included 'O-Mika', based on the choreography of Japanese dancer, Sadi Yaco; 'Bakawali', based on a Hindu love story; and the spectacular dance pageant of Egypt, Greece and India at the University of California's Greek Theatre – all demonstrating what Joseph H. Mazo calls '[a] mind that revelled in mysticism and understood dance as a religious experience [but] also had a remarkable appreciation of popular taste'.[37]

In 1914, she met her future husband, Ted Shawn, who would

Figure 4.2 Ruth St Denis as the Courtesan in *O-Mika*, 1913. Denishawn Collection. Jerome Robbins Dance Division, The New York Public Library for the Performing Arts, Astor, Lenox and Tilden Foundations.

pioneer modern dancing for men. The American ballet had assigned all male roles to women by the late nineteenth century and, by the 1910s, dance critics were bewailing that 'a man himself would as a rule rather be caught in the act of stealing than of dancing alone or with his fellows'.[38] In time, Shawn would choreograph several innovative all-male dance pieces, but his first major contribution was helping St Denis set up their school Denishawn in 1915. Licensing its syllabus for $500, schools based on their system sprang up across the country, training a generation in the techniques of free dance, yoga and oriental choreography which Shawn and St Denis had developed.[39]

Little Theatre

In a business prone to spectacular failures, American theatre began with a particularly influential one in the 1910s. The New Theatre held the ambition of being a national theatre to rival those of Europe, and aimed to produce high-quality repertory productions of classic theatre and opera, maintained by subscriptions from wealthy patrons. Opening in 1909 in a ceremony which included Woodrow Wilson, Thomas Edison and J. P. Morgan, it was conceived by the director of the Metropolitan Opera, Heinrich Conried, and housed in a purpose-built 2,500-seat luxury theatre on Central Park West. It was a disaster from the outset, slammed for incoherent programming, bad acoustics, overly complex scenery, a total lack of the intimacy which new styles of acting demanded and for having no compelling vision of what exactly was 'New' about its productions. Its size meant it quickly ran up huge losses, and it closed in 1911.[40]

The New Theatre's collapse made clear that the economies of scale for art theatre in the United States would be small and dispersed rather than huge and central. Accordingly the decade saw a spate of 'little theatres' initiated across the country, devoted to providing alternatives to mainstream commercial theatre. Often launched in contrast to the risk-averse trends of Broadway and a high cultural fidelity to European classics, most of these were run by dedicated amateurs as repertory, non-profit organisations. By 1920 there were hundreds across the country, in cities such as Boston, Philadelphia, Cleveland, Madison, Pasadena, Los Angeles and Galesburg, Illinois.[41] The most important of these radiated out from the centres of avant-garde and bohemian intellectual activity in Chicago and Greenwich Village; particularly influential were Maurice Browne's Chicago Little Theatre, with its innovative impressionistic stage-designer, C. Raymond Johnson, and the Washington Square Players (which transformed into the influential Theatre Guild in 1919).[42] These theatres produced the new European writing of playwrights such as Shaw, Maeterlinck, Chekhov, Wilde, Ibsen and Galsworthy, as well as encouraging native writing.

As well as performing the works of these modern European playwrights, the little theatres were also inspired by the so-called 'New Stagecraft'. Developed by Europeans such as Edward Gordon Craig, Adolphe Appia and Max Reinhardt, this new aesthetic provided sets which relied on symbolism, abstraction, and bold, simple lighting and colour schemes. Its aim for psychological affect through abstraction contrasted strikingly with the realist recreation of detail that was the norm in Broadway productions in the first half of the 1910s, a realism most associated with David Belasco (famously, in Belasco's production of *The Governor's Lady* in 1912, the entire interior of a Childs' restaurant – the 1910s equivalent of Macdonald's – was recreated on-stage). Particularly influential in bringing the New Stagecraft to American attention were The Irish Abbey Players' 1911–12 American tour, and also Max Reinhardt's 1912 New York production of the oriental pantomime *Sumurun* – which drew on Japanese kabuki theatre in presenting backdrops without perspective, the extensive use of bold silhouettes and vivid blocks of single colour. As a contemporary reviewer admiringly noted – and in a dig at Belasco – Sumurun's staging 'hits the imagination instead of merely filling the eye'.[43] Wide notice was also given to visiting productions such as Harley Granville Barker's 1915 version of *A Midsummer Night's Dream*, and the tour of Jacques Copeau's Théâtre du Vieux Colombier in 1917, both of which presented a 'neo-Elizabethan' staging of Shakespeare which featured an essentially bare stage and little scenic detail.[44] Innovative American set designers, such as Robert Edmond Jones (who had trained under Reinhardt in Europe) as well as Rollo Peters, Sam Hume, Lee Simonson and Cleon Throckmorton, brought these stylistic influences to both Broadway plays and to the little theatres. This also fed the development of the American expressionist aesthetic which would flower in the 1920s, particularly in the plays of Eugene O'Neill and Elmer Rice.[45] Significantly, Jones was a founding member of the Provincetown Players, arguably the company with the firmest place within the modernist romance of the 1910s.

The Provincetown Players' 1916 Season

By 1915 the small town of Provincetown, at the tip of Cape Cod, had become a popular summer retreat for the constellation of writers, dramatists, political activists and salon hostesses which characterised 1910s radicalism. The idea for a small theatre was driven by George Cram Cook, a stalwart of 1910s bohemianism: by 1915 he had been twice divorced, had held teaching positions in Greek at Iowa and Stanford, had run for Congress on the socialist ticket, had worked on the pioneering Friday Literary Supplement of the *Chicago Evening News* and had settled in Greenwich Village.[46] In 1915 he and his wife, Susan Glaspell, had co-authored 'Suppressed Desires', a one-act skit on Freudian psychoanalysis which gently mocked the enthusiasm for Freud in Greenwich Village, particularly its tendency to interpret narrowly his theories as a green light for sexual promiscuity. This was performed in a Provincetown living room in the summer of 1915, along with Neith Boyce's satire on John Reed and Mabel Dodge's affair in her playlet 'Constancy'. So successful was this that the bill was repeated in an old fish shed at the end of a local wharf; patrons brought their own chairs. The shed was owned by the socialist and suffragist activist Mary Heaton Vorse and, after the performance, Cook extracted her promise to lend them this venue for the following summer.

The narcissistic tenor of 'Constancy' and 'Suppressed Desires' remained a staple of the Provincetown Players' programme; subsequent bills were peppered with comic playlets about the mores of marriage, the affectations of idealist poets or the sexual double standards implicit in bohemian celebrations of freedom. This introversion was later defended by Hutchins Hapgood as the only adequate response to global war; he claimed that 'without self-knowledge and honest reconsideration our political and economic effort is useless . . . without a truthful effort for a deeper culture, all our large social purposes are impossible'.[47] Cook's vision for that culture was the guiding force, and emphasised collaborative creativity and the emotional and practical models of Greek theatre. Particularly important was 'the triple province of Dionysus – intoxication, sexual rites, and theatre: different forms of release from routine and morality which he saw not as a social safety valve, but rather as the basic building material of a creative community'.[48] Cook's fascination with Greece also fed a culturally nationalistic approach to theatre, and the Provincetown Players held a distinctive ambition to cultivate what he called a 'native stage for native plays', which would 'prove that the finest culture is a possibility of democracy'.[49] Utopian in ideology and structure, the Players reflected Cook's ambition – shared so widely on the 'lyrical left' in the decade – to reimagine a national culture, as well as his hopes of orchestrating 'a theatre of collective ecstasy and pure space'.[50]

For the 1916 season, the company adopted the subscription system much utilised by little theatres; this guaranteed regular income and allowed the flexibility to take risks with experimental work. With some of this money, they refitted the shed with seating, electric light, and a flexible staging space which had four movable sections and a 10 foot by 12 foot stage (the backdrop – revealed by a rolling door – was the Atlantic).[51] This season is principally remembered for introducing individual works by two of the century's great American dramatists: Susan Glaspell and Eugene O'Neill. O'Neill, who met the group earlier in the summer and would become its most powerful influence aside from Cook, saw his one-act play,

Bound East for Cardiff (1914), performed in the company's second bill of the season – the first ever performance of his work. Later incorporated into his *S. S. Glencairn* cycle, which featured three other short plays literally in the same boat – *In the Zone* (1917), *The Long Voyage Home* (1917) and *The Moon of the Caribbees* (1918) – it takes place on a tramp steamer travelling between New York and Cardiff. An emotionally taut and unsettling play, *Bound East for Cardiff* follows the slow death of Yank, a sailor, following a heavy fall – and his increasingly desperate deathbed conversation with his best friend, Driscoll. The play features many themes and devices which mark O'Neill's later career, including a homosocial setting, a focus on morbidity and self-pity, the harshness of working-class life at sea, an exploration of working-class speech, and ideals of familial happiness which can never be realised in the face of life's brutal realities. Perhaps most important, as Sarlós notes, was its ability to substitute mood for plot, a feature which underpinned other plays in the cycle and would be crucial to the expressionist aesthetic which O'Neill went on to explore more radically in later plays such as *The Hairy Ape* (1921, 1922) and *The Emperor Jones* (1920).

The other memorable piece of the season was Glaspell's *Trifles*, a play exploring the investigations of a crime scene after a farm housewife kills her husband, apparently without motive. Set in the farm kitchen, the county law officials – all men – laughingly dismiss the 'trifles' of the wife's domestic existence – her baking, her sewing, her solitude – while searching for 'real' evidence which will lead them to her reasons for murder. It is left to the two women who accompany them to piece together the details of her domestic isolation and the abuse she suffers from her husband; it is they who 'know what stillness is', and who consequently come to understand her motive.[52] As they do so, they feel their own complicity in creating the isolation which drove her to murder, and ultimately this empathy leads them to conceal evidence from their husbands and lawmen which would further incriminate her. In keeping the male characters off-stage for most of the play, and in having her female characters afford the murderess, Minnie Foster, this degree of protection, Glaspell implicitly questions the patriarchal assumptions and privileges in contemporary systems of law and marriage – and in who gets to define what constitutes meaningful labour or meaningful evidence. The irony of the title is not merely that it is the 'trifles' of Minnie's kitchen which explain the murder; it is that Mrs Hale and Mrs Peters 'trifle' with a system which seeks the death penalty for women who fight back when subjected to domestic abuse. For these reasons, and along with her fictional version of the play, the short story 'A Jury of Her Peers', *Trifles* has become a much-anthologised feminist classic from the period.[53]

The following season the players moved to Greenwich and leased a property on Macdougald Street, naming it the Playwrights' Theatre (at O'Neill's insistence). Over the next six years the Provincetown Players produced fourteen plays of O'Neill's and eleven of Glaspell's, and a further sixty-eight by another forty-five American dramatists. In 1920 O'Neill leapt to fame as *The Emperor Jones* transferred to Broadway, and *Beyond the Horizon* won him his first Pulitzer Prize. This commercial breakthrough marked the end of Cook's vision of a communal theatre defined by its opposition to commercial success, and he broke up the theatre's original constitution by fleeing to Greece in 1922.[54] In a letter written at the time, Cook recalled his promise 'to let this theatre die rather than let it become another voice of mediocrity', bewailing its failure to 'create a soul under the ribs of death in the American theatre'.[55] Yet the Provincetown Players had nurtured personnel and stylistic innovations which would transform the commercial American stage, and would shape the indigenous theatre he had longed to develop.

Broadway and Commercial Theatre

The Provincetown Players and other little theatres continued to perform avant-garde work in the decade, including verse drama from poets such as Alfred Kreymbourg and Edna St Vincent Millay (whose 'Aria da Capo' of 1917 presented a poignant and insightful symbolic rendering of the futility of war). Yet it was O'Neill who quickly emerged as the pioneer of a serious native drama alive to innovative techniques of staging – an effort that has sometimes been read as an Oedipal rejection of the mode of theatre of his father, James O'Neill.[56] O'Neill senior had played Edmond Dantes in *The Count of Monte Cristo* – to which he held the rights – over six thousand times in his career and, although the melodramatic 'points'-based acting style he had been famous for was falling out of favour by the 1910s, other elements of his theatre were still a staple of the commercial mainstream.

Broadway was the focus for the national theatre. As well as being the centre of America's highly centralised and syndicated theatre business, it was there that shows gained a large portion of their receipts, as well as competed for the chance to go on national tours. These shows were committed to 'combination' companies assembled for a single show rather than the repertory companies of the little theatres, a company style based around the economics of the long run. Shows typically had a target of one hundred continuous performances; forty to eighty would represent a modest run; and fewer than thirty counted as a failure.[57] Traditionally, these hit shows then embarked on lucrative 'road' tours to other major American cities although, during this period, a glut of theatres nationwide and rising transport costs saw audiences tail off and production costs rise. Consequently, the great days of 'the road' were in decline, with touring shows falling from 289 in 1909 to around forty by 1920.[58]

Part of the reason for that glut of theatres was the fierce

competition in the early part of the decade between rival theatrical conglomerates. Since the 1890s, the considerable logistical complexity of managing road tours for booking agents, producers, and theatre managers had been rationalised and controlled by the Theatrical Syndicate. Formed in the wake of the financial panic of 1893, this was a nationwide partnership of separate booking circuits headed by Marc Klaw and Abraham Lincoln Erlanger, who held a virtual nationwide monopoly on the booking of first-class theatres and productions. This worked in a similar way to the Keith-Albee circuit in vaudeville (see Chapter 1), and its practices of dictating content to its artists and forcing out opposition were later copied by the growing power of Paramount Studios in films. At the beginning of the 1910s, however, another syndicate organisation, run by the Shubert Brothers, had used its foothold in a chain of theatres in upstate New York to challenge this stranglehold by offering a refuge to theatres dissatisfied with the syndicate's coercive and bullying tactics. In the 1910s, the Shuberts would grow to eclipse the Theatrical Syndicate in importance.

These structural changes did not diminish the chance for hit shows to generate enormous runs on the road, though. *Peg O' My Heart* (1912) and *Lightnin'* (1918), the two most successful shows in the decade, had 603 and 1,291 Broadway performances respectively and, counting road tours and overseas transfers, *Peg O' My Heart* had racked up 10,232 performances by 1918. *Peg O' My Heart* was indicative of the taste of the time for light, domestic comedy; a Cinderella story, it starred Laurette Taylor in the role of Peg, an Irish American girl staying with her snobbish and selfish English aristocratic relatives. J. Hartley Manners's play relies for its appeal on cocking a snook at fusty English aristocrats, and on the charms of the feisty Peg, as she discovers – in the play's swooning final line – 'love's young dream'.[59] Peg is – as James Joyce would ironically remark of his character Gerty MacDowell early in the next decade – 'as fair a specimen of winsome Irish girlhood as one could wish to see', but the role came to imprison Taylor just as Dantes had imprisoned James O'Neill: she would not escape it for a further twenty years.[60] It also flirted with sexual impropriety; Peg's dissolute cousin Ethel contemplates an affair with a married man as a means of dispelling her *ennui* in the English countryside, only to be rescued by the virtuous Peg. This foreshadowed the rise of another popular dramatic genre in the 1910s, the sex farce, which achieved a hit production every year from 1915 to 1921. Many of the most successful were written by Avery Hopwood, who generated a series of suggestive titles for his works – *Fair and Warmer*

(1915), *Double Exposure* (1918) and *The Girl in the Limousine* (1919); other playwrights produced works such as *His Bridal Night* (1916), *The Naughty Wife* (1918) and *Up in Mabel's Room* (1919). As Ronald Wainscott notes, the plays worked through *double entendre*, near escapes, misunderstandings, and by presenting attractive female actors – often ridiculed for their lack of acting talent – in various situations of vulnerability and undress.[61] Nonetheless, they appealed through titillation rather than through explicitness, and traditional sexual and marital mores would generally be endorsed in the play's closing scenes.

Critics saw these types of productions as indicative of a theatrical business model which discouraged a serious, experimental native drama in favour of lightweight confections – or, as George Jean Nathan put it in 1922, had delivered a 'drama deaf' theatrical culture which ran on 'legs, lewdness and sentimentality'.[62] This was partly a swipe at Florenz Ziegfeld and David Belasco for, while the economics of the theatres had been dominated by trusts, the aesthetics had been highly influenced by these two independent producer–impresarios. Ziegfeld launched his annual Follies show in 1907 and, for much of the 1910s, it played at Klaw and Erlanger's showpiece Times Square theatre, the New Amsterdam. From 1915 he also ran the Ziegfeld Midnight Frolic cabaret revue on the Amsterdam's roof theatre, and lucrative road tours took the Follies nationwide. The Follies was part revue, part vaudeville, and featured comics such as Bert Williams, Eddie Cantor, W. C. Fields, and Fanny Brice, but its popular appeal and publicity focused on what the *New York Times* drolly called the 'undraped entertainment' provided by its chorus line of 'Ziegfeld Girls'.[63] The aesthetics of the show worked on their worshipful objectification; Ziegfeld's avowed intent was 'to glorify the American girl'. Working with brilliant costumiers, stage designers, and choreographers such as Joseph Urban and Ned Wayburn, Ziegfeld's Follies figured a grand spectacle which presented the chorus girls not just as images of erotic pleasure but as icons of sexual and stylistic modernity.[64] Film stars such as Louise Brooks, Marion Davies, and Mae Murray came through their ranks and, as Julie Malnig notes, by the end of the decade the chorus girl had become a 'lower-class competitor to the Aristocratic Gibson Girl' – an aspirational typology of the new woman, and one widely celebrated in film, dance magazines, and theatre.[65] Yet as the historian of Times Square, Anthony Bianco, has noted, this aspirational appeal of the chorus girl had frequently disastrous consequences for the thousands of young single women who arrived in New York seeking places in Broadway's chorus lines. There were 10,000 unemployed chorus girls in New York in 1904, many of whom became involved in the enormous sex industry which grew up around 42nd Street; and, although public morality campaigns had forced much of this trade underground by the time of the war, its presence remained a feature of the area.[66]

David Belasco, in contrast, had made his reputation in drama, particularly sentimental melodrama; he worked as a writer, director and producer, usually producing his own work. Hits such as *Madame Butterfly* (1900) and *The Girl of the Golden West* (1905) – both later adapted into operas by Giacomo Puccini – and *The Return of Peter Grimm* (1911) demonstrated his taste for the exotic and the supernatural, as well as his tendency to focus on the emotional struggles of a central woman character.[67] He was important in launching several theatrical stars of the period, as well as developing a dramaturgy of unparalleled realism, particularly in his pioneering use of lighting to simulate sunsets or sunrises and in the staging of crowd and mob scenes.[68] He was suspicious of the New Stagecraft – dismissing 'modern, wild, high colors' in 1916 as inferior to the eternal verities of 'the simple things' – and this anti-modern attitude led to his staging gradually falling from favour in the 1910s.[69] His presentation of strong (or at least suffering) women in highly sentimental situations was also challenged and extended by several writers of 'problem' plays in the period; as contemporary commentator Charles Klein noted, 'the real play begins with marriage, for the reason that all real problems in life begin at that time'.[70] Particularly notable were Edward Sheldon and Rachel Crothers. Sheldon – who had trained at George Pierce Baker's playwriting Workshop at Harvard (which O'Neill would later attend) – built on his enthusiastically received social play *Salvation Nell* (1908) with *The Boss* (1911), a Dreiserian play about big business and machine politics.[71] Crothers addressed issues such as the sexual double standard, workplace and career freedoms for women, the efficacy of progressive campaigns against 'white slavery', and the limits of how far even supposedly 'feminist' men would go in accepting female autonomy and power. Plays such as *A Man's World* (1909), *He and She* (1912), and *Ourselves* (1913) even prompted 'answer' plays defending the double standard – Augustus Thomas, for example, responded to *A Man's World* with *A Man Thinks* in 1911.[72] Crothers's ability to generate debate such as this – as well as her tenacity and versatile capacities as actor, director, and producer (she revived *He and She* in 1920 after it had failed in its initial production, and acted in it herself) established her as an important early feminist voice in American drama. She also achieved commercial success in the 1920s with a series of social comedies that continued to address the issues of marriage, the family and divorce.[73]

As theatre often hesitatingly mediated some of the debates around women's place in society in the decade, so the class and ethnic tensions of the era were also visible. The cultural critic Waldo Frank, bewailing the middle-class turgidity of mainstream theatre in 1919, saw hope in New York's small ethnic theatres, where 'still unassimilated cultural groups – Jewish, Italian, German – have their playhouses where dramas, actors, audiences meet on a common mental and emotional level', and where 'from under the shoddy surface of the plot come gleams of folk-lore, racial confessionals to clash with the cheap *patter* of the American assimilation'.[74] Both Italian and Jewish theatres in urban working-class districts were highly popular in the period, and served as centres for community identity and socialisation – Italian theatres, for example, had lights half dimmed so that conversation, eating and meeting friends could go on more easily in the auditorium. Particularly popular in both were melodramas, which often recurred to the problems of anti-immigrant prejudice and persecution, or dwelt on the hardships of being a 'greenhorn' in a new city.

Indeed, in an era where these communities had little political power in civic life and their members often worked in non-unionised industries, theatre played an important part in discussing political issues, articulating a sense of group solidarity, and venting anger at situations of social disempowerment. Jewish melodramas – often derided as 'onion plays' or 'three-hankie' plays for their tear-jerking qualities – even took plays from the classic repertoire and adapted them to Jewish situations (Hamlet as a young scholar and Claudius as a lecherous rabbi, for example, or Uncle Tom's Simon Legree figured as a bloodthirsty Cossack).[75] In the Italian theatre the comedian Eduardo Migliaccio, commonly known as Farfariello, was the star of the era for his comic sketches, or *machiette*, featuring stock characters drawn from the *commedia dell'arte*. The most beloved of these was the *cafone*, the clueless country immigrant in the New World who, like Chaplin's Little Tramp, was a 'little guy full of good intentions and ambitions but was victimized by both society and his own ineptitude'.[76] So important were these theatres to their communities that Jewish fan clubs for popular actors – known as *patriotn* – would fight each other outside theatres, and the funerals of Jewish actors attracted thousands of mourners.[77]

Theatre also did not escape the wave of industrial action in 1919. The struggle of actors to unionise had taken a decisive step forward when the Actors' Equity Association – formed in 1913 – affiliated to the American Federation of Labor in 1916. In August 1919, when the Producing Managers' Association refused to recognise either Equity or actors' rights to collective bargaining, Equity called its members out on the first strike in the history of American theatre. By the beginning of September, thirty-seven shows had been closed and only five theatres remained open on Broadway; before long the PMA called an end to the strike by agreeing to most of Equity's demands.[78] By the end of the 1910s, the unparalleled financial supremacy of Broadway, the increasing turn towards serious native drama and the development of expressionistic and innovative staging, and the growing sophistication of the little theatres had formed the conditions that would underpin arguably the greatest decade in the history of American theatre.

Art Music

The fruitful tension between modernism and more conservative forms that was such a feature of art, photography, literature and drama in the decade was much less palpable in music. Art music continued to be well funded, well supported and decentralised; in the 1910s major symphony orchestras, which existed as unparalleled symbols of highbrow civic pride, were established in San Francisco, Houston, Baltimore, Cleveland, Detroit and Philadelphia. Music clubs – run predominantly by women – existed in their hundreds, and were responsible for three-quarters of concert bookings outside the main cities.[79] Yet, as Michael Broyles observes, when the French avant-garde composer Edgard Varèse arrived in America in 1915 he was distressed at the staleness of American composition, and the reliance of its art music on European composers.[80]

Even as America's symphony orchestras moved decisively to reduce the German and Austro-Hungarian repertoires (and personnel) which had dominated their output before World War I, it was not American music which filled the vacuum.[81] America's great classical composer of the time, Charles Ives, was working in isolation in Massachusetts throughout the decade, after early performances of his work had been poorly understood. As well as his masterful art songs, works like his First Orchestral Set (1911–14), his Fourth Symphony (1910–16) and his Concord Sonata (completed c.1912) would later be praised for their ability to accommodate America's vernacular music

– its hymns, fiddle songs, marches, and patriotic songs – into 'intricately interlocking thematic relationships, implying that all music is part of a single tonal universe'.[82] It also seemed to establish a folk basis for a truly indigenous American classical music, a goal which had been a preoccupation for American composers for at least thirty years. Ives's complex experimentalism in tone clusters, polytonality, rhythmic complexity, dissonance, and cumulative setting also paralleled developments in European music, particularly that of Stravinsky, although Ives would dismiss this as an influence. He had only one performance of his work in the decade, at the Carnegie Chamber Music Hall in 1917, and his work did not receive widespread performance until the 1930s.

Tin Pan Alley

In this situation, the vitality of the decade's American music was most immediately evident in popular song, and particularly in the music of its recent immigrants. In the 1900s, the Broadway musical revue was dominated by the Irish American George M. Cohan, whose brash, patriotic march music and vernacular vigour were epitomised in songs such as 'The Yankee Doodle Boy' and 'Give My Regards to Broadway', both from *Little Johnny Jones* (1904), and 'You're A Grand Old Flag', from *George Washington Jr* (1906). Shows such as *Broadway Jones* (1912) and his patriotic contributions to the war effort, especially the song 'Over There', kept him firmly a part of the Broadway scene in the 1910s. Yet, despite this success, it was Jewish composers who took popular music in new directions in the decade, none more so Jerome Kern and Irving Berlin. American born to German Jewish parents, Kern wrote the music to an influential series of musicals staged at the small Princess Theatre in Manhattan between 1915 and 1918. The most memorable of these, *Oh, Boy!* (1917) and *Oh, Lady! Lady!!* (1918) featured lyrics and librettos by Guy Bolton and the British humorist P. G. Wodehouse. In fully integrating the songs to the narrative of the plays, and in blending Kern's classically trained, sophisticated handling of Tin Pan Alley formula with P. G. Wodehouse's erudite and witty wordplay, they charted the future direction of the American musical.[83] As Philip Furia notes, young lyricists such as Cole Porter, Ira Gershwin, and Lorenz Hart were entranced by Wodehouse's lyrics, which often gently and ironically undercut the clichés of the romantic ballad – an approach they followed in their own songwriting. Kern was also a central figure in developing the staple form of the show tune, the thirty-two-measure modulator which became the norm by the 1920s (so much so that Theodore Adorno would later lambaste it as the perfect formal example of capitalist, mass cultural standardisation in popular music).[84] In this development, Kern was joined by Berlin, whose long and illustrious career took off in 1911.

Irving Berlin, 'Alexander's Ragtime Band' (1911)

In 1911 Irving Berlin scored his first big hit with 'Alexander's Ragtime Band', his first major contribution to the American songbook in a career which spanned six decades and almost nine hundred songs registered for copyright. It was also the biggest-selling song ever up to that point, with over one million copies sold by the end of the year and a further million from domestic and overseas sales the next.[85] Read by some critics as the quintessential call to American youth to participate in a new musical culture of urban modernity – it begins with the invocation to 'come on and hear' the 'ragged meter man' – Berlin himself saw the song's success as reliant on 'that idea of *inviting* every receptive auditor within shouting distance, [which] became a part of the happy ruction'.[86] It is a transitional song, which marks a movement of the Tin Pan Alley song towards a mass culture of urban entertainment where popular music would be primarily for dancing rather than for singing, and away from the ethnic novelty song which had played such a role in the vaudeville stage.

Berlin was born Israel Baline in 1888 in Siberia and, as a boy, watched his town burned in one of Tsar Alexander III's pogroms. His family migrated to the United States in 1893, and by 1907 he was a singing waiter in Pelham's Café in Chinatown in New York's Lower East Side: it was a dive popular with tourists interested in ethnic slumming in the United States' most famous immigrant district. His job involved making risqué versions of popular Broadway hits, and his skill in witty lyrical adaptation, suggestive humour and melodic invention soon led him to write and publish his own songs. His first – 'Marie from Sunny Italy' – was copyrighted in 1907 and, like many of his early productions, was an ethnic novelty song. These made comic capital out of ethnic and racial stereotypes: Berlin's titles from this time included 'Sweet Italian Love' (1910) 'Oh, How that German Could Love' (1910), 'Yiddisha Eyes' (1910) and 'Abie Sings an Irish Song' (1913). Several of Berlin's early songs were coon songs, presenting African Americans as sexually lascivious (as in 'Do your Duty Doctor!', 1909) or absurd in their affected appropriation of an Anglo-American high culture they did not really understand (as in 'Colored Romeo', 1910). Part of that affectation was the supposed tendency of African Americans to assume pretentious names, of which Alexander was one.

'Alexander's Ragtime Band' had traces of the coon song, then, in both the bandleader's name and in its use of African American dialect terms such as 'honey' and 'the best band what am'. It did not have much to do with the musical forms of classic piano ragtime as perfected by Scott Joplin, though; a form of two-step march, 'Alexander' had only subtle references to rag (its thirty-two bar chorus, for example, in a subdominant key).[87] While the purists of the later ragtime revival dismissed it as being unworthy of the name, it obviously counted as a ragtime song in 1911. As the songwriter and publisher Harry von Tilzer put it in 1912, rag was not necessarily 'a type of song: it is a type of song treatment', a treatment which 'reflects the spirit of the American people', as any composition could be 'ragged'. Ragtime was more about a syncopated rhythm, infectious melody, and an energy and exuberance in performance than about any precise formal style, and Berlin's song had that attitude in abundance.[88]

The fact that 'Alexander' dispensed with many of the more obvious and demeaning racial features of the coon song – as well as the formal features of classic ragtime – indicates Berlin's interest in transforming African American cultural forms into this new, 'American' musical attitude. As Jeffrey Magee observes, after 1911 none of Berlin's ragtime songs featured a black protagonist – even though the African American dialect of 'baby' and 'honey' remained a feature of his lyric writing, as it does in popular song today. For Magee, this indicates Berlin's ambition to deracinate ragtime, to broaden its appeal by removing its more ethnocentric features and treating it as a medium through which 'an ethnically diverse population can be united, Americanized, and modernized'.[89] The counterargument, however, is to see such 'deracination' not as Americanisation but as cultural theft. Right from the outset of the song's popularity, Berlin faced accusations that he had stolen the song from a black musician; later rumours even suggested this was Scott Joplin.[90] Philip Furia suggests this type of rumour could have prompted Berlin's 'unfortunate denials that ragtime was the indigenous music of African-Americans', as he traced its genealogy instead to the traditions of Russian folk music.[91] Such dynamics indicate the unease and suspicion, but also the deep interconnection, fruitfulness and syncretism, which marked the relationship between Jewish and black performers and styles in the popular stage and song of the 1910s – as well as, perhaps, Berlin's own sense of American insecurity as an immigrant Russian Jew. Even at the height of his early success, at a reception hosted by his peers in 1913, his hero George M. Cohan taunted him as a 'Jew Boy'.[92]

Regardless of the song's racial politics, the institutional pattern of how it achieved its phenomenal success indicates just how interconnected and geographically centralised was the business of popular song in vaudeville, burlesque and the fledgling recording industry. It was published in March, by Berlin's Tin Pan Alley firm the Ted Snyder Company, and was pioneered by the German-born Emma Carus in vaudeville in Chicago in April, with such success that it was rapidly adopted by other vaudeville acts, such as Al Jolson and Eddie Cantor. In late May, Berlin himself sang the song at the Friar's Frolic, and a road tour took this to twelve other major cities over the next ten days. In June it was the big hit of the Broadway burlesque show

The Merry Whirl, which was a smash all summer – despite unusually hot temperatures in New York, which in the days before air conditioning usually killed off theatrical receipts. It was recorded in June by Arthur Collins and Byron G. Harlan and then, in November, by Billy Murray. By September, *Variety* was calling it the 'musical sensation of the decade', and rival music publishers were holding back other releases because it was the only song that was selling.[93] Berlin's peerless ability to fuse the elements of the music of his times perfectly to fit (and develop) the public taste, as well as his ability to craft quickly memorable melody and lyrics, would be evident in the extended life of this song: it would be recorded by Bing Crosby, Ethel Merman, Al Jolson, Bessie Smith, Benny Goodman, Louis Armstrong and Ella Fitzgerald, among many others.

Berlin's career was also closely intertwined with the considerable technological and institutional changes taking place in the American music industry in the 1910s. At the beginning of the decade, sheet music was the dominant form for music sales: it sold in music stores as well as in five-and-dimes like Woolworth's and Kresge's, and was printed in newspapers and song anthologies. Sales of pianos paralleled that of sheet music throughout this period: upright pianos as well as player pianos, which had been perfected by 1904, sold in huge numbers, with 1909 seeing the all-time peak for American piano production. Recordings were also growing in popularity, however. There were one million cylinder players in the United States in 1913 (the technology favoured by Edison), and the Victor Talking Machine Company, which utilised disc-playing phonographs, sold 124,000 of its players in 1911 – rising to 560,000 in 1920.[94] By the end of the decade, the Berlin hit 'You'd Be Surprised' (1919), sung by Eddie Cantor, had sold as many recordings – 800,000 – as it had copies in sheet music and, by the end of the 1920s, the piano industry was in sharp decline.[95] Berlin was also a keen supporter of the the American Society of Composers, Authors, and Publishers, which was founded in 1914 with a view to gaining royalties from all public performances of composers' material rather than just from music sales. In 1917 the United States Supreme Court decreed that songwriters were entitled to payment for the use of their compositions in hotels, restaurants, cabarets, vaudeville theatres, cinemas and dance halls, and a system of licensing was devised to distribute payments to members of the ASCAP. In time, with radio and television royalties, this would become the major income stream for composers like Berlin.[96]

Blues and Jazz

In a story of racial bias and neglect which would be repeated in the history of rock'n' roll and jazz, it was Berlin who carried the title the 'Ragtime King' in the decade, rather than the composer responsible for writing the majority of the most enduring ragtime songs over the previous twenty years, Scott Joplin. Indeed, Joplin's ambitions in the decade outran what the white industry or public would finance from a black composer: he saw his opera project, *Treemonisha*, fold after only one read-through performance in 1915. Despite this prejudice, the most innovative and, in the long term, the most influential developments in popular music in the decade would be produced by black musicians. These took place in working-class juke joints, barrelhouses, saloons, brothels, and small venues; at fish-fries and picnics; at dances and on steamboats; and on the nation's vaudeville circuit. They happened predominantly in the 'tenderloin' districts of southern cities such as Memphis and especially New Orleans, and in the rural black belt communities of the Mississippi Delta, East Texas and the Piedmont. Yet the distance of this music from the centres of power in the music and publishing industries means that how it was conceived, performed and received in these early days is poorly documented – making the histories of this process often reliant on anecdotal evidence collected long after the fact. As pioneering jazz documents illustrate – Frederic Ramsey Jr and Charles Edward Smith's *Jazzmen* (1939) or Allan Lomax's recordings of Jelly Roll Morton for the Library of Congress, for example – this has often delivered a history as prone to romantic exaggeration as the music once was to contemptuous dismissal.

These musical developments would subsequently be known as blues and jazz, although often the line between them would be hard to draw. Blues developed in the 1890s as a coalescence of African American rural worksong, field hollers and ballads: it was also conditioned by the songs African American convict labourers sang in the South's extensive system of prison farms. Indeed, one of the most influential East Texas blues musicians of the period – Huddie Ledbetter, or 'Lead Belly', served time in Texas's prison system, and later in Louisiana's notorious Angola Farm.[97] By the 1910s, some of the most influential innovators of this rural blues were at work, usually performing solo with a guitar accompaniment, and already performing the twelve-bar, AAB stanza structure which would remain the staple blues form. Secular songs of loss, heartbreak, travel and hard work – what Langston Hughes memorably called songs from 'black, beaten, but unbeatable throats' – at its heart, the blues was a powerful and often brutally realistic lyrical meditation on the sexual relationship in impoverished and often itinerant communities.[98] A sharp contrast to the sentimental and saccharine portrayal of love and sex in most Tin Pan Alley songs, it was this sexual candour that gave 'the blues its tension and ambiguity, dealing simultaneously with togetherness and loneliness, communion and isolation, physical joy and emotional anguish', in the words of Giles Oakley. [99] It was also central in embedding its status as a vital subculture for working-class black Americans for over fifty years.

In parts of the rural South in the decade it was performed at house parties, barrelhouses, and juke joints; in the Delta, Charely Patton would move from plantation to plantation performing his characteristic guttural, shouting (and often incoherent) deep-toned singing style of often autobiographical lyrics. This was enhanced by his emotive slide-guitar – which made the guitar sound like an additional, crying, vocal accompaniment.[100] At the same time, musicians such as Lead Belly and Blind Lemon Jefferson were developing a distinctive East Texas style, lighter and often more poetic in its vocalisation. The two sometimes performed together in Dallas and other Texas towns; Lead Belly's skill on the twelve-string guitar was characterised by bass-heavy strums, and Jefferson's singing – which made him the most recorded 'country' blues singer in the 1920s – was distinguished by what Paul Oliver calls a 'high-voiced, lean toned' style.[101] Also central to this music was the blue note which, according to European styles of notation, was flatted or 'bent' at the third or seventh note of the scale – although this notation was incapable of capturing how the blue notes gave the 'wailing slurring tones of a real blues song', as Hughes put it.[102]

Often contrasted to these rural bluesmen are the 'classic' female blues singers who were the first to record this music in the 1920s, such as Gertrude 'Ma' Rainey, Ida Cox, Alberta Hunter, Ethel Waters, Mamie Smith and Bessie Smith. In the 1910s, many of these women toured theatres and vaudeville houses in small towns and cities, frequently booked through the African American vaudeville agency which had formed in 1909 – the (in)famous Theatre Owners' Booking Agency, or TOBA (often ruefully referred to as 'tough on black artists', or 'asses').[103] Although owned by white entrepreneurs, it offered an unprecedented chance for black performers to get into the concert halls of the biggest southern, midwestern and eastern cities – as well as to perform in front of white audiences. This allowed blues singers like Gertrude 'Ma' Rainey to make the transition from the rural, southern, travelling minstrel tent show, where she began her career, to become an urban blues icon who had recorded ninety-two records by the end of the 1920s. A performer with the Rabbit Foot Travelling Minstrel show, an all-black minstrel troupe, Rainey combined a mixture of earthy humour, emotional plaintiveness and sexual confidence that brought her adoring audiences. She also cultivated an on-stage persona that would be the model for later blueswomen – she was full figured, with a smile full of gold teeth, and kohled eyes; she wore extravagant clothing of headdresses, beads, satin gowns, ostrich feathers and necklaces of gold coins. Both she and her fans revelled in her bisexual (and extramarital) promiscuity. She nurtured the career of Bessie Smith, who was possibly her lover; and, in what Buzzy Jackson calls her 'renegade moral style' she presented a form of black feminism – based in creative and financial autonomy, freedom of movement and a celebration of female sexual desire – which was largely unavailable to the small and precarious black American middle class.[104] Moreover, as Hazel Carby has noted, the performances of women like Ma Rainey expressed the problems and resilience not just of working-class black women, but of black women in the midst of the enormous cultural and social upheaval of the great migration. In this situation, women's blues offered both 'social models for women who aspired to escape from and improve their conditions of existence', and also formed what Carby sees as the major cultural mediation of the often dislocating experience of urban migration.[105]

Just as blues was moving with southern rural migrants into the cities – especially Memphis and Chicago, where it would flourish in the 1920s – so the dispersal of jazz was inseparable from the great migration. A style steeped in both blues and ragtime, jazz emerged as a phenomenon in the decade; the first appearance of the word 'jazz' in connection with music was in 1915 and, by 1920, it was already being played in Helsinki, London and Sydney. It had ragtime's lightness and melodic variety but also the emotional range and blue notes of blues. It drew on ragtime's reliance on syncopation but departed from ragtime's steady, left-hand beat by 'swinging' the fundamental rhythm; as Burton Peretti notes, 'many observers attribute both the seductive, sensual element in jazz and its special excitement in fast tempi to this swinging of the beat'.[106] It was primarily a band music rather than music for a solo pianist and, unlike ragtime's stress on notation, it relied on improvisation – extending and complexifying the improvisatory character of blues. Several of its early standards were the blues

songs published in the 1910s, especially those of the self-proclaimed 'father of the blues', W. C. Handy, whose 'Memphis Blues' (1912) and especially 'St Louis Blues' (1914) did much to popularise this new genre. Jelly Roll Morton – who claimed to have heard blues first performed in New Orleans in 1902 and who, as a light-skinned Creole, was one of the few early jazzmen to play in white bordellos in the city – published what has been hailed as the first true jazz composition in 1915, 'Jelly Roll Blues'.[107]

The heart of this music was in New Orleans, where a range of musical cultures fed into the creation of jazz in the early part of the century. The city's unrivalled brass band tradition, the importance of ragtime piano in the city's bars and brothels, and the polyrhythmic drumming of slaves and their descendants in Congo Square informed this development (drumming in Congo Square lasted until 1885, and pioneering jazz clarinettist and saxophonist Sidney Bechet would claim that his grandfather had played there). Jazz was led by the cornetist Buddy Bolden in the 1900s and, by the 1910s, the distinctive early New Orleans style of jazz had emerged, based in small-group, polyphonic collaboration – wherein the lead instruments, most often cornet, clarinet and trombone, engaged in complex counterpoint. This was punctuated by short, improvised 'breaks', and an obsession with brass tones which approximated the human voice; as Ted Gioia observes, the cornetist Joe Oliver claimed to have spent ten years working on his.[108] After Bolden came successive cornet 'Kings', whose bands sometimes fended off claims to their supremacy from rivals in open-air 'ballyhoo' battles of musical skill.[109] Formed of about six people, these bands were often very badly paid – gigs in the poorer, black sections of New Orleans sometimes offered only $1.25 a night. Along with the Navy crackdown on the brothels of the Storyville district in 1917, this was a major factor informing what came to be known as the New Orleans Jazz diaspora, as the city's best musicians moved on to higher-paid work elsewhere.[110]

Conventional wisdom holds that this took place primarily in the late 1910s and early 1920s, as musicians such as Joe 'King' Oliver, Louis Armstrong, Jimmy Noone, Sidney Bechet, Johnny Dodds and Jelly Roll Morton followed the principal direction of black migrants from Mississippi and Louisiana by relocating to Chicago (although this was highly temporary for some of these artists). Certainly the music of Oliver and Armstrong, who collaborated in 1922 at Chicago's Royal Gardens in the Creole Jazz Band and recorded in 1923, is rightly celebrated as the greatest surviving early example of the New Orleans style, along with Morton's Chicago-based Red Hot Pepper sessions of 1926–7. But recently jazz historians such as Alyn Shipton have questioned this story, noting that Morton left New Orleans in 1908, and cornetist Freddie Keppard in 1914 – and that both played and toured extensively on the nationwide variety circuits. This included stays in California, and the tour of Keppard's Original Creole Orchestra on the Orpheum Theatre Circuit also took in Chicago and New York. In addition, the first jazz recordings by a black artist were made in California, not Chicago, by the New Orleans trombonist Kid Ory and his Creole Orchestra, who set down six tracks for the Sunshine label in 1921; the five thousand copies pressed sold predominantly at The Spikes Brothers' record store in Los Angeles, which was already doing a large trade to the city's black population in blues records.[111] It seems fair to assume, then, that this diaspora was more peripatetic and possibly earlier than has often been claimed, and that early jazz was gaining a nationwide audience well in advance of the first recordings by black artists in the early 1920s. It was also undergoing important developments elsewhere, particularly in the New York-based 'stride' style of piano, which built on the complex right-hand melodic work of ragtime to present a virtuosic, orchestral style of playing which would be widely influential. James P. Johnson's 'Carolina Shout' of 1918 was the *locus classicus*, serving as a test piece for aspiring jazz pianists for years to come, and forming part of the repertoire of classic stride musicians such as Willie 'The Lion' Smith and Fats Waller.[112]

Nonetheless, the rapid and international spread of jazz would have been inconceivable without its early recordings. The best early groups would not record until the 1920s, in part because of the racism of the American recording industry, and so it fell to the Original Dixieland Jazz Band to pioneer jazz recordings in 1917. An all-white group from New Orleans, their frenetic first side, 'Livery Stable Blues', demonstrated jazz's early connections with the novelty record by being peppered with instruments imitating animal noises. It went on to sell a million, and was heard by a generation of young musicians who otherwise would have had very limited access to the music – the young Bix Beiderbecke, for example, listened to the ODJB on his family's Columbia Gramophone in Davenport, Iowa in 1918 and decided on the spot to become a jazz cornetist.[113] The ODJB's recordings sound dogged and predictable when placed against the crop from the first great year of jazz recordings by black artists in 1923, and their leader Nick LaRocca's aggressive insistence that jazz was solely their invention and had nothing to do with black musicians or styles clouded early understandings of the music. Indeed, their tour of England in 1919 meant that the full importance of black Americans to the development of jazz was not fully understood there for a decade.[114]

Nonetheless, the ODJB did more to popularise and disseminate jazz than any of the other early acts. Their success meant that by 1919 the jazz age was indisputably underway: the *New York Times* would be referring to Einstein's theory of relativity as the scientific equivalent of jazz, and ran pieces talking about the old-fashioned decorum of ragtime.[115] And whether seen as war's antidote or war's consequence, a music of youthful, joyous abandon or a music of menacing, primitive anarchy, it was widely understood as the music of a postwar world: the word itself entered American English at the same time as barrage, camouflage, tank, smoke screen, and zero hour.[116]

Conclusion

With its startling novelty, its mixture of impiety, aural assault and unpredictability, jazz reflected in a way no other mainstream cultural form could match the new circumstances for experiencing the world that the war had imposed on millions. As the following chapter will consider, American culture was uniquely placed to assume a more global role in the postwar world: not only did its culture industries emerge strengthened from the conflict, but European fantasies of American idealism and youthful energy – which seemed to offer a rejuvenating tonic to a weary and battered continent – led to the first global 'American moment' in cultural tastes. A key part of that was the exposure Europeans had to American culture during the war: American troops went off to battle singing George M. Cohan's 'Over There', or Berlin's 'Oh! How I Hate to Get Up in the Morning'; regimental bands introduced jazz and ragtime to thousands of doughboys and Europeans alike. This cultural export also betokened a new maturity in American mass culture: dance, music, and film-going increasingly took place in what David Nasaw calls an unprecedented 'culture of civic sociability,' a 'common commercial culture . . . where social solidarities were emphasized and distinctions muted'.[117] Moreover, Woodrow Wilson had signalled the changing attitude among political elites towards leisure by declaring during the war that 'a reasonable amount of amusement' was not 'a luxury but a necessity'; by 1933 the sociologist Jesse Frederick Steiner could remark that 'during the past

thirty years the earlier prejudices against sports and amusements have
been replaced by an almost equally intolerant belief in their value'.[118]
Yet, during the war, the tensions that resided in American culture in
the decade, and which were sharply manifest in dance, theatre and
music – between service and self-fulfilment, industry and artistry,
modernism and the market, and who could lay claim to the label of
being an 'American' – were often brutally exposed. This was because
the stakes were high: culture had a vital importance to the American
war effort and, as public amusements gained in popularity and influence, so they became of increasing interest to those seeking to shape
public opinion and national identity.

Chapter 5

The Great War and American Culture

On 2 April 1917, Woodrow Wilson asked Congress to support his declaration of war against Germany and its allies. Pledging that America would fight 'for a universal dominion of right by such a concert of free peoples as shall bring peace and safety to all nations and make the world itself at last free', his message was met with clamorous approval in the House, Senate, and national press.[1] Germany had gambled it could win the war with the aid of unrestricted submarine warfare before the United States had a chance fully to mobilise its resources, a fair bet given the pitiful state of the United States army – ranked by experts as nineteenth in the world in size and capacity in 1914 – and the demoralisation of French and British forces in 1917.[2] Indeed, initially it was believed America's contribution might remain financial, as it had been during its period of nominal neutrality: by 1916 Britain was receiving 40 per cent of its military supplies from America, and was totally reliant on US credit.[3]

By the Armistice of November 1918, however, twenty-four million American men had registered for the draft, two million had travelled to France, and 1,400,000 had seen active front-line service. In terms of casualties, the United States got off relatively lightly, with 50,300 battle deaths – compared to 1.6 million for Germany, 1.7 million for Russia, 1.38 million for France, and nine hundred thousand for Britain.[4] (Most of these American fatalities occurred in two engagements for the American Expeditionary Forces, at Château-Thierry in July–August 1918 and at the Meuse–Argonne in October). Yet its associated costs were enormous: the Federal budget leapt from $0.75 billion in 1916 to $19 billion in 1919, and with the continual need for veterans' support and pensions it would never again see prewar levels of frugality.[5] Civil liberties were greatly curtailed, and the postwar upheaval of a year of strikes, labour activism and the spectre of Bolshevism in Russia prompted America's first-ever Red Scare in 1919. America's refusal to join the League of Nations, its new role as a massive international creditor and the disillusionment with erstwhile Allies felt by thousands of returning doughboys all helped set the tone for America's relationship with the rest of the world for a generation. The war for America was not the apocalypse it had been for Europe, but its transformative effects were substantial and long lasting.

Those effects were closely related to American culture. As John T. Matthews notes, the remoteness of the war – fought in a Europe most had never visited and few understood – meant that, for most Americans, representations of war *were* the war.[6] Consequently, the cultural products from America in wartime often show the strain of ordinary Americans attempting to understand their nation's strategy and the implications of their involvement in this global war. A good initial example is the novel *The Desert of Wheat*, written by America's most popular author, Zane Grey, in 1919. In many ways it was conventional and unsurprising: it centres on a farmer-hero from the Northwest who performs heroic military service in France, and returns to marry his sweetheart. Echoing staple narratives of many wartime films and patriotic stories, their home community bands together for the good of the country in raising gargantuan quantities of wheat to feed the Allied forces, and crushes the local Industrial Workers of the World (IWW) through the action of local patriotic vigilantes. Such action is regrettable but necessary: the IWW has been infiltrated by German spies and saboteurs bent on hindering the United States war effort. The novel also features typical Zane Grey motifs of the flawed but almost superhuman male hero, a mytho-poetic rhapsody over the western landscape, and the synecdoche of woman and homeland which was such a powerful trope in American propaganda during the war. In all this, it demonstrates prevalent attitudes in American life during the war years: a zealous patriotism on both home and battle fronts; a fierce condemnation of any dissent from the war effort; and a rigorous policing – by vigilante violence if necessary – of any ethnic and political difference from what was deemed '100% Americanism'. The crushing of imperial Germany – described here, as in many other instances, as a nation racially inclined to tyranny and atrocity – is represented as a noble and necessary cause.

Yet Grey's novel is not quite this simple. In his fight with the IWW, the young Kurt Dorn finds men who have been evicted from their farms by the big money interests, and find their only refuge in radical socialism. Brave volunteers from Oregon die in unsanitary training camps in the East because of inadequate medical care, overlooked by a state apparatus so vast it has lost any apprehension of individual suffering. The representation of vigilantism is finely balanced between heroic self-reliance and a reversion to a wild west of lawlessness and ugly violence; the newly instituted Bureau of Investigation (surveillance of enemy alien operations during World War I had been assisted by a young J. Edgar Hoover) is represented as both all-knowing and sinister in its faceless power. Dorn suffers the loss of an arm, an injury that unmans him in the face of his sweetheart Lenore – a woman who assumes more of the business and organisational running of the farm than either he or her father is completely comfortable with. She even ruminates that 'if women could help govern the world there would be no wars' – and the novel seems uncertain whether or not this would be a good thing.[7] Moreover, Dorn himself is half German, and has bitter arguments with his intransigent German father over the validity of the war. Grey's book seems muddled because of the acute conundrums the war presented to American political and cultural life; it questioned how their vaunted individualism could be compatible with the enormous state necessitated by 'total war', and exactly what the long-term effects of this expanded state would be. It wonders whether the war would change relationships between men and women, labourer and owner. And it contains the troubling realisation that reliance on persuasion and voluntarism rather than on legal sanction could whip up a vicious patriotism and xenophobia, a xenophobia that threatened huge numbers of immigrant Americans whose labour had helped build the country.

Preparedness and Early Responses to the War

The situation in 1919, however, was far different from the days of 1916 and early 1917. To begin with, many American writers and intellectuals welcomed the war, for a variety of reasons. Those who had been the fiercest critics of the increasingly bureaucratised and standardised workplace, with its concomitant cultural apparatus of mass production and aesthetic conformity, saw the war as offering the escape of manly adventure. As Sherwood Anderson put it, 'boys . . . are right when they are thrilled by the tales of war and are not thrilled by the tales of the stock-exchange', a sentiment also apparent in his militaristic and proto-fascist novel *Marching Men* (1917).[8] For the twenty-four-year-old poet, Charles Reznikoff, war offered a romantic purification from the degradations of the mundane: as he

wrote of the heroic troops 'riding by', 'they touch the dust in their
homes no more / they are clean of the dirt of shop and store / and they
ride out clean to war'.[9] Arthur Train's popular novel *The Earthquake*
(1918) posited the hope that American involvement in the war would
reverse the nation's social and moral decline, resolving the simmering
class and racial conflicts assailing the United States by asserting the
primacy of national unity, and predicted that a mutual respect would
be fostered by communal sacrifice.[10] Such romantic notions extolled
what T. J. Jackson Lears has called the 'martial ideal'. This ideal
functioned as one of the most potent models buttressing the spirit
of anti-modernism, a spirit attractive for its offer of an alternative to
what he calls the 'weightless modernity' of corporate and standardised
America. The martial ideal appealed both to certain traditionalists and
also – perversely – to certain modernists, concerned as they were with
retrieving a sense of the authentic. For Lears,

> to bourgeois moralists preoccupied by the decadence and disorder
> of their society, the warrior's willingness to suffer and die for duty's
> sake pointed the way to national purification; to those who craved an
> authentic selfhood, the warrior's life personified wholeness of purpose
> and intensity of experience. War promised both social and personal
> regeneration.[11]

Such attitudes were particularly apparent in the Preparedness
movement, which urged an expanded military in response to the
European war well before 1917. Preparedness became an increasingly
popular cause after the sinking of the *Lusitania* in 1915 and, by June
1916, 350,000 people were willing to march in support of it in ten
cities across the country. In 1915 Theodore Roosevelt, its most vocal
proponent, chastised the United States for having played an 'ignoble
part' in world affairs, for having 'declined to take action for justice
and right'; for him, war was a righteous endeavour which also held the
promise of national regeneration.

Other literary supporters of war were less convinced of its regenerative powers, but urged American participation out of a deep sense
of connection to France and England. The young poet, Alan Seeger,
volunteered immediately for the French Foreign Legion in 1914,
motivated by a fierce sense of protectiveness towards French republicanism; his 'I have a Rendezvous with Death', the most famous
American poem of the war, was first published shortly after his own
death on the Somme in 1916. Edith Wharton, who by this point lived

permanently in France, was awarded the Legion of Honour for her work with war refugees and wounded veterans. She delivered medical supplies to Verdun, Ypres, and the Vosges, and wrote about these experiences for Scribner's magazine, articles later collected in *Fighting France* (1915). For Wharton, France was a 'luminous instance', a country typified by 'intellectual light and . . . moral force', menaced by a militarism which was 'stupid, inartistic, unimaginative and enslaving'.[12] Moreover, fighting to save France equated to fighting against what she saw as the most corrosive forces of modernity; the war involved the similar threats of tastelessness, crude materialism, challenges to established elites and naked self-interest that appalled her on the American scene.[13] Her great friend, Henry James, had similar views, adopting British citizenship in 1915 partly in protest at America's persistent neutrality, and expressing his great dismay at 'the awful proposition of a world squeezed together in the huge Prussian fist and with the variety and spontaneity of its parts oozing in a steady trickle, like the sacred blood of sacrifice, between those hideous knuckly fingers'.[14] Wharton, along with Willa Cather, whose cousin died at Cantigny in May 1918, would later fictionalise the conflict as a clash of civilisations. Her *A Son at the Front* appeared in 1923; Cather's *One of Ours* (1922) won the Pulitzer Prize that same year.

For many Progressive intellectuals, the war was conditionally welcomed not as a refuge from modernisation, but as a mechanism, however unfortunate, for building a more perfect version of it. In the pages of *The New Republic*, figures such as John Dewey and Walter Lippmann laid out their hopes for the war, hopes much buttressed by Woodrow Wilson's idealistic pronouncements about the shape of the postwar peace. As Alan Dawley has argued, 'the dual quest for improvement at home and abroad was at the heart of what it meant to be a progressive', and Wilson's call for a 'concert of nations' for arbitrating international disputes, and support for the self-determination of peoples, put the flesh on his pronouncement that America's war aim was to 'make the world safe for democracy'.[15] Such a bold and idealistic vision for reshaping the world sat well with Progressive hopes for a global environment shaped by representation and dialogue rather than by militarism and imperialism. Lippmann heralded the war as a time when 'new sources of energy are tapped, when the impossible becomes possible', when 'an access of spiritual force [has opened] a new prospect in the policies of the world'. The effect would be not only global but would mean 'we shall stand committed as never before to the realization of democracy in America . . . . we shall turn with fresh interest to our own tyrannies'.[16] Dewey dismissed appeals to 'Home and hearth, defense of ancestral altars and graves, glory and honor, bravery and self-immolation' as helpful motivating factors for the war; instead, he argued, the war presented 'a task ... to be accomplished to abate an international nuisance, but in the accomplishing there is the prospect of a world organization and the beginnings of a public control which crosses national boundaries and interests'. These hopes were no 'sugar coatings of the bitter pill of war', but 'objects of a fair adventure', a gamble that Wilson's Progressive credentials would win out over the devastating exigencies of war waged on such a colossal scale.[17]

Propaganda in Wartime

Lippmann put his energies at the service of the Wilson administration, advising the president, helping with Allied propaganda missions in Europe, and even getting involved in interrogating German prisoners. He also participated in the Committee on Public Information, the huge wartime organisation set up to manage governmental communication – and exhortation – about the war to the American people.

The CPI found arguably its most eager partner during the war years in the American film industry, which saw a rush to the colours as both patriotic and lucrative. Stars such as Douglas Fairbanks, Theda Bara and Mary Pickford campaigned to raise war bonds; Pickford took in two million dollars in a tour of California alone, and Chaplin even produced a promotional short, *The Bond* (1918), which featured Charlie hitting the Kaiser over the head with a Liberty Bond mallet.[18] A string of 'Kaiser movies' were produced demonising the German autocrat. In the most popular, *The Kaiser: The Beast of Berlin* (1918), an Omaha dispatch noted that 'Wild cheering marked every show when the young captain soaked the Kaiser on the jaw.'[19] Such films were occasionally too much for the authorities; Raoul Walsh's *The Prussian Cur* (1918) was withdrawn because of its encouragement of lynching as an appropriate punishment for disloyal German Americans.[20] Major directors, such as D. W. Griffith, Cecil B. De Mille and Charlie Chaplin, also produced war films, with their *Hearts of the World* (1918), *The Little American* (1917) and *Shoulder Arms* (1918) respectively. Griffith's film, which had been produced at the request of British propaganda chief Lord Beaverbrook, took place in an occupied village in France and copied many of the motifs he had deployed in *The Birth of a Nation* – 'the same family structure,

The Committee on Public Information

As noted in the introduction to *Propaganda* (1928) by Edward Bernays – the virtual inventor of public relations (PR) in the 1920s – the word propaganda was not used as a pejorative term before World War I.[21] Before American entry, British propaganda had been highly influential in moulding American support for the allies and demonising Germany, especially over its supposed atrocities in Belgium. Yet the activities of Wellington House in the United States – and its later notoriety – were dwarfed by the American organisation formed to organise governmental information and mould public opinion: the CPI, otherwise known as the 'Creel Committee'.

Just a week after declaring war, Wilson established this information agency: given the course of American war policy, such a body was imperative. There would be no steep rises in taxation, but the war would instead be heavily funded by bond issues sold to the public; there would be no food rationing; there would be no mass internment. The reluctance to practise such European methods of putting the state on a war footing called for a reliance on persuasion rather than on coercion to raise money or to conserve food and fuel; consequently, American success in the war would rest on the ability to consolidate public opinion. This endeavour called for a massive cultural apparatus to get the message across: at its peak the CPI employed 150,000 people in an assemblage of what the first CPI historians called 'as brilliant and talented a group of journalists, scholars, press agents, editors, artists, and other manipulators of the symbols of public opinion as America had ever seen united for a single purpose'.[22] By its own standards, it would be phenomenally successful. The draft was accomplished with little protest; all the bond issues were oversubscribed; and targets for Red Cross contributions were met, as well as drives for food and fuel conservation.[23]

The committee was headed by the flamboyant and zealous muckraker George Creel. Creel held with the Progressive faith in publicity which, as David Kennedy notes, had the 'crowning appeal [of] the assurance that informed public opinion could substitute for radical institutional reordering or for the naked brandishing of state power as a solution to the problems of the day'.[24] As Creel would boast in his smug postwar memoir, *How We Advertised America*, 'we had no authority . . . yet the American idea *worked*. And it worked better than any European *law*.'[25] The 'American idea' was marketed with blanket application by the CPI: Mock and Larson identify twenty-four separate divisions within the organisation. The division of news issued press releases and appeared in around 20,000 newspaper columns per week. The foreign language division translated CPI publications into foreign languages, and monitored the foreign-language press in America; the division for work with the foreign born strove to promote patriotism in various immigrant communities. The division of industrial relations and the labour publications division worked with unions and developed patriotic literature to appeal to the working class. The division of civic and educational co-operation distributed pamphlets in schools, and reached a staggering circulation of seventy-five million. The film division liaised with Hollywood and made pictures of its own. The bureau of war expositions organised expositions of trophies captured from the Germans and displays of war equipment, and even put on sham battles employing the services of three thousand soldiers, sailors and marines; the exposition at Chicago was visited by two million people alone. The bureau of pictorial public-ity produced seven hundred poster designs for all divisions of the CPI, some of which remain the most memorable cultural products of the war. The four-minute men division recruited an army of seventy-five thousand volunteer speakers, who spoke on the US war effort across the nation for a strict four minutes (approximately the time it took to change a reel of film) in theatres, cinemas and other public venues. Many of these activi-ties were duplicated by the foreign section which handled the distribution and collection of American news and propaganda overseas, including the distribution of American films, news features and photographs.[26]

Culturally, its impact was huge. Advertising space donated to the CPI filled newspapers with warnings about the dire consequences of German victory, and exhortations to buy bonds and conserve food. Famous authors such as Booth Tarkington, the western writer Rex Beach, and Wallace Irwin worked for the Division of Syndicate Features, producing fiction for the CPI. The division of pictorial publicity, headed by America's favourite illustrator, Charles Dana Gibson, produced posters which defined the visual language of patriotism for a generation – much of it consisting of virginal, white young girls in attitudes of heroic inspiration. In film, the War Cooperating Committee, including prominent figures such as Adolph Zukor, Carl Laemmle, D. W. Griffith, Jesse Lasky and Marcus Loew, liaised with the CPI over how Hollywood could make patriotic films; CPI personnel wrote scenarios for Hollywood films; and commercial distributors handled CPI documentaries about the war effort. Its own films, such as *Pershing's Crusaders*, were successes at home and abroad.[27] Yet this organization of public discourse about the war was as restrictive as it was productive. Although Creel often pronounced the CPI's opposition to censorship, he sat on the censorship board, and the CPI's 'voluntary' codes with news and media outlets regulated highly what the American people could learn of the war. Material which breached such codes was harshly dealt with: the film *The Spirit of '76*, for example, was finished just before the war by the producer Robert Goldstein, who hoped to emulate D.W. Griffith's portrayal of the Civil War with his own War of Independence film. Featuring British soldiers in the War of Independence killing women and children and carry-ing off young girls, it was seized under the Espionage Act, and Goldstein was jailed for ten years.[28] In schools, many classrooms that used the CPI's *National School Service* magazine, or its pamphlet *Conquest and Kultur: Aims of the Germans in Their Own Words*, had banned the teaching of German.

The legacies of such a vast institution and its extensive cultural outputs are inevitably complex but, for succeeding generations, two factors stood out. The CPI produced often virulently xenophobic material: leaflets for distribution in colleges proclaimed that, in Germany, students educated 'in the vicious guttural language of Kultur' received A.B. degrees denoting 'Bachelor of Atrocities'; Gibson produced posters depicting Uncle Sam lynching the Kaiser; adverts in magazines carried maps of America under conquest, renamed 'New Prussia', with New York as New Berlin and the Gulf of Mexico as the Gulf of Hate.[29] Such material contributed to a mood of xenophobic intolerance overtaking much of the nation, and fuelled the intimidation and intrusive surveillance of foreign-born or left-wing Americans by powerful vigilante organisations such as the American Protective League (and, later, many sections of the newly formed American Legion). It transpired that there was a narrow line between a progressive ideal of rational citizens persuaded to support the war because of the legitimacy of the Allied cause, and mobs goaded into horrific acts of vigilante violence by a cultural torrent of racial hatred.[30] Across the nation, the worst excesses of this saw German Americans lynched, as were IWW organisers and African American veterans. Moreover, the powerful swings in public sentiment orchestrated by the CPI brought a lively awareness on the part of corporate America that public tastes and desires could be shaped with surprising effectiveness through modern communicative methods. As Bernays – who learnt his trade as a CPI operative – put it in his celebration-cum-sales-pitch of the profession of public relations, the 'logical result of the way in which our democratic society is organized' meant 'we are governed, our minds molded, our tastes formed, our ideas suggested, largely by men we have never heard of'.[31] Such a view was anathema to the Progressive dream of 'publicity' as an enabling agent in an ideal democracy, and as an important check on corporate power; yet the ethos of men like Bernays fuelled the advertising boom of the 1920s. Equally destructive to the idealism of much of the Progressive project of the 1910s was the widespread loss of faith in public political discourse caused by the activities of the CPI. Despite the CPI's stated credo of being scrupulous over facts, even language itself seemed degraded by the war; in 1915, Henry James would bemoan that 'the war has used up words; they have weakened, they have deteriorated like motor tires'.[32] John Dos Passos – in the first of several novels bitterly decrying the change in the public sphere ushered in by the war, and especially by the CPI – expressed a common sentiment through the mouth of a disillusioned American ambulance driver:

> I shall never forget the flags, the menacing, exultant flags along all the streets before we went to war, the gradual unbaring of teeth, gradual lulling to sleep of people's humanity and sense by the phrases, the phrases. . . America, as you know, is ruled by the press. And the press is ruled by whom? Who shall ever know what dark forces bought and bought until we should be ready to go blinded and gagged to war? [author's ellipsis][33]

Figure 5.1 The Christy girl goes to war: Howard Chandler Christy's 'Clear-The-Way-!!' promotes the fourth Liberty Loan drive. Courtesy of the Library of Congress, LC-USZC4-2011.

the same separations and reunions, [and] the same editing patterns'.[34] It also utilised the same moral absolutes, with a fierce anti-German sentiment that was heavily edited for its final release (which came after the Armistice). Interestingly, Griffith found World War I difficult to film; its nature as a primarily defensive war of attrition did not provide the dynamic movement that had stunned viewers in his Civil War epic, and he commented that 'a modern war is neither romantic nor picturesque . . . It's too colossal to be dramatic.'[35] Chaplin's film was in a quite different vein. He had been warned against producing a comedy of life in the trenches, but his playing out of a doughboy fantasy – capturing the Kaiser and winning a pretty French girl – made the film a hit in the United States and in Europe.

Patriotic as these films were, the CPI exerted a firm say over their content. Creel had asked studio bosses to produce films presenting 'the wholesome life of America', and he exerted leverage to give force to this request. In 1918 the film industry managed to gain draft exemptions for its employees from the War Industries Board by having them classified as 'essential workers' – but on the condition that 'wholesome' films were the order of the day. Just as important was the power of the CPI to grant or to withhold export licences to American films. As Steven Ross notes, films showing labour strikes and riots, or hunger and poverty – such as *The Eternal Grind* (1916) and *Little Sister of Everybody* (1918) – were denied export licences by the CPI on the grounds that they were a 'bad testimonial to the value of democracy'. By 1918, the most powerful man in films, Paramount boss Adolph Zukor, had pledged to 'produce only plays of a cheerful nature', and 'select only such subjects for production as will dictate to the people of foreign nations the qualities and spiritual texture which have been developed in American manhood and womanhood by the institutions which we are now striving to preserve'.[36]

Export licences were ever more central to American studio profits, given the enormous opportunity in global markets caused by the collapse of the European film industry in the war. Leslie Midkiff Debauche opens her recent *Reel Patriotism: The Movies and World War I* (1997) with an astonishingly callous editorial from *Moving Picture World*, the United State's major film trade paper, less than two weeks after the conflict had begun in Europe; it mused that 'the war now in progress in Europe will undoubtedly affect the situation here . . . insamuch as we have in the past suffered from overimportation of cheap features so-called the situation is not without its compensating advantages'.[37] In 1914, the United States made about half of the world's films; by 1919 the collapse of the European film industry meant that 90 per cent of films screened in Europe, and virtually all shown in South America, were made in the United States.[38] Moreover, the war consolidated California and Hollywood's dominance as the major production centre, partially accelerated by the fuel shortages of the winter of 1918–19 (which made the balmy California climate particularly appealing). Although a rash of New York studio construction would follow the war, by 1922 Hollywood accounted for 84 per cent of American film production (with New York on 12 per cent), and the mythos of Hollywood was on the brink of becoming a national obsession.[39]

The war also altered elements of content: Steven Ross's research demonstrates the decline in pro-labour films in postwar Hollywood, a decline exacerbated by Hollywood's increasing industrialisation and its own consequent conflicts with organised labour. Heroine-based serials, such as the *Perils of Pauline*, also went out of fashion. Partly this paralleled the postwar retrenchment of wartime opportunities for women, who were generally pushed out of the manufacturing jobs they had occupied in wartime (although gains made in advertising, design and sales were more permanent).[40] The war also dominated 1920s Hollywood as a theme: blockbusters such as *The Big Parade* (1925), *What Price Glory* (1926) and *Wings* (1927) brought some of the biggest returns of the decade. Moreover, they brought a more even-handed treatment to the consequences of war, and the humanity of America's antagonists. By 1925, when the American hero of *The Big Parade* shares a cigarette in a foxhole with a dying German soldier, the time of bestial Huns threatening the American homeland seemed long past.

If the war and the CPI had a shaping influence on films, that influence was replicated in America's embryonic radio industry. The day after the declaration of war Wilson effectively nationalised the airwaves, with commercial radio telegraphy stations either being closed or taken over by the naval authorities, and amateur operators being banned from transmitting. At this time radio was generally understood as useful for point-to-point communication, especially at sea, and not as a medium for public broadcast; and, since the beginning of the decade, control of its key patents, as well as the discourse over its public and social function, had passed from inventors and small-scale companies into large communications corporations such as AT&T and General Electric.[41] In the war, a government-instigated moratorium on patents meant that these corporations collaborated in their research and development as they worked to fill huge navy contracts, a process which greatly accelerated the rate of radio's technological advance. Secretary of the Navy, Josephus Daniels, believed that the future of radio and radio regulation in the United States rested firmly with the Navy and, as well as its monopoly on broadcasting, he oversaw the Navy's acquisition of key patents for radio's postwar development. Although the turn against public ownership of utilities would thwart that ambition, the Navy, along with General Electric and American Marconi, was heavily involved in the creation of the Radio Corporation of America in 1919, and RCA soon became the cornerstone of the 'radio trust' that dominated the radio boom of the 1920s. As Susan Douglas notes, the Navy's monopoly on radio in the war years did much to structure that corporate trust: it bequeathed it 'improved radio components, a trend towards consolidation and centralisation of the industry, and a legitimation in the press of monopolistic control'.[42] During the war, the CPI liaised with the Navy over broadcasting their propaganda content, and both Wilson's speech outlining his fourteen points and later his speech to the German people in September 1918 were broadcast to Germany from the Navy station in New Brunswick.[43]

The patriotic turn in the films and the radio was echoed in many other cultural forums. In 'slick' large-circulation magazines such as the *Ladies' Home Journal* and the *Saturday Evening Post*, illustrations, reportage, fiction, poetry and advertisements combined to represent and encourage patriotic service in multiple ways. In the *Ladies' Home Journal*, tips for food conservation rubbed shoulders with reportage from the front lines and advertisements for 'patriotic' products. Fictionalised letters from women to their menfolk both encouraged women to write and gave them a formula for doing so. The illustrators who had defined the cover art of the family national magazine in the decade – Howard Chandler Christy, Harrison Fisher, J. C. Leyendecker and James Montgomery Flagg – transposed their already iconic young men and women into the poses of national service and patriotism for the CPI Pictorial Divison. In the *Saturday Evening Post*, popular pre-war writers such as Ring Lardner turned their brand of folksy humour and sensitivity to dialect to the fictional experiences of a typical doughboy 'over there', and the exploits of the air corps were regaled in romantic fashion. Its war fiction regularly drew on the narrative structures and characterisations familiar from Hollywood and westerns in order to present a reassuring framework for martial heroism in the face of a very different style of war. It also scorned modernist experimentalism in wartime – one parody mocked writers congregating in 'a mauve mildewed hole / full of sawdust and soul' in Greenwich Village, 'whose rare inspirations / Were limited mostly to rare publications / With small circulations.'[44] Lewis Hine turned his hand from work with the National Child Labor Committee to working for the Red Cross; he spent a year in Europe in 1918–19 taking photographs in France, Italy, Serbia, Greece and Belgium. He published patriotic and supportive photos of army camps and postwar reconstruction in periodicals such as the *Red Cross Magazine* and *The Survey*; as he said, 'In Paris, after the Armistice, I thought I had done my share of *negative* documentation. I wanted to do something *positive*.'[45] Tin Pan Alley also played its part: popular songs included 'How Ya Gonna Keep 'em Down on the Farm (After They've Seen Paree?), by Sam Lewis and Joe Young in 1918, and the comic 'Hunting the Hun', by Archie Gottler and Howard E. Rogers (1918). Irving Berlin was drafted as a private, and wrote the tunes 'When I get Back to the USA' (1917) and the hugely popular 'Oh! How I Hate to Get up in the Morning' in 1918, which gave vent to his loathing of a military discipline that expected him to get up at the hour at which he usually went to bed. He also wrote the revue *Yip! Yip Yaphank* (partly as a way to get out of reveille) which was based on the comedies of army life and starred his comrades at Camp Upton; it raised $83,000 for the army from its Manhattan production.[46] The most ubiquitous song, however, was George M. Cohan's 'Over There' (1917), which resurfaced as a popular anthem in World War II, helping Cohan to the Congressional Medal of Honor.

Cultures of Protest

Other Americans were less enthusiastic about the war. Before 1917, large numbers of socialists, pacifists and suffragists had all argued strongly against US involvement. Prominent Progressives such as Jane Addams, Lillian Wald, Carrie Chapman Catt and Crystal Eastman were active in giving a feminist tenor to the peace movement; they also had the ear of the president in the years when he was committed to non-intervention. Firmly of the view that war was contrary to women's nurturing instincts, Addams helped found the American Union Against Militarism, the pre-eminent anti-war organisation; she also chaired the Women's Peace Party (WPP), and led an American delegation to an international peace conference in the Netherlands in 1915 (on a liner chartered by Henry Ford).[47] Alfred Bryan and Al

Piantadosi's hit song 'I Didn't Raise My Boy to be a Soldier', perhaps the defining American cultural statement of maternal pacifism, sold a huge 650,000 copies in the same year, and the WPP was active in producing pacifist poetry.[48] Debates around how the conflict would shape women's duty and supposed nurturing instincts became sharply drawn in the war years; Theodore Roosevelt thundered that 'women who do not raise their boys to be soldiers when the country needs them are unfit to live in this republic', and many stories and poems appeared extolling 'valiant mothers' prepared to sacrifice both domestic comforts and their menfolk for the sake of the nation.[49] Much of the CPI's propaganda was targeted at women, explaining how the correct management of the home would aid the war effort, especially in the area of food conservation. As Jennifer Haytock explores, such rhetoric did much to reinscribe a notion of separate and complimentary gendered spheres – of war front and home front, public and private, military and domestic. Yet women did much to resist that division, seeing food management, sending supplies to soldiers, and their emotional labour as ways that previously private activities gave them a degree of control over events on the battlefield.[50] Struggles over the gendered definitions of war also played an important role in the fashioning of American modernism; Hemingway infamously accused Cather's novel *One of Ours* of lifting its battle scenes from *The Birth of a Nation*, a critique designed to establish a terrain of masculinised authenticity for war writing which sought to exclude all those who had not physically experienced the front. More recent critics have been interested in dismantling this exclusivity, and in exploring the ways women participated in the war both physically and aesthetically. This interest has encompassed examination of several memoirs of women's service in nursing or as assistance in the YMCA in France, as well as an interest in how wartime texts concerned with the domestic quotidian interrogate rather than reinforce dualistic notions of separate spheres.[51]

The Seven Arts

Elements of the intellectual left were also arraigned against the war. Most famous was the group of cultural critics known as the 'Young Americans', sometimes also referred to as the lyrical left, which had constellated around the *Seven Arts* journal. Running from November 1916 to October 1917, the journal emphasised the need for a revaluation of the role of culture in social life, urging the formation of an American culture that was unsentimental, organic, democratic and characterised by what their leading critic, Randolph Bourne, called 'abounding vitality and moral freedom'.[52] This was a politicisation of culture and an enculturation of politics which argued that 'a revitalized American culture could only be realized . . . in a society that returned aesthetic experience to the center of everyday life by reversing the industrial division of labor'.[53] As Waldo Frank phrased it, 'we were all sworn foes of capitalism, not because we knew it would not work, but because we judged it, even in success, to be lethal to the human spirit'.[54] Beginning with an awareness – as Van Wyck Brooks noted – that 'for two generations the most sensitive minds in Europe – Renan, Ruskin, Nietzsche . . . have summed up their mistrust of the future in [the] one word' – 'Americanism' – *The Seven Arts* analysed American cultural potential through reference to other cultural nationalist movements, especially the Russian literary renaissance of the nineteenth century and the Celtic Revival in Ireland.[55] Equally important for Brooks was the work of British critics such as John Ruskin, Matthew Arnold and particularly William Morris on how an organic and enriching culture could coexist with industrial capitalism. They were closely aligned with French intellectuals such as Romain Rolland and carried articles on the nascent spirit of cultural nationalism in other countries in a series of articles on 'Young Japan', 'Young Spain', 'Young India' and 'Youngest Ireland.' Its editors, Waldo Frank and James Oppenheim, were Jewish; and, as Thomas Bender has noted, the magazine was 'the first example of an ethnic collaboration, Christian and Jew, that sought to speak for an American national culture embracing "different national strains"'.[56] Their project was a bold one: their major critic, Casey Nelson Blake, characterises their unifying objective as 'a communitarian vision of self-realization through participation in a democratic culture', what Bourne called the 'good life of personality lived in the environment of the Beloved Community'.[57]

Critics such as Bourne, Brooks, Frank and James Oppenheim promulgated this vision before the war, championing cultural figures such as Sherwood Anderson, Theodore Dreiser and Alfred Stieglitz; *The Seven Arts* also published work by Robert Frost, Amy Lowell, Kahlil Gibran and Carl Sandburg. They also often allied themselves with pragmatic and progressive thinkers – especially John Dewey's attempts to theorise a democratic and individualising practice of education. Yet, as America entered the war, Bourne produced in *The Seven Arts* a series of articles which broke with these theories, articles that subsequently became central to the canon of pacifist literature in America. In pieces such as 'War and the Intellectuals', 'A War Diary' and, in the last ever edition of *The Seven Arts*, his 'Twilight of Idols', he chastised his former mentor, Dewey, and other Progressive intellectuals for viewing war as an opportunity for democratisation and liberal reforms. War was inexorable, Bourne noted, and governments had to crush everything which might deflect them from victory; given this, the fantasy that, when faced with the inexorable, Progressives could 'somehow tame it and turn it to [their] own creative purposes' was outright naivety.[58] As he wryly observed, 'the soldiers who tried to lynch Max Eastman showed that current patriotism is not a product of the will to remake the world'.[59] Moreover, he interpreted Dewey's faith in the trained expert's ability to exert a control over war policy as profoundly anti-democratic; pragmatism, he contended, had trained a generation of horrifying Progressive technocrats who were thrilled by the opportunity the war afforded to exercise their professional expertise. Yet their failure to be led by values rather than by technique was inimical to the good life; as he warned, 'there is nothing in this outlook that touches in any way the happiness of the individual, the vivifying of the personality, the comprehension of social forces, the flair of art, – in other words, the quality of life'. Dewey's pragmatism would no longer suffice: he had earlier characterised Dewey's instrumentalist approach of testing all moral values experimentally rather than relying on received moral law as 'revolutionist,' praising its ability to 'slash up the habits of thought, the customs and institutions in which our society had been living for centuries'.[60] Now, he saw it differently: instrumentalism's tendency to work 'against concern for quality of life as above machinery of life' involved an acquiescence to existing facts, including facts such as imperialism, militarism, and capitalism, which a steadfast commitment to what he called 'spiritual values' would never allow.[61] It was a devastating critique which – as James Livingston has noted – has underpinned left-wing criticism of pragmatism ever since.[62]

In keeping with The Seven Arts's insistence on the symbiotic relationship between culture and politics, Bourne also fulminated that the war was a disaster for American culture. Pragmatism's failure had been its inability to accommodate what he called 'poetic vision', or, elsewhere, 'creative desire'.[63] Detesting the shallow jingoism of wartime writing, he also predicted that 'creative and constructive activities will suffer not only through the appalling waste of financial capital in the work of annihilation, but also in the loss of emotional capital in the conviction that war overshadows all other realities'.[64] The danger that warfare might make all cultural, social and creative endeavour seem insignificant expressed Bourne's own fears that the dwindling public sphere made his own voice irrelevant; but it also buttressed his strongest criticism of the conflict, namely that far from epitomising American idealism, the war represented its gravest threat. As he lamented, a war 'so blithely undertaken for the defence of democracy, will have crushed out the only genuinely precious thing in a nation, the hope and ardent idealism of its youth'.[65] The choice was stark: 'The war – or American promise: one must choose.'[66] As with much other dissent from war, the journal did not survive 1917; The Seven Arts was shut down because of the squeamishness of its major investor, Annette Rankine, over the anti-war invectives of Bourne and John Reed. Waldo Frank registered as a conscientious objector in 1917, an action which Dewey had publically criticised. Bourne himself died in the influenza epidemic of 1919, at the age of thirty-two, an early death which did much to cement his later status as an icon of the American left.

Labour and the War

Many working-class Americans were also unenthused by the war, seeing the conflict as a 'rich man's war, poor man's fight', and interpreting Wilson's idealistic pronouncements as a smokescreen for the real reason for American intervention – to safeguard the enormous loans made by J. P. Morgan, Jr which were at risk in the event of an Allied failure. The IWW believed that war was inevitable under a capitalist system and that, consequently, negotiation with capitalist governments was futile in preventing it. This fed an attitude of cynicism towards the war which manifested itself in songs and poems insistently parodying overblown nationalistic and patriotic rhetoric. Its famous 'little red song book', a key part of how it inducted and socialised new members to the organisation, contained several examples of this type.[67] Socialist writers and intellectuals were horrified at the sight of working-class Europeans facing each other across no-man's-land, and by the seeming ease with which patriotic fervour had swept away working-class internationalism; many exhorted American workers not to follow the same route. The day after war was declared, the Socialist Party of America (SPA) passed a motion condemning America's entry into the war as a 'crime against the people of the United States', and urged resistance to the draft. Although such resistance did not occur in any great numbers, hundreds of farmers and socialists forcibly refused conscription in Oklahoma in August in what became known as the Green Corn Rebellion.[68]

Nonetheless, after America entered the war, much of this outright opposition evaporated; even Jane Addams spoke at Liberty Loan Rallies in 1918. Given their experiences of wage exploitation and the increasing disruption of free speech and assembly, many socialists continued to resent the hypocrisy of a war being fought to preserve democracy. They also abhorred the huge profits being made from the war by American manufacturers. Yet many lent tepid support to it, often with a spirit of pragmatic resignation tuned to exacting what they could in the way of improved industrial relations from the war, during a period when the price of their labour was at a premium. The American Federation of Labour had lent its support to preparedness in 1916; a year later prominent socialist literary figures such as Carl Sandburg and Upton Sinclair split with the SPA leadership and supported the war, even though the equivocation of that support is clear from the tortured work they produced in the war years.

A good example is Sinclair's novel, *Jimmie Higgins* (1919), which tells the story of a committed socialist and working-class machinist buffeted between conflicting opinions and allegiances. Sinclair piles up a bewildering set of contradictions which progressively enmesh Jimmie and assail his fierce commitment to the class struggle. A pacifist, he is arrested for organising a strike in the local munitions factory – but it is the factory where he has consented to work. Jimmie is blacklisted as a union agitator but, when he does find work, he gets higher wages than ever before. He respects the idealism and patriotism of a friend and Civil War veteran, yet is horrified when that friend brands his socialist colleagues traitors. He sees Germany as the cradle of socialism, yet is aghast when his German socialist friends are convicted of sabotaging a local munitions plant. He accedes to his wife's argument that the home is a sanctuary from the violence of war, only to see his entire family killed by an explosion on a munitions railway that runs behind his house. And finally, he chooses to enlist after German soldiers march on the new Bolshevik state in Russia, and yet is sent to Archangel in the later stages of the war as part of America's abortive campaign against the Soviets. Horribly tortured by his own officers for distributing Bolshevik leaflets, in a waterboarding scene with uncomfortable resonances for our own era, he ends the novel mad and incarcerated; and yet that madness also reflects the difficulty of balance and equivocation in such a polarising political environment. As Jimmie reflects on hearing the roar of artillery:

> Millions of dollars every hour were being blown to nothing in that fearful inferno; a gigantic meat-mill that was grinding up the bodies of men and had never ceased day or night for nearly four years. You could be a violent pacifist in sound of those guns, or you could be a violent militarist, but you could not be indifferent to the war, you could not be of two minds about it.[69]

Sinclair's novel is a tragedy, a comment on the difficulties of remaining committed to a principle of working-class solidarity in such nationalistic times – difficulties which echoed his personal dilemmas. Such strains were even more evident in poet Carl Sandburg's work during the war years, as he invented an alter ego to manage his contrary viewpoints. He wrote pro-war pieces under his own name for the American Alliance for Labor and Democracy, a government-backed body with close connections to the CPI. At the same time, he invented the pseudonym Jack Phillips to publish numerous articles lambasting government war policy in the anti-war *International Socialist Review* – a publication committed to direct action and the revolutionary overthrow of the government.[70] His poetry also reflected this split; *Chicago Poems* (1916) contained a section lamenting the huge waste of life in Europe, and looked forward to a time of socialistic government when monarchies would be abolished. His 'Planked Whitefish' depicts graphic atrocities committed by German soldiers not as a rationale for fighting – as was a frequent tactic in British and American propaganda – but as an argument against war itself. In contrast, poems such as 'The Four Brothers', which first appeared in *The Chicago Evening Post* in October 1917, celebrate the 'four big brothers', the 'four republics' of Russia, France, Britain and America (a particularly awkward shoe-horning for Britain, especially given the poem's prediction that the war will bid 'good-night to the kings'). Intoning that 'only fighters today will save the world', the poem consoles that despite the 'death-yells of it all, the torn throats of men in ditches calling for water, the shadows and hacking lungs in dugouts', 'look, child! the storm is blowing for a clean air'.[71] Despite this support for American belliger-ence, he saw the most promising source of the postwar 'clean air' as the new Bolshevik state in Russia; indeed, he was briefly incarcerated and questioned by US Military Intelligence for carrying Bolshevik leaflets back into the United States in 1919. Sandburg was not alone in seeing the new socialist republic as the one Progressive ray of light to emerge from the war: Upton Sinclair, W. E. B. Du Bois, Randolph Bourne and, most famously, John Reed were of the same opinion.

In contrast to the acquiescence of figures like Sandburg and Sinclair, the IWW kept up its protests. In an impish parallel to the cultural barrage of the CPI, in spring 1917 it embarked on a huge 'stickerette' campaign to distribute over a million 'stickerettes' to be plastered up in workplaces across America. Urging revolutionary unionism, the stickerettes frequently parodied recruitment posters produced by the CPI. According to a lyric in the magazine *Solidarity* (the eastern organ of the IWW), they would mean

Now all the bosses and their stools will think they're out of luck
To see the spots of black and red where Stickerettes are stuck;
And after they have scratched them off and shook their fists and swore
They'll turn around to find again about a dozen more.

Upon the back of every truck, on packages and cards,
Upon the boats and in the mines and in the railroad yards,

From Maine to California and even further yet,
No matter where you look you'll see a little stickerette![72]

As these examples suggest, poetry was one of the key media
wherein cultural debate over the war occurred, and huge quantities
of it were published during the war years. Mark Van Wienen's work
has been crucial in uncovering the range and extent of this 'partisan
poetry', from the 'sock songs' produced for a *Boston Globe* contest
to stimulate the knitting of socks for soldiers, to poems in praise of
conscientious objectors, to work produced by major figures such as
Robert Frost, Amy Lowell and Wallace Stevens. Eighty anthologies
of war poetry were published in the United States between 1914 and
1920, and eighty-six different periodicals carried war poems; over a
thousand war poems appeared in the *New York Times* alone during
the course of the war.[73] Poetry had the advantage of being quick to
write, and therefore responsive to fast-moving events; of being short
and easily reproducible, which saw many popular poems syndicated
and frequently reproduced in many different periodicals; and carrying
a unique cachet of cultural, intellectual and moral authority that was
very helpful in buttressing political positions. Moreover, these poems
often entered into dialogue with one another, or dialogue with other
public discourse about the war. Poetry's sensitivity to tone and its
flexible irony meant that this dialogue encompassed homage, imitation, parody and mimicry. Rudyard Kipling, Edgar Allan Poe and
especially Wilson's speeches – none was safe. As Van Wienen notes,

> the subject of this dialogue was not literature but history: poems sought
> to interpret what the events reported in the papers meant, what the
> lived experience of war mobilization meant, and what role the United
> States played, and should play, in those events and in the lives of its
> citizens.[74]

The cultural work these poems enacted was often highly organised;
particularly important was that of The Vigilantes, a group of patriotic
writers and artists who worked closely with subcommittees of the CPI
and organised their own press syndicate to distribute their poetry.
Their recruitment campaign of 1917 elicited pledges to join from
328 writers, including prominent figures such as Edward Arlington
Robinson, Amy Lowell, Vachel Lindsay, Edgar Lee Masters and
Hamlin Garland.[75] Setting down strict rules, which insisted poets
produce patriotic work on the demand of the leadership, the group

was particularly important in exhorting housewives to follow the
guidelines on food conservation produced by Herbert Hoover's Food
Administration.[76]

African Americans in Wartime

Other groups had particularly partisan positions to adopt. Many
African American workers in the South were indifferent to the war,
and used the high labour mobility it ushered in to slip away from local
draft boards – as well as to migrate to the North to the better-paid,
industrial jobs long denied to them by cheap immigrant labour. Some
small black periodicals protested against the war; *The Messenger*,
which was funded and promoted by the Socialist Party, saw its
editors, Chandler Owen and A. Philip Randolph, arrested under
the Espionage act for an editorial entitled 'Pro-Germanism amongst
Negroes'. In the end, only the actions of a paternalistic judge, who
refused to believe two such 'boys' could write the offending editorials and dismissed the case, saved them from potentially lengthy jail
time.[77] Federal authorities harassed and intimidated a number of other
publications, including the NAACP journal *The Crisis*; after the war,
Wilson himself worried that returning black soldiers would be the
'greatest medium in conveying bolshevism to America'.[78]

For the most part, however, African American newspapers and
intellectuals had little choice but to vociferously support the government, and urge it to allow African Americans to contribute fully to
every aspect of the war effort. By such enthusiasm for the burdens of
citizenship, they hoped to secure more of its rewards once the war was
over. Around four hundred thousand served in the US forces during
the war, two hundred thousand of them overseas; and, although
African Americans were generally allocated to labour battalions – the
white South in particular had been greatly alarmed by the prospect of
the mass combat training of black draftees – around forty thousand
African Americans fought in France. The most famous unit involved
in this fighting was a former National Guard unit, the New York
15th – which became the 369th Infantry of the 93rd Division, or more
colloquially the 'Harlem Hellfighters'. Drawn from Harlem, they
were brigaded with the French, and, once equipped with French rifles
and helmets, they spent more time on the front lines than any other
American unit. Soldiers from the unit were the first to win Croix de
Guerre; it were also the first Allied unit to reach the Rhine. The unit's
fame was cemented by its rapturous welcome home in February 1919,

when thousands of New Yorkers turned out to witness their victory march up Fifth Avenue and into Harlem. Yet their fame was not just a result of their military exploits but was also due to their regimental band, led by James Reese Europe.

James Reese Europe

Europe was already a celebrity by the time he landed in France with the 369th at the head of the largest – and best-paid – regimental band in the American Expeditionary Force. He had worked as the personal bandleader for Vernon and Irene Castle, providing the ragtime orchestration which underpinned their success; he had also helped them develop the foxtrot step, which became a staple of popular dancing for the next fifty years. He had begun the Clef Club, a support organisation and booking agent for black musicians in New York which became a crucial factor in the increasing dominance of African American bands on the New York music scene. He had also been the first African American bandleader to sign a contract with a major recording company, recording the Castles' signature tune, 'Castle Rock', in 1914; and he is often cited as an important figure in the early development of jazz. Like many prosperous black men in America's cities at the time, however, he was also active in politics and community affairs. Following the model of civic (and sometimes martial) service known to the African American community as the 'race man', Europe had volunteered for service in the 15th New York. The high-profile public role of the 'race man' was a prominent feature of the discourse of 'uplift', a key strategy in the early twentieth-century civil rights struggle; such men, it was hoped, would both encourage other black men to similar efforts of civic and racial service and convince a sceptical white America of black male competence and valour. As Europe remarked, 'Our race will never amount to anything, politically or economically in New York or anywhere else, unless there are strong organizations of men who stand for something in the community.'[79] He was also committed to synthesising a new American music, employing ragtime as well as the newly emergent styles of jazz, and placing especial emphasis on distinctive African American rhythms through a powerful percussion section.[80] So innovative was his band's inflection of traditional military and patriotic songs with syncopated, ragtime orchestration that when the band played the Marseillaise on the docks at Brest on the day of the regiment's arrival, it took the French audience eight or ten bars to recognise their own national anthem.[81]
    This began the band's tours in Europe and, later, in the United States. They played for French and American audiences at rest areas for American troops, and in front of the top brass of the American General Staff – who regularly broke army rules to keep the band together. They played in concerts alongside the best British, Italian, and French regimental bands; the French band of the Garde Républicaine insisted

on inspecting the 369th band's instruments, convinced that the sounds Europe's musicians had produced were not possible with standard brass.[82] Moreover, they were not solely in France for entertainment; in the spring of 1918 Europe became the first African American officer to see combat, taking part with a French officer in a raid on German trenches and coming under fire. (The experience led him to write 'On Patrol in No-Man's Land', which became a staple of the band's performances.) Europe was hospitalised after a German gas attack shortly afterwards, which saw him withdrawn from active service.[83]

The band has gone down in musical folklore; as well as Europe, it featured stellar performers such as drum major and singer Noble Sissle, and Bill 'Bojangles' Robinson, who achieved fame starring as a tap dancer in a string of 1930s Hollywood films. Its major claim was being a pioneer of jazz in Europe, particularly in France. As Sissle recalled, French audiences greeted this new music with almost involuntary abandon; at one performance 'the audience could stand it no longer; the "Jazz germ" hit them, and it seemed to find the vital spot, loosening all muscles and causing what is known in America as an "Eagle Rocking Fit".'[84] Bands like Europe's, and other regimental outfits in the all-black 92nd and 93rd divisions, did much to pave the way for black musicians to establish themselves in Paris in the 1920s, and assisted in creating the vogue of French 'Negrophilie' in the decade. This was an interdisciplinary movement, wherein celebrations of the supposedly 'primitive vitality' of African dance, music, spectacle and visual art became fashionable in a time desperate for alternatives to a European cultural heritage tarnished by its associations with the war. Such Negrophilie made superstars out of African American performers such as Bricktop and Josephine Baker, and helped construct a place for jazz and blues in French popular culture which persists to this day. American jazz bands were in great demand in 1920s Paris, a fact resented in certain French circles. French bands complained about the loss of work (it was regularly suggested throughout the 1920s that they could not play jazz); certain French critics saw jazz as a primitive, racially inferior *musique nègre*; some regarded it as standardising, machine-age music; and others saw it as a leading force in American cultural imperialism. Yet, by the end of the 1920s, the process of transnational musical dialogue was well underway, and various groups had inaugurated the vibrant French tradition of jazz.[85]

The final significance of the band was in its return. After playing standard martial marches all the way up Fifth Avenue through white New York, when they reached the Harlem reviewing stand they switched style – to the upbeat jazz number 'here comes your daddy now'. Several influential historians choose this moment to begin their histories of the Harlem Renaissance: they see it as indicative of the new mood which characterised 1920s African American culture. In producing such a moment of urban and urbane sophistication and pride, of masculine self-assurance which military experience had undergirded, and an innovative and unashamed adaptation of vernacular African American cultural form, Europe's band foreshadowed much that would follow in the efflorescence of literature, sculpture, painting, music and photography that emerged from African America's new urban communities in the 1920s. Moreover, it demonstrated the increasing importance that culture would assume in the civil rights struggle. As Europe said, 'We won France by playing music that was ours and not a pale imitation of others.'[86] Such a bold assertion of the centrality of African American music to an American cultural nationalism would be typical of the way African American artists and intellectuals increasingly deployed specifically cultural arguments to assert their full citizenship rights in the decade that followed.

1. Lieut. James Reese Europe and Men of the 15th New York.   2. Band Master Oliver Mead.   3. Band of the 815th Pioneer Infantry, with Men on leave, at Challes-les-Eaux.

Figure 5.2 James Reese Europe and the band of the 369th Infantry, 1918–19. Courtesy of the General Research and Reference Division, Schomburg Center for Research in Black Culture, The New York Public Library, Astor, Lenox and Tilden Foundations.

Nativism and the Red Scare

The model of heroic citizenship which the war so often invoked was, of course, one of the most potent mechanisms for defining who was truly an American. Yet, even as men such as James Reese Europe used their music to stake a new claim for full African American participation in national life, many branches of the newly established veterans' association, the American Legion, refused to accept black members.

The legion's racial protectionism was just one example of a growing intolerance towards displays of ethno-racial diversity in American life by the end of the war, and of a narrowing set of criteria for who could claim the cultural and civic mantle of American citizenship. In the early stages of the war, the work of what John Higham calls 'Liberal Americanizers' was prominent; their view held 'the nation as great in the universal range of its ties and sympathies' rather than 'great in the purity of its separateness'. Institutionally, such liberal Americanisers offered citizenship classes and English lessons in factories, community halls and schools, in a generally sincere effort to equip recent immigrants with the linguistic and cultural tools to succeed in their new home.[87] Figures such as Teddy Roosevelt voiced the hope that the army would be a democratising and Americanising experience for its immigrant draftees. The CPI's Division of Work with the Foreign-Born produced propaganda for distribution in immigrant communities; one particularly famous poster carried a list of names – Du Bois, Smith, O'Brien, Cejka, Jancke, Pappandrikopoulos, Andrassi, Vilotto, Levy, Turovich, Kowalski, Chriczanevicz, Knutson, and Gonzales – under the slogan 'Americans All'. Lewis Hine published photoessays celebrating the 'the many nationalities within our army', showing the resilience of wounded American soldiers in a Red Cross hospital in Paris as well as their 'picturesque' constellation of ethnicities.[88] As the war progressed, however, nativism became an increasingly resurgent force. An article in the *Saturday Evening Post* in June 1918 reflected a dominant mood in proclaiming that 'deleting the hyphen' should be 'the doctrine of 1918'; fears about imported German 'Kultur' rapidly spread to encourage hostility to all non-anglophone culture.[89] The association of immigrant communities with Bolshevism from 1918 onwards only sharpened a spirit of 100 per cent Americanism which harassed, surveilled and assaulted the institutions and cultural practices of America's cultural diversity. As David Kennedy notes, 'by the time of the Armistice, the 100 per cent spirit, so distant from the original Americanizing aims of people like Jane Addams and Frances Kellor, reigned supreme'.[90]

As much of the foregoing suggests, the war has often been remembered as the end of an era of intellectual freedom and idealism, political reform, and ethno-cultural diversity. For Blanche Wiesen Cook, 'The Red Scare carved the heart out of American liberalism, and charted the course of twentieth-century politics.'[91] David Kennedy, reflecting on the disillusionment of the Progressives who had supported the war, suggested that 'the war had killed something precious and perhaps irretrievable in the hearts of thinking men and women'.[92] In cultural terms, the war certainly did much to extinguish the remarkable reformist energies that connected up socialism, feminism, modernism and psychoanalysis in bohemias in Greenwich Village and Chicago, constellations which had determined the culture of the most innovative poetry, drama and little magazines in the decade. It shut down much of the engagement of American cultural work with legislative politics, and dampened the utopian tenor of much Progressive culture of the 1910s.

Yet Bourne's fear that the war would destroy the nation's cultural vitality was misplaced. The role of radio in wartime conditioned its blossoming into a major mass cultural form in the 1920s. The war provided a foundational theme for the great generation of American modernist prose writers, many of whom had served in World War I. It provided the financial grounding for Hollywood's golden era of silent movies, and it put in place the demographic and cultural conditions for the Harlem Renaissance. As the conclusion will discuss, the widespread sense of the war as marking an epochal shift was perhaps the major cultural legacy of the 1910s; and if that shift was more partial or less dramatic than was often claimed by those who defined their generation through the war, nonetheless it was real enough to shape much of the culture of the 1920s.

Conclusion

In 1927, the American Legion celebrated the tenth anniversary of the United States entering the war with a parade in Paris. Some 25,000 legionnaires and their families travelled to France on fifteen specially chartered liners and, after visiting battlefields, military cemeteries, and the fully licensed bistros and cafés of Paris, they reprised the victory march of 1919 down the Champs-Elysées.[1] Watched by a million Parisians, they dropped flowers on the tomb of the Unknown Soldier in a display the *New York Times* compared to 'a "co-ed" college celebration after the year's biggest football victory'.[2] Yet their French hosts were not universally thrilled by this invasion of what was dubbed the 'second American Expeditionary Force'. Some felt the gaiety of the visit inappropriate to the scale of the bitter losses France (but not their former Allies) had suffered in the war. Communists had tried to sabotage railway lines carrying the legionnaires travelling around France, and the reverberations of the controversial executions of the Italian anarchists Ferdinando Nicola Sacco and Bartolomeo Vanzetti in Massachusetts in August were still palpable; protests targeting the legionnaires' parade had been suppressed by the French authorities. Liberal commentators at the time wondered about the picture of the legacy of the war this presented: was it 'the old America France had learned to honor; pioneer America, generous, brave, simple, sincere in faith and modest in achievement?'[3] Or was it an America whose respect for political freedoms had been eviscerated by the Red Scare, whose isolationism had hampered European recovery from the ravages of war, and whose crass triumphalism and insensitivity to global concerns had shattered the Allied coalition in reordering the postwar world?

The War and the 1920s

These questions were much addressed in the immediate cultural after-math of the 1910s. They particularly preoccupied the many veterans who came to the fore in fiction and theatre in the 1920s, many of whom sought to articulate the war as a schism in generational attitudes. According to Ernest Hemingway, Gertrude Stein famously labelled this a 'génération perdue', or lost generation, which had 'no respect for anything'.[4] Although Hemingway disliked the label, it correctly iden-tified a shared agenda among a younger, male generation of writers, many of them with battlefield experience. They sought to break sharply from the jingoism which had dominated cultural discourse during the war years, as well as the idealism of both prewar bohemian modernism and Progressive technocracy. Many of them were volun-teer ambulance drivers who had seen the psychological physiologi-cal and spiritual wounds of war at first hand, and they worked these experiences into some of the most important fiction of the 1920s.

The depiction of the war in John Dos Passos's *1917: One Man's Initiation* (1920) and *Three Soldiers* (1921), e.e. cummings's *The Enormous Room* (1922), and Ernest Hemingway's *In Our Time* (1925), *The Sun Also Rises* (1926) and *A Farewell to Arms* (1928) showed lives overseen by a state apparatus too vast and indifferent for any single individual either to understand or to change. Indeed, the first three chapters of *Three Soldiers* are entitled 'Making the Mould', 'The Metal Cools', and 'Machines', suggesting how men had been coerced into the amoral, mechanistic and dehumanising production methods of industrial capitalism by the wartime state. Dismissing the wave of veterans' activism which followed the war – the lobbying of politically active citizen-soldiers led to the groundbreaking adjusted compensation award in 1924 for all veterans – these writers saw the war instead as an alienating break with the civic sociality that had undergirded the Progressive ideal of public life. Other veterans, such as Thomas Boyd, Laurence Stallings and Hervey Allen, produced plays, fiction and autobiography which critiqued the war, as did work by writers who joined up but never made it to France, such as William Faulkner and F. Scott Fitzgerald. In the New Negro Renaissance, novelists and poets such as Jessie Redmon Fauset, Walter White, Langston Hughes, James Weldon Johnson and Edward Christopher Williams dwelt on the heroism that black servicemen had displayed, and the prejudice which continued to block their accession to full citizenship despite the sacrifices they had undergone.

The sense that the war had forced a decisive break from an earlier set of aesthetics and politics was widely articulated, both at the time and in much subsequent criticism. This prompted a wave of often anxious self-scrutiny in the cultural criticism of the 1920s, marked by a particular obsession with the concept of 'civilization', as Warren Susman has noted. Several essay collections evaluating American civilisation appeared in the decade, attempting 'a sort of balance sheet for the American people'.[5] Some continued the pre-war tendency to see failures of civilization in gendered terms, but often in even sharper language; in one of the most influential, Harold Stearns's *Civilization in the United States* (1922), Stearns's essay on 'The Intellectual Life' blasted the 'extraordinary feminization of American social life', and the 'intellectual anemia or torpor that seems to accompany it'.[6] He was not alone; Ezra Pound famously referred to a pre-war 'botched civilization' as an 'old bitch gone in the teeth', responsible for 'wastage as never before'.[7] Such arguments sometimes took a racial turn, too: the 'vogue of the Negro' of the 1920s carried a sense that a supposedly primitive culture was untainted by the industrial killing of the war, and represented a cultural haven of innocent physicality and unimpaired male virility. In the centerpiece volume of the New Negro movement, the African American critic Joel Rogers would praise jazz in exactly these terms, seeing it as a music which had flourished 'when minds were reacting from the horrors and strain of war' by allowing a 'temporary forgetfulness'. Its value, he suggested, was 'a recharging of the batteries of civilization with a primitive new vigor'.[8]

The sharp resurgence of masculinism, and a dampening of a utopian spirit which had animated the earlier part of the 1910s, was partly a result of the dissolution of the pre-war coalition of political and aesthetic radicalism which would become mythologised as the Greenwich Village spirit. This bohemian coalition held feminism, sexual freedom and campaigns for the legalisation of birth control as core principles, but a new generation of writers would often sharply distance their own aesthetic objectives from the political concerns of pre-war writers. As Malcolm Cowley (another wartime ambulance driver) put it, this generation had learned a 'spectatorial attitude' from the war, and rather than 'assault[ing] our American puritanism', they were more interested in 'form, simplification, strangeness, respect for literature as an art with traditions'. They certainly 'were not bohemians'.[9] In consequence, he and his compatriots – who had all 'lost our ideals at a very early age' – believed that 'female equality was a good idea, perhaps, but the feminists we knew wore spectacles and

flat-heeled shoes'.[10] Feminism, like Progressivism, did not evaporate
in the 1920s but, by and large, it moved from legislative to social and
cultural terrain, often to the chagrin of older activists. For example,
in the 1920s Charlotte Perkins Gilman bemoaned 'the lowering of
standards in sex relations, approaching some of the worst periods in
ancient history'.[11] More broadly, there was a shift in how cultural producers of the 1920s conceptualised the relationship of art to politics.
Although recent scholarship has redressed Fitzgerald's blithe assertion that 'it was characteristic of the Jazz Age that it had no interest in
politics at all,' the interest in collective action to effect social change
evident in the work of Sherwood Anderson, Upton Sinclair, Charlotte
Perkins Gilman, Carl Sandburg and W. E. B. Du Bois attracted few of
the new generation.[12]

Moreover, despite the internationalism of expatriation which
several writers of the 1920s pursued, the protectionist spirit of
1920s American politics dovetailed with a new nativism in American
culture. Alfred Stieglitz's internationalist gallery '291', with its huge
and continually changing cast of contributors and exhibitors from
around the world, was replaced by a second circle in the 1920s devoted
to the spiritualisation of national culture; by the end of the decade, it
was based at Stieglitz's 'An American Place'. This focused on a much
narrower, and all-American, cast. In literature, Walter Benn Michaels
has influentially discussed the preoccupation with family, identity and
belonging in much postwar modernist writing, preoccupations gen-
erative of a 'nativist modernism' which coalesced in the 1920s. He has
noted 'the way in which newly revised categories of collective identity
– and, in particular, of collective national identity – began in the 1920s
to occupy . . . a central position in American culture', revisions which
sought to reframe and exclude in a similar way to the Johnson-Reed
Immigration Restriction act of 1924.[13] In contrast, for Michaels, 'the
major writers of the Progressive period – London, Dreiser, Wharton
– were comparatively indifferent to questions of both racial and
national identity.'[14]

This nativism was coextensive with the spur the war provided to
American cultural boosterism and imperialism. Ann Douglas argues
that the American literary tradition and the American language
became the most suitable versions of literary English for representing
this postwar terrain of shocking newness, violence, unpredictability
and the sudden obsolescence of older traditions of discourse. For her,
Hemingway is the greatest writer in English of World War I because
as a 'culturally impoverished' American, he 'could fashion with little

resistance or waste the new literary tools the modern experience demanded'.[15] American protectionism forced European business – including cultural business – out of its markets; immediately after the war, the Wilson government and the Navy pressured the British-owned Marconi firm to relinquish control of its American radio assets in the formation of the Radio Corporation of America, which would become the bedrock of the 'radio trust' of the 1920s.

Such aggressive cultural economics were taking place in music and in cinema as well, aided by the economic dominance the American mass-entertainment industry had been able to open up in the war, as well as the exposure to American cultural products which many Europeans had gained from American servicemen. By 1925, the year New York took over from London as the world's largest city, British officials estimated that only 5 per cent of films on British screens were British made.[16] Such expansion brought conflicting views. For example, although the American-made war film *The Big Parade* was reviewed poorly by the *Times* in 1926, which sniffed at the 'indiscipline . . . shown which will seem strange to British ex-service eyes', and tutted at the appearance of 'more than a touch of American film methods', it ran for a huge twenty-seven weeks at London's flagship Tivoli theatre – and followed on from a series of performances by the jazz band leader, Paul Whiteman.[17] In Germany, Metro-Goldwyn-Mayer had to overcome protests that the film was anti-German – just as the German film industry railed against the 'Europäische Monroe-Doktrin' blocking European films from American markets.[18] Such a situation led several European countries to introduce quotas guaranteeing a certain amount of home-made film time on screen in its cinemas, but this did not dent Hollywood's global dominance. By 1934, with the advent of talkies, Wyndham Lewis bemoaned that 'the "Americanizing" process is far advanced', as 'the cinema has brought the American scene and the American dialect nightly into the heart of England'.[19] The reverential tenor of the transatlantic literary relationship was altered, too; what Henry James called the 'superstitious valuation' of Europe by American authors was greatly reduced from when his generation had travelled across the Atlantic. The strong dollar, the 'dollar imperialism' of 1920s global finance, and a sense of having saved an anachronistic civilisation in the war fed a sense of cultural and economic confidence in American travellers to Europe. As Fitzgerald said, 'we were the most powerful nation. Who could tell us any longer what was fashionable and what was fun?'[20]

1910s: The Legacy

The political and cultural legacies of the 1910s have been most reso-
nant in subsequent periods of American history eager for reform; they
also set inspiring precedents for later generations of grass-roots activism. This was most obvious in the 1930s, when Progressive ideas and
figures re-emerged to guide America through the Great Depression.
Franklin Roosevelt had served under Wilson as assistant secretary in
the navy, and he recruited old Progressives such as Josephus Daniels,
Cordell Hull, Harold Ickes and Donald Richberg to his administration. His interest in conservation and public power projects bore
the hallmark of the earlier movement; his 'brain trust' of academics
informing his first hundred days were steeped in Progressive theories
of governmental regulation of financial and corporate structures; and
it was his second administration which finally enacted strict federal
controls on child labour with the 1938 Fair Labor Standards Act.[21]
Yet Roosevelt had learned from Progressive failures, and presented
a platform which was much less zealous in trying to reform personal behaviour than his 1910s forerunners had been. One of his
first acts as president was to repeal prohibition; as McGerr summa-
rises, Roosevelt's view of 'the task of government was to make sure
Americans could afford pleasure, and then get out of the way'.[22]

Cultural figures on the left who had swum against the Republican
tide in the 1920s also re-emerged to take prominent positions in
New Deal agencies. At times, these included members of the old
left who had sharply criticised Progressive reluctance adequately to
confront big capital. Floyd Dell joined the WPA in 1935 as an editor
and ghostwriter, for example, and Claude McKay worked for the
Federal Writers' Project. Others joined the Popular Front to the
left of Roosevelt's New Deal, a movement which united 'industrial
unionists, Communists, independent socialists, community activists, and émigré anti-fascists around laborist social democracy, anti-
fascism, and anti-lynching.'[23] Waldo Frank, Theodore Dreiser and
Sherwood Anderson all became involved with publicising the cases
of striking miners and textile workers in flashpoints such as Gastonia,
North Carolina and Harlan, Kentucky. Frank was the first president of the communist-affiliated League of American Writers, and
John Reed Clubs sprang up around the country in the early 1930s,
attracting young leftist intellectuals inspired by Reed's campaigning
reportage on the class war in the United States and on the Russian
Revolution.[24]

Emerging as the literary champion of this 'Popular Front' was John Dos Passos, whose epic sweep of contemporary history in his three-volume *U.S.A.* served as the defining statement of what Michael Denning has called the elegy for the Lincoln republic. As he observes,

> its greatness at the time of publication was that it narrated in a powerful and convincing way the history of its present: the history of the Lincoln republic, of how the promise of a continental nation of small producers, full of Yankee ingenuity, tinkerers like the Wright brothers and even Henry Ford, was betrayed by the 'big money', ending in the Wall Street crash and the depression.[25]

Central to that narrative was a 'nostalgic evocation of the pre-war world of Wobblies, anarchists, Eugene Debs, and Jack Reed', often celebrated as martyrs to the cause of labour when the struggle with the 'big money' seemed capable of going in a different direction.[26] *U.S.A.*'s much-praised biographical sections dwell disproportionately on figures who defined the 1910s, and who serve as polarised antagonists in this conflict: Debs, Bill Haywood, William Jennings Bryan, Robert La Follette, Jack Reed, Randolph Bourne on one side; Andrew Carnegie, J. P. Morgan, Frederick Winslow Taylor, William Randolph Hearst, and Woodrow Wilson on the other. The pivotal year of 1919 is the title of the middle book, which ends with a biographical portrait of the Unknown Soldier – whose youth, death and anonymity, as well as the pontificating hypocrisy of those who officiate at the ceremony of his burial, epitomise the death of the promise of a young republic and the utter failure of public language to guarantee the universal freedoms and opportunities which that idealised republic had promised. The final sections of *U.S.A.*, haunted by the execution of Sacco and Vanzetti, conclude with the resignation that 'all right we are two nations', and 'we stand defeated America', a defeat cemented by the failures of the labour movement to overcome the 'big money' in the struggles of 1919.[27]

Dos Passos's gloomy interpretation of the obsession in the 1910s with social mobility was echoed in several 1930s and early 1940s film adaptations of 1910s novels. Marion Gering's *Jennie Gerhardt* (1933) and Orson Welles's *The Magnificent Ambersons* (1942) are in this vein – before its final release, Welles's film had fifty minutes hacked out by RKO and its ending reshot because test audiences found the original version too depressing. Other leftist figures followed Dos

Passos's tendency to romanticise socialist martyrs of the 1910s: the Industrial Workers of the World songwriter and martyr, Joe Hill, executed in 1915, would be celebrated and referenced by generations of leftist singer-songwriters, including Woody Guthrie, Pete Seeger, Bob Dylan, Joan Baez and Billy Bragg. Allan Ginsberg waxed fondly about the IWW as part of his counter-cultural discourse in the 1950s, admitting 'America I feel sentimental about the Wobblies', and reprising the chant of 'free Tom Mooney'.[28] In the Oscars ceremony of 1982, at the outset of the Reagan era, the film *Reds* scooped three awards; Warren Beatty directed and starred as John Reed in a three-hour epic reprisal of Reed's pro-labour campaigning during the 1910s, his reportage on the Bolshevik Revolution of 1917, his founding role in the Communist Party of America, and his relationship with Louise Bryant (played by Diane Keaton). Switching between Greenwich Village, Provincetown, Croton-on-Hudson, and Petrograd, and featuring an illustrious cast including Jack Nicholson as Eugene O'Neill and Maureen Stapleton as Emma Goldman (for which she won an Oscar), the film is the major evocation of the era in contemporary Hollywood (along with Milos Forman's 1981 film *Ragtime*).

Beatty clearly felt an affinity with Reed's struggle to relate art to politics, and also with Reed's effortless charm and playboy reputation (even in the 1910s Reed's friend Walter Lippmann had scoffed at 'legendary John Reed', and mocked 'what many people believe to be the central passion of his life, an inordinate desire to be arrested').[29] Beatty was also clear that he was making a film about communism, one that aimed both to reclaim the legacy of Reed from Soviet Communism, and to redress an American paranoia about communism which Vietnam had reinvigorated for his generation. It also exemplified the fascination of Beatty's generation with an earlier moment of American political, sexual and artistic radicalism. Yet, although the film is faithful to the radical demands of Reed and his allies for an overthrow of American capitalism, by 1982 this was seen as a rather toothless period piece; the film was bankrolled by Gulf and Western, and Beatty even arranged for a screening at the White House for Ronald and Nancy Reagan.[30]

What critics have called the 'cultural turn' in labour history, a tendency for recent labour history to be taken up with the cultural rather than the institutional forms of the American working class, has been a source of contemporary enthusiasm for the IWW. That enthusiasm is not restricted to academia: *Reds* begins with a piece of ragtime music, and its conjunction of nostalgia for the innovations in popular culture of the 1910s with nostalgia for its leftist politics is echoed elsewhere in contemporary culture, most notably in E. L. Doctorow's novel *Ragtime* (1975). A charming work of historical metafiction, it interweaves invented characters with real historical figures (including Harry Houdini, Sigmund Freud, Emma Goldman, J. P. Morgan and the showgirl Evelyn Nesbit). Its imagined characters live through real events such as the Lawrence textile strike, Peary's polar expedition and the Mexican Revolution; and its historical characters do fictional things, such as Houdini performing a flying demonstration in front of Archduke Franz Ferdinand. The book's charm often rests on a kind of anecdotal quaintness, anecdotes hilarious to those who get the joke: examples include Sigmund Freud and Carl Jung taking a boat through the Tunnel of Love at Luna Park on Coney Island during Freud's one visit to the United States; how Taft's fatness made corpulence unfashionable; the wildlife body count of Theodore Roosevelt's African safari; and the ugliness of J. P. Morgan's nose. These anecdotes appeal through their difference from contemporary mores; a running joke is the Victorian stuffiness of the central family in the plot, who are only ever referred to as 'mother', 'father', and 'the little boy'. This quaintness is closely connected to innocence (and its corollary, prudishness); it follows Frederick Lewis Allen and Henry May's characterisations of this era as charming for being simultaneously so close in temporal terms and so distant in moral ones. That this represents the last moment of modern America's supposed 'prehistory' is emphasised by the familiar milestone of the novel finishing with the early days of World War I.

The book also revels in the love of Americana that characterised the 1970s, the decade which invigorated the academic study of American vernacular culture. In many ways, this reprises the cultural nationalism alive in the 1910s, but on different terrain; whereas the cultural arbiters of the time (with a few exceptions) were deeply unsure about the social and artistic merits of mass culture, *Ragtime* shows it as innovative, enthralling, fun, exhilaratingly new and often profoundly beautiful. Moreover, vaudeville, ragtime and, above all, cinema provide characters with both social mobility and the ability to develop their own, distinctive identities as Americans, even as they struggle against the racial, ethnic and class strictures of the time – strictures Doctorow never tries to conceal.

For example, the immigrant Jewish figure 'Tateh', a street pedlar on the Lower East Side, becomes a Hollywood director and mogul; his transition from a silhouette-maker to a flick-book artist to film director pays affectionate homage to the long pre-cinematic history of visual illusion which so inflected the culture of early film. The 'New Negro' Coalhouse Walker is a smart, wealthy and talented ragtime pianist who lives in the newly African American district in Harlem, and disdains the nineteenth-century musical traditions of minstrelsy and 'coon songs'. The novel clearly chimes with the 'ragtime revival' of the 1970s, one which saw Scott Joplin receive a posthumous Pulitzer Prize in 1976 for his services to American music. Moreover, in common with other major historical novels looking back to this period written in the 1970s – such as Ishmael Reed's *Mumbo Jumbo* (1972) and Michael Ondaatje's *Coming Through Slaughter* (1976) – Doctorow sees ragtime and jazz as not just providing a soundtrack to contemporary America, but a sensibility. This sensibility was located in improvisation, racial plurality, sensuality and a fundamental change in the rhythms of popular music and dance; it was both mass culture and folk culture. Also, it is a music that draws on disparate and often antagonistic sources for an ingenious and often irreverent synthesis, and the novel follows a similar formal pattern through interweaving the narratives of three families: White Anglo-Saxon Protestant, Jewish, and African American. The stark ethnic and racial diversity of America's cities in the era – so often perceived as a catastrophic social problem in the 1910s – is here celebrated as a foundational fact of America's rich cultural heritage. This was a very 1970s narrative of American exceptionalism: exceptional for its industrial mastery of entertainments which were popular and endlessly reproducible but not trite or inauthentic; exceptional in how its social mobility and ethnic diversity created a synthetic society of exhilarating novelty and promise.

This indicates another source of contemporary nostalgia for the 1910s, a nostalgia for the 'golden door' era of mass European immigration which ended with World War I. Whether in the sweeping scenes of a young Vito Corleone's arrival past the Statue of Liberty and into Ellis Island in Francis Ford Coppola's *The Godfather Part II* (1974), the cartoon treatment with the 1986 film *An American Tail* (about a family of immigrant Russian mice), or the converted immigrant reception centre at Ellis Island, a visitor centre since 1990 with 1.7 million visitors a year (and sixteen billion annual hits on its website), the golden door is firmly (and warmly) ingrained in America's cultural memory. Indeed, as the cover to this book suggests, such nostalgia was operative even within the 1910s.[31] Yet others argue this approach sentimentalises and depoliticises the very raw tensions and fierce nativism provoked by mass immigration in the 1910s, partly to cocoon this legacy from contemporary debates over immigration.[32]

A similar duality attends the memory of the great migration of African Americans to the northern cities which began in the decade. In 1930 James Weldon Johnson praised the newly-black neighbour-hood of Harlem as a 'Mecca for the sightseer, the pleasure-seeker, the curious, the enterprising, the ambitious, and the talented of the entire Negro world'; and similar celebrations of the migration as a moment of urban magnetism for black enterprise, promise and creativity animate several recent cultural memories of the era. These include Toni Morrison's *Jazz* (1992), films such as Isaac Julien's *Looking for Langston* (1988), recent exhibitions such as the 1997 travelling art exhibition 'Rhapsodies in Black: Art of the Harlem Renaissance', and the recovery of the work of Harlem Renaissance photographer James VanDerZee.[33] That romance of the migration north, however, its promise of greater opportunities, safety and prosperity, would be rejected by many black writers after the Depression; for Langston Hughes it was a 'dream deferred' by poverty and inequality, as Meccas became slums; and for James Baldwin the only difference between the 'nervous, hollow, ringing city' of New York and the South was that 'the North promised more'.[34] The phenomenon of rapidly expanding black urban districts in the northern and midwestern states simulta-neously breeding new forms of social exclusion, as well as some of America's most innovative and significant culture, is a defining feature of twentieth-century African American cultural history, and it is one rooted in demographic shifts that began in the 1910s.

Ragtime's evocation of Jewish social mobility within the film industry was an affectionate nod to figures like Adolph Zukor, Carl Laemmle, Samuel Goldwyn and Marcus Loew, men who helped build the industry structure and film style that would dominate the next fifty years of global cinema. Memorialised in nostalgic biopics such as *Chaplin* (1992) and Gore Vidal's novel *Hollywood* (1990), the 'classical era' of Hollywood, which began in the 1910s, established a remarkably consistent approach to narrative film style and continuity editing which lasted until (at least) the 1960s. Indeed, though some critics argue that Hollywood films entered an era of 'post classical' style in the 1960s, others – most notably David Bordwell – main-tain that the dominant style of contemporary Hollywood cinema is instead a form of 'intensified continuity', wherein 'nearly all scenes in nearly all contemporary mass-market movies (and in most "inde-pendent" films) are staged, shot, and cut according to principles which

crystallized in the 1910s and 1920s'.[35] Certainly the institutional structure of vertical integration and the dominance of the majors in all aspects of film production, distribution and exhibition lasted until the anti-trust Paramount Decree in 1948, which broke up the Hollywood majors. Moreover, the dominance in American markets Hollywood established in the 1910s still accounts for America's economic dominance in global film, and its ability to produce films with an average budget higher than any other national film industry. Although in 1919 'Hollywood' was still a few years away from becoming a byword for fantasy, glamour and opportunity, the institutional and formal structures that had been established there in the decade would inform its centrality to the twentieth-century cultural imagination.

Writing almost a century after this decade, and at a moment when the American economic future looks very different to the rosy optimism of 1910, the United States of 1910 to 1919 can seem very distant. Yet any close examination reveals continuities everywhere: in debates over how mass immigration will change the cultural tenor of the nation; in how new media will affect the moral and social fabric of the country; or in the implications of waging idealist wars for democracy abroad. In the 2008 presidential election campaign John McCain regularly identified Teddy Roosevelt as one of his heroes, whereas Barack Obama – the first university professor president since Wilson – raised much of his campaign money from the kind of grass-roots, middle-class donors keen for reform that fuelled the Progressive movement. Indeed, Obama was happy to assume the label of Progressive – and at times had to defend a distinction between Progressive and socialist in the face of attacks exploiting the scaremongering toxicity of the word 'socialism', a toxicity which first entered the American political lexicon in 1919. Hillary Clinton frequently articulated her campaign in the terms of a long history of female participation in the American political process, a history which arguably had its defining moment in the 1910s. That the election was decided in part because politicians could talk about the devastating consequences of 'Wall Street' on 'Main Street' indicates that a feature Robert Wiebe identified of the Progressive era – that of 'attributing omnipotence to abstractions' – was still politically powerful; the complex inscrutability of big corporate capital, combined with a resentment over its huge impact on ordinary lives, were vital election issues then and now.[36]

This intense concern with civic sociality, which was perhaps the decade's defining feature, was also imprinted on its culture. The success of Charlie Chaplin's Little Tramp indicated the fascination with how the marginal and 'unimportant' could relate to the impersonal, intimidating and often terrifyingly new forces of mechanisation, law and corporate finance. That the Little Tramp met those forces with balletic grace, resilience, humour and occasionally triumph perhaps explains why he is the cultural icon of the decade we remember most fondly today.

Notes

Introduction

1. 'New Year's Eve Gay in Hotels, Quiet on Streets', *New York Times* (1 January 1920), p. 1.
2. 'The Old and the New', *New York Times* (1 January 1920), p. 14.
3. As well as Henry May, *The End of American Innocence: A Study of the First Years of Our Own Time, 1912–1917* (New York: Columbia University Press, [1959] 1992), see Merion and Susie Harris, *The Last Days of Innocence: America at War, 1917–1918* (New York: Random House, 1997), and Brian Lee and Robert Reinders, 'The Loss of Innocence, 1880–1914', *Introduction to American Studies*, ed. Malcom Bradbury and Howard Temperley, 3rd ed. (London: Longman, 1998), pp. 178–96.
4. Henry May, *The End of American Innocence*, p. xxiii.
5. Dominic Sandbrook, 'Why We Love History in Ten-Year Chapters', *The Observer* (19 April 2009), available at http://www.guardian.co.uk/books/2009/apr/19/decaditis-cultural-history.
6. Ann Douglas, *Terrible Honesty: Mongrel Manhattan in the 1920s* (London: Papermac, 1997), p. 182.
7. Isabel Leighton, 'Preface', *The Aspirin Age: 1919–1941*, ed. Isabel Leighton (New York: Simon and Schuster, 1949), p. xi. Frederick Lewis Allen, *Only Yesterday: An Informal History of the 1920's* (New York: Harper & Row, 1931), p. 1.
8. See Warren Susman, '"Personality" and the Making of Twentieth-Century Culture', *Culture as History: The Transformation of American Society in the Twentieth Century* (Washington DC: Smithsonian, 2003), pp. 271–85; T. J. Jackson Lears, *No Place of Grace: Antimodernism and the Transformation of American Culture, 1880–1920* (New York: Pantheon, 1982), pp. 32–3, 52–5.
9. John Milton Cooper Jr, *Pivotal Decades: The United States 1900–1920* (New York: Norton, 1990), pp. 133–4.
10. Frederick Winslow Taylor, *The Principles of Scientific Management* (New York: Norton, [1911] 1967), p. 5.
11. See Steven J. Kern, *The Culture of Time and Space 1880–1918*, 2nd edn (Cambridge MA: Harvard University Press, 2003); and Cooper, *Pivotal Decades*, p.136.

12. See Lee and Reinders, 'The Loss of Innocence', p. 180.

13. Edna Kenton, 'Mothers and Daughters', *The Seven Arts* (December 1916), pp. 185–92.

14. Robert H. Wiebe, *The Search for Order 1877–1920* (New York: Hill and Wang, 1967), p. xiii.

15. *The Quest of the Silver Fleece* (New York: Broadway Books, [1911] 2004), p. 259.

16. Helpful overviews of these debates can be found in the introductions to Alan Dawley's *Changing the World: American Progressives in War and Revolution* (Princeton NJ: Princeton University Press, 2003), and Kristofer Allerfeldt's edited collection *The Progressive Era in the USA: 1890–1921* (Aldershot: Ashgate, 2007).

17. Michael McGerr, *A Fierce Discontent: The Rise and Fall of the Progressive Movement, 1880–1920* (Oxford: Oxford University Press, 2003), p. 43.

18. Wiebe, *The Search for Order 1877–1920*, p. 113.

19. David Nasaw, *Going Out: The Rise and Fall of Public Amusements* (New York: Basic Books, 1993), pp. 4–5.

20. Michael McGerr, *A Fierce Discontent*, p. xiv.

21. Ibid., p. 158.

22. Nell Irving Painter, *Standing at Armageddon: A Grassroots History of the Progressive Era* (New York: Norton, 2008), pp. 275–6.

23. Wiebe, *The Search for Order*, pp. 116, 119.

24. See James Chace, *1912: Wilson, Roosevelt, Taft and Debs – The Election that Changed the Country* (New York: Simon and Schuster, 2004), p. 8; Cooper Jr, *Pivotal Decades*, p. 175.

25. Chace, *1912*, p. 8.

26. Cooper Jr, *Pivotal Decades*, p. 188.

27. John Dewey, *Democracy and Education: An Introduction to the Philosophy of Education* (New York: Macmillan, [1916] 1938), p. 101.

28. Eric Schocket, *Vanishing Moments: Class and American Literature* (Ann Arbor: University of Michigan Press, 2006), p. 123.

29. Walter Lippmann, *Public Opinion* (Filiquarian Publshing, [1922] 2007), p. 33.

30. See McGerr, *A Fierce Discontent*, pp. 107–14.

31. 'Introduction', *Photo Story: Selected Letters and Photographs of Lewis Hine*, ed. Daile Kaplan (Washington DC: Smithsonian Institution Press, 1992), pp. xvi–xxxvi, xxv.

32. Vicki Goldberg, *Lewis W. Hine: Children at Work* (Munich: Prestel, 1999), p. 16.

33. Daile Kaplan, *Lewis Hine in Europe: The Lost Photographs*, p. 44, quoted in Alan Trachtenberg, *Reading American Photographs: Images as History, Matthew Brady to Walker Evans* (New York: Hill and Wang, 1989), pp. 198–9.

34. Trachtenberg, *Reading American Photographs*, p. 168.

35. Ibid., p. 204.

36. George Dimock, 'Children of the Mills: Re-reading Lewis Hine's Child Labour Photographs', *Oxford Art Journal* 16 (1993), pp. 37–54.

37. Ibid., p. 52.

38. Lewis Hine, 'Social Photography', *Classic Essays on Photography*, ed. Alan Trachtenberg (New Haven CT: Leete's Island Books, 1980), p. 110.

39. Quoted in T. J. Jackson Lears, *Fables of Abundance: A Cultural History of Advertising in America* (New York: Basic Books, 1994), pp. 271–2.
40. Quoted in Lears, *Fables of Abundance*, p. 223.
41. Richard L. McCormick, 'Public Life in Industrial America, 1877–1917', in *The New American History*, ed. Eric Foner (Philadelphia PA: Temple University Press, 1977), pp. 107–32, p. 123.
42. Antonia Lant and Ingrid Periz, *Red Velvet Seat: Women's Writings on the First Fifty Years of Cinema* (London: Verso, 2005), p. 547.
43. Painter, *Standing at Armageddon*, p. 249.
44. Ibid, p. 271; McGerr, *A Fierce Discontent*, p. 296.
45. Kris Allerfeldt, 'Introduction', *The Progressive Era in the USA 1980–1921*, p. xviii.
46. Introduction, *The Jane Addams Reader*, ed. Jean Bethke Elshtain (New York: Basic Books, 2002), p. xxv.
47. 'The Settlement as a Factor in the Labor Movement', *The Jane Addams Reader*, pp. 46–61, p. 59.
48. See Painter, *Standing at Armageddon*, p. 251; also http://www.law.umkc.edu/faculty/projects/ftrials/triangle/trianglefire.html.
49. Emma Goldman, 'The Tragedy of Women's Emancipation', *Anarchism and Other Essays* (Filiquarian Publishers, [1910] 2005), pp. 165–75, p. 166.
50. Ann J. Lane, *To Herland and Beyond: The Life and Work of Charlotte Perkins Gilman* (New York: Pantheon, 1990), pp. 333–4, p. 231.
51. Charlotte Perkins Gilman, *Herland* (London: Dover, [1915] 1998), p. 57.
52. Lane, *To Herland and Beyond*, p. 298.
53. Gilman, *Herland*, p. 50.
54. Ibid.
55. Lane, *To Herland and Beyond*, p. 4.
56. Gilman, *Women and Economics* (London: Dover, [1898] 1998), p. 21, p. 3.
57. Sandra Gilbert and Susan Gubar, *No-Man's Land: The Place of the Woman Writer in the Twentieth Century*, Vol. 2: *Sexchanges* (New Haven CT: Yale University Press, 1989), p. 73.
58. These observations were made in Nolan's research paper at the 2008 British Association for American Studies Conference, entitled 'Charlotte Perkins Gilman and Early Twentieth Century Women's Magazine Culture'.
59. Addams, 'Contrast in Post-War Generation', *The Jane Addams Reader*, pp. 294–306, p. 298.
60. See, for example, Lane, *To Herland and Beyond*, p. 305; Sandra Gilbert and Susan Gubar, *No-Man's Land*, p. 82.
61. Gilman, *Herland*, p. 118.
62. McGerr, *A Fierce Discontent*, p. 266.
63. Margaret Anderson, 'Incense and Splendor', *Little Review* (June 1914), pp. 1–3, p. 1, p. 3.
64. Ibid., p. 1.
65. Painter, *Standing at Armageddon*, p. 295.
66. McGerr, *A Fierce Discontent*, p. 16.
67. Chace, *1912*, pp. 85, 87.
68. Painter, *Standing at Armageddon*, p. 264.
69. Patrick Renshaw, *The Wobblies: The Story of the IWW and Syndicalism in the United States* (Chicago: Ivan R. Dee, 1999), p. xix.

70. Ibid., p. 97.
71. Eugene E. Leach, 'The Radicals of the Masses', *1915: The Cultural Moment*, ed. Adele Heller and Lois Rudnick (New Brunswick NJ: Rutgers University Press, 1991), pp. 27–45, pp. 28–9.
72. Quoted in Steven Watson, *Strange Bedfellows: The First American Avant-Garde* (New York: Abbeville Press, 1991), p. 165.
73. Floyd Dell, 'Feminism for Men', *The Masses* (July 1914), pp. 19–20, p. 19.
74. Sandford Gifford, 'The American Reception of Psychoanalysis 1908–1922', *1915: The Cultural Moment*, pp. 128–45, p. 136.
75. Watson, *Strange Bedfellows*, p. 161.
76. Ibid., p. 148; see pp. 138–49 for Watson's account of the strike and the pageant.
77. Renshaw, *The Wobblies*, p. 115.
78. Watson, *Strange Bedfellows*, p. 149.
79. Max Eastman, 'In Case of War', *The Masses* (April 1917), pp. 7–8, p. 7.
80. Max Eastman, 'Conscription for What?' *The Masses* (July 1917), pp. 18–19, p. 18.
81. John Reed, 'One Solid Month of Liberty', *The Masses* (September 1917), pp. 5–6, p. 5.
82. Chace, *1912*, p. 257.
83. Watson, *Strange Bedfellows*, pp. 322–3.
84. Floyd Dell, *Intellectual Vagabondage* (Chicago: Ivan R. Dee, [1926] 1990), pp. 260, 257.
85. See Elizabeth W. Burt, 'Introduction', *The Progressive Era: Primary Documents on Events from 1890 to 1914* (Westport CT: Greenwood, 2004), p. 7.
86. Ibid., p. 9.
87. Marion Elizabeth Rodgers, 'Introduction', *The Impossible H. L. Mencken: A Selection of His Best Newspaper Stories* (New York: Anchor, 1991), pp. xxxvii–lviii, p. xlvii.
88. H. L. Mencken, 'Theodore Dreiser' (1916), in *The Vintage Mencken*, ed. Alistair Cooke (London: Vintage, 1955), p. 46.
89. H. L. Mencken, 'The Archangel Woodrow' (1921), in *The Vintage Mencken*, p. 120.
90. Robert M. Crunden, *American Salons: Encounters with European Modernism 1885–1917* (New York: Oxford University Press, 1993), p. 184.
91. Ibid, p. 387.
92. Janet M. Lyon, 'Gender and Sexuality', in *The Cambridge Companion to American Modernism* (Cambridge: Cambridge University Press, 2005), pp. 221–41, p. 236.
93. Ezra Pound, 'Salutation the Second', *Selected Poems* (London: Faber and Faber 1975), pp. 42–3, p. 43.
94. Walter Lippmann, 'The White Passion', *The New Republic* (21 October 1916), pp. 293–5, p. 294; Jane Addams, 'Women's Conscience and Social Amelioration', *The Jane Addams Reader*, pp. 252–63, p. 263.
95. Wiebe, *The Search for Order*, p. 296.
96. T. J. Jackson Lears, *No Place of Grace: Antimodernism and the Transformation of American Culture, 1880–1920*, pp. 296–7.
97. 'This Older Generation', [1915] *Randolph Bourne: The Radical Will, Selected Writings 1911–1918*, ed. Olaf Hansen (Berkeley: University of California Press, 1992), pp. 159–68, p. 160.

98. Van Wyck Brooks, *Van Wyck Brooks, The Early Years*, ed. Claire Sprague (New York: Harper and Row, 1968), p. 83, p. 88.

99. George Santayana, 'The Genteel Tradition in American Philosophy', *The Genteel Tradition: Nine Essays by George Santayana*, ed. Douglas L. Wilson (Lincoln, NB: Bison Books, 1998), pp. 37–64, p. 40.

100. Henry Adams, *The Education of Henry Adams*, ed. Ernest Samuels (Boston: Houghton Mifflin, [1918] 1973), pp. 385, 387.

101. Brooks, *The Early Years*, p. 128.

102. H. L. Mencken, 'More Notes for a Work Upon the Origin and Nature of Puritanism' (1916), in *The Impossible H. L. Mencken: A Selection of His Best Newspaper Stories*, ed. Marion Elizabeth Rodgers (New York: Anchor-Doubleday, 1991), pp. 30–5, p. 32.

103. Brooks, *The Early Years*, p. 132.

104. Ezra Pound, 'A Pact' (1913), in *Ezra Pound: Selected Poems 1908–1959* (London: Faber, 1975), p. 45.

105. R. J. Coady, 'American Art', *The Soil* (January 1917), pp. 54–6, pp. 54–5.

106. Matthew Frye Jacobson, *Barbarian Virtues: The United States Encounters Foreign Peoples at Home and Abroad, 1876–1917* (New York: Hill and Wang, 2001), p. 4.

107. Timothy Prchal, '"The American of the Future:" Fictional Immigrant Children and National Ethnic Identity in the Progressive Era', in Kristopher Allerfeldt, ed., *The Progressive Era in the USA: 1890–1921*, pp. 142–60, p. 142.

108. John Higham, *Strangers in the Land: Patterns of American Nativism, 1860–1925* (New Brunswick NJ: Rutgers University Press, 2002), p. 198.

109. Randolph Bourne, 'Trans-National America', *War and the Intellectuals: Collected Essays 1915–1919*, ed. Carl Resek (Indianapolis IN: Hackett Publishing, 1964), pp. 107–23, p. 122.

110. See 'Introduction', Werner Sollors, Mary Antin, *The Promised Land* (London: Penguin, 1997), p. xxxv.

111. *The Promised Land*, p. 1; Higham, *Strangers in the Land*, p. 121.

112. *The Promised Land*, pp. 144–5.

113. Higham, *Strangers in the Land*, p. 213.

114. Arthur E. Barbeau and Florette Henri, *The Unknown Soldiers: African-American Troops in World War I* (New York: Da Capo Press, 1996), p. 176, p. 174.

115. *The Crisis* (November 1910), p. 10.

116. Carol Marks, 'The Social and Economic Life of Southern Blacks During the Migration', *Black Exodus: The Great Migration from the American South*, ed. Alferdteen Harrison (Jackson: University Press of Mississippi, 1991), pp. 36–50, p. 46.

117. 'The New Negro – What is He?' *The Messenger* (August 1920), p. 74.

118. Gary Mead, *The Doughboys: America and the First World War* (London, Penguin, 2000), p. 358.

1. Film and Vaudeville

1. David Bordwell, Janet Staiger, and Kristin Thompson, *The Classical Hollywood Cinema: Film Style and Mode of Production to 1960* (London: Routledge, 1985), p. 3.

2. This was Charlie Chaplin's salary at Mutual.

3. Roy Rosenzweig, 'From Rum Shop to Rialto: Workers and Movies', *Moviegoing in America*, ed. Gregory A. Walker (Oxford: Blackwell, 2002), pp. 27–45, p. 30.

4. Lewis Mumford, 'The City', *Civilization in the United States*, ed. Harold Stearns (New York: Harcourt, Brace and Co., 1922), pp. 3–20, p. 13.

5. Steven J. Ross, *Working-Class Hollywood: Silent Film and the Shaping of Class in America* (Princeton NJ: Princeton University Press, 1998), p. 24.

6. Ibid., p. 19.

7. Louise de Koven Bowen, 'Five and Ten Cent Theatres', 1901 and 1911, in *Red Velvet Seat: Women's Writing on the First Fifty Years of Cinema*, ed. Antonia Lant and Ingrid Periz (London: Verso, 2006), pp. 303–8, p. 304.

8. Quoted in Jane Addams, 'The House of Dreams' (1909), in *Red Velvet Seat*, pp. 297–303, p. 299.

9. See Kristin Thompson, 'The Formulation of the Classical Style, 1909–1928', *The Classical Hollywood Cinema: Film Style and Mode of Production to 1960*, p. 159.

10. 'What the Public Wants in the Picture Theater', Samuel L. 'Roxy' Rothapfel, *Moviegoing in America*, pp. 100–3.

11. Richard Koszarski, *An Evening's Entertainment: The Age of the Silent Feature Picture, 1915–1928* (Berkeley: University of California Press, 1990), pp. 9, 55–61.

12. Staiger, 'The Central Producer System: After 1914', *The Classical Hollywood Cinema: Film Style and Mode of Production to 1960*, p. 132.

13. Quoted in Eileen Bowser, *The Transformation of Cinema, 1907–1915* (New York: Scribner's, 1990), p. 95.

14. Thompson, 'Formulation of the Classical Style', p. 191.

15. Ibid., p. 194.

16. Linda Arvidson Griffith, *When the Movies Were Young* (New York: Dover, 1969), p. 252.

17. See Richard Sklar, *Movie Made America: A Cultural History of American Movies* (London: Chappell and Co., 1978), p. 58.

18. See Michael Rogin, '"The Sword Became a Flashing Vision": D. W. Griffith's The Birth of a Nation', *Representations* 9 (1985): pp. 150–95.

19. 'Brotherly Love', *The New Republic* (20 March 1915), p. 185; Johnson quoted in Lawrence J. Oliver and Terri L. Walker's 'James Weldon Johnson's *New York Age* Essays on *The Birth of a Nation* and the "Southern oligarchy"', *South Central Review* 10 (1993): pp. 1–17, p. 12.

20. 'Brotherly Love', p. 185.

21. *D. W. Griffith and the Origins of Narrative Film: The Early Years at Biograph* (Urbana: University of Illinois Press, 1991), p. 204.

22. Quoted in Rogin, '"The Sword Became a Flashing Vision"', p. 164.

23. See Eileen Bowser, *The Transformation of Cinema 1907–1915*, p. 187.

24. Richard Koszarski, *An Evening's Entertainment*, p. 276.

25. Richard deCordova, *Picture Personalities: The Emergence of the Star System in America* (Urbana: University of Illinois Press, 1990), p. 36.

26. Ibid., p. 109.

27. Charles J. Maland, *Chaplin and American Culture: The Evolution of a Star Image* (Princeton NJ: Princeton University Press, 1989), pp. 9–11.

28. See Austin Briggs, 'Chaplin's Charlie and Joyce's Bloom', *Journal of Modern Literature* 20 (1996), pp. 177–86.

29. See, for example, John Montgomery, 'A Brief Overall View', in *Focus on Chaplin*, ed. Donald W. McCaffrey (Englewood Cliffs NJ: Prentice-Hall, 1971), pp. 11–26, p. 17.

30. Charlie Chaplin, 'Making Fun', *The Soil*, 1 (December 1916), pp. 4–7, p. 6.

31. Ibid., p. 6.

32. Angela M. Blake, *How New York Became American, 1890–1924* (Baltimore MD: Johns Hopkins University Press, 2006), pp. 127–30.

33. Chaplin, 'Making Fun', p. 5.

34. Koszarski, *An Evening's Entertainment*, p. 71.

35. *An Evening's Entertainment*, pp. 99–104.

36. Kristin Thompson and David Bordwell, *Film History: An Introduction* (New York: McGraw-Hill, 1994), p. 55.

37. See M. Alison Kibler, *Rank Ladies: Gender and Cultural Hierarchy in American Vaudeville* (Chapel Hill: University of North Carolina Press, 1999), p. 8.

38. Ibid., p. 15; David Nasaw, *Going Out: the Rise and Fall of Public Amusements* (New York: Basic Books, 1993), p. 20.

39. Kibler, *Rank Ladies*, p. 17.

40. B. F. Keith, 'The Vogue of Vaudeville', 1898, rpt in *American Vaudeville as Seen by its Contemporaries*, ed. Charles W. Stein (New York: Da Capo, 1984), pp. 15–20, p. 17.

41. Quoted in Lawrence Levine, *Highbrow/Lowbrow: The Emergence of Cultural Hierarchy in America* (Cambridge MA: Harvard University Press, 1990), p. 196.

42. Ibid., p. 199.

43. Kibler, *Rank Ladies*, p. 11.

44. Nasaw, *Going Out*, p. 30; Stein, *American Vaudeville*, p. 109.

45. Robert C. Toll, *On With the Show: the First Century of Show Business in America* (New York: Oxford University Press, 1976), p. 283.

46. Ibid., p. 278.

47. Richard Koszarski gives salary figures for Hollywood stars in the period on pp. 114–16 of *An Evening's Entertainment*: for example, in 1916 Henry Walthall received $500 a week at Essanay, whereas Valeska Suratt was receiving $5,000 a week at Fox.

48. 'Thrown Overboard Manacled in a Box', *New York Times* (8 July 1912), p. 6.

49. Toll, *On with the Show*, p. 280.

50. Quoted in Charles Hamm, *Irving Berlin: Songs from the Melting Pot: The Formative Years 1907–1914* (New York: Oxford University Press, 1997), p. 31.

51. Nasaw, *Going Out*, p. 51.

52. Toll, *On With the Show*, pp. 247–53; George Chauncey, *Gay New York: Gender, Urban Culture, and the Making of the Gay Male World, 1890–1940* (New York: Basic Books, 1994), p. 47.

53. Toll, *On With the Show*, p. 252.

54. Nasaw, *Going Out*, p. 54.

55. Michael Rogin, 'Blackface, White Noise: The Jewish Jazz Singer Finds His Voice', *Critical Inquiry* 18 (1992), pp. 417–53, pp. 430, 447.

56. Louis Chude-Sokei, *The Last 'Darky': Bert Williams, Black-on-Black Minstrelsy, and the African Diaspora* (Durham NC: Duke University Press, 2006), p. 165.

57. Ann Charters, *Nobody: The Story of Bert Williams* (New York: Da Capo, 1983), p. 126.
58. Chude-Sokei, *The Last 'Darky'*, p. 2.
59. Ibid.
60. Charters, *Nobody*, p. 9.
61. 'The Original and the Echo', Bert Williams and Eddie Leonard, in *American Vaudeville as Seen by its Contemporaries*, ed. Charles W. Stein (New York: Da Capo, 1984), pp. 241–7, p. 242.
62. Ibid., pp. 241–2.
63. 'Bert Williams', *The Soil* 1 (December 1916), pp. 19–23, p. 19.
64. Chude-Sokei, *The Last 'Darky'*, pp. 18–19.
65. See, for example, Charters, *Nobody*, pp. 8–9; Toll, *On with the Show*, p. 131; Caryl Phillips, *Dancing in the Dark* (London: Vintage 2005).
66. 'Bert Williams', *The Soil*, p. 19.
67. Susan Gubar, *Racechanges: White Skin, Black Face in American Culture* (Oxford: Oxford University Press, 1997), p. 114.
68. Chude-Sokei, *The Last 'Darky'*, p. 5.
69. David Krasner, *A Beautiful Pageant: African American Theatre, Drama and Performance in the Harlem Renaissance, 1910–1927* (New York: Palgrave-Macmillan, 2002), p. 10.
70. Ann Douglas, *Terrible Honesty: Mongrel Manhattan in the 1920s* (London: Papermac, 1997), p. 329.
71. Walter Benjamin, 'The Work of Art in the Age of Mechanical Reproduction', *Illuminations*, ed. Hannah Arendt and trans. Harry Zohn (New York: Schocken, 1968), pp. 217–51, p. 231.

2. Visual Art and Photography

1. Theodore Roosevelt, 'An Art Exhibition', in *History as Literature and Other Essays* (New York: Scribner's, 1913), pp. 303–10.
2. Marsden Hartley to Alfred Stieglitz, February 1913, *My Dear Stieglitz: Letters of Marsden Hartley and Alfred Stieglitz, 1912–1915* (Columbia: University of South Carolina Press, 2002), p. 61.
3. See Steven Watson, *Strange Bedfellows: The First American Avant-Garde* (New York: Abbeville, 1991), p. 376.
4. William B. Scott and Peter M. Rutkoff, *New York Modern: The Arts and the City* (Baltimore MD: Johns Hopkins University Press, 1999), p. 61. See also Watson, *Strange Bedfellows*, p. 166.
5. Quoted in Susan Herbst, *Politics at the Margin: Historical Studies of Public Expression Outside the Mainstream* (Cambridge: Cambridge University Press, 1994), p. 108.
6. William Innes Homer, *Robert Henri and his Circle* (New York: Hacker Art Books, 1988), p. 175.
7. Scott and Rutkoff, *New York Modern*, p. 27.
8. Watson, *Strange Bedfellows*, p. 170.
9. Wanda Corn, *The Great American Thing: Modern Art and National Identity, 1915–1935* (Berkeley: University of California Press, 1999), p. xv.
10. Ibid.

11. Carolyn Kitch, *The Girl on the Magazine Cover: The Origins of Visual Stereotypes in American Mass Media* (Chapel Hill: University of North Carolina Press, 2001), p. 95.

12. Ibid., pp. 7–8.

13. Frances M. Naumann and Beth Venn, *Making Mischief: Dada Invades New York* (New York: Whitney Museum, 1996), p. 143.

14. See http://news.bbc.co.uk/1/hi/entertainment/4059997.stm. Accessed 30/4/2007.

15. Michael North, *Camera Works: Photography and the Twentieth-Century Word* (Oxford: Oxford University Press, 2005), p. 4.

16. 'Dada's Daddy *c.*1917: Duchamp in New York and the Art of Woman/Women', *European Journal of American Culture* 19 (2000), pp. 84–95, p. 95. Goody stresses the significant role played in New York Dada by women poets and artists such as Beatrice Wood, Clara Tice, and Mina Loy. See also *Women in Dada: Essays on Sex, Gender and Identity*, ed. Naomi Sawelson-Gorse (Cambridge MA: MIT Press, 2001).

17. Naumann and Benn, *Making Mischief*, p. 62.

18. Arturo Schwarz, *Man Ray: The Rigor of Imagination* (New York: Rizzoli, 1977), p. 35.

19. Ibid., p. 39.

20. Andreas Huyssen, *After the Great Divide: Modernism, Mass Culture, Postmodernism* (Bloomington: Indiana University Press, 1986), p. 11.

21. Roland Penrose, *Man Ray* (London: Thames and Hudson, 1975), pp. 42–3.

22. Quoted in Marjorie Perloff, *21st Century Modernism: The New Poetics* (Oxford: Blackwell, 2002), p. 83.

23. Schwarz, *Man Ray*, p. 39.

24. Harold Clurman, 'Alfred Stieglitz and the Group Idea', *America and Alfred Stieglitz: A Collective Portrait*, ed. Waldo Frank et al. (New York: Doubleday, 1934), pp. 267–80, p. 274.

25. Wanda Corn, *The Great American Thing*, p. 17.

26. Sheldon Reich, 'John Marin: Paintings of New York, 1912', *American Art Journal* 1 (spring 1969): pp. 43–52, p. 44.

27. Dorothy Norman, 'John Marin: Conversations and Notes', *College Art Journal* 14 (1955): pp. 320–1, p. 325.

28. Marcia Brennan, *Painting Gender, Constructing Theory: The Alfred Stieglitz Circle and American Formalist Aesthetics* (Cambridge MA: MIT Press, 2001), p. 8.

29. 'Art and the Camera', *The Nation* (16 April 1924): pp. 456–7.

30. Patricia Johnston, *Real Fantasies: Edward Steichen's Advertising Photography* (Berkeley: University of California Press, 1997), p. 1.

31. See Patricia Holland, '"Sweet it is to Scan. . .": Personal Photographs and Popular Photography', in *Photography: A Critical Introduction*, ed. Liz Wells, 2nd edn (London: Routledge, 2000), pp. 117–64, p. 145.

32. Paul Rosenfeld, *Port of New York* (New York: Harcourt, Brace and Co., 1924), pp. 245–6.

33. Ibid., p. 266.

34. Alfred Stieglitz, 'Our Illustrations', *Camera Work* 49–50 (June 1917); rpt in *Stieglitz on Photography: His Selected Essays and Notes*, ed. Richard Whelan (New York: Aperture, 2000), p. 223.

35. 'Photography', Paul Strand, *The Seven Arts* (August 1917), pp. 524–6; rpt in *Classic Essays on Photography*, ed. Alan Trachtenberg (New Haven CT: Leete's Island Books, 1980), pp. 141–2.

36. The fullest account of Strand's work in 1916 and 1917 can be found in Maria Morris Hambourg's *Paul Strand: Circa 1916*, (New York: Metropolitan Museum of Art/Abrams, 1998).

37. Ibid., p. 34.

38. Maria Morris Hambourg, 'From 291 to the Museum of Modern Art: Photography in New York, 1910–1937', in *The New Vision: Photography Between the World Wars*, Maria Morris Hambourg and Christopher Phillips (New York: Metropolitan Museum of Art–Abrams, 1994), pp. 3–63, p. 47.

39. Johnston, *Real Fantasies*, p. 13.

40. Alan Trachtenberg, *Reading American Photographs: Images as History, Matthew Brady to Walker Evans* (New York: Hill and Wang, 1989), p. 169.

41. See Constance Rourke, 'Artist in the American Tradition', rpt in *Photography in Print: Writings from 1816 to the Present*, ed. Vicki Goldberg (Albuquerque: University of New Mexico Press, 1981), pp. 273–5, p. 273.

42. Theodore E. Stebbins Jr, 'Sheeler and Photography', *The Photography of Charles Sheeler, American Modernist* (Boston MA: Bulfinch Press, 2002), pp. 9–25, p. 15.

43. Ibid., p. 13.

44. Quoted in Elaine Dines-Cox with Carol McCusker, 'Directorial Modernist: The Life and Art of Paul Outerbridge', *Paul Outerbridge 1896–1858*, ed. Manfred Heiting (Köln: Taschen, 1999), p. 18.

45. Jim Haskins, *James Van DerZee: The Picture-Takin' Man* (Trenton NJ: Africa World Press, 1991), p. 157.

46. See, for example, Mick Gidley's 'Pictorialist Elements in Edward S. Curtis's Photographic Representation of American Indians', *The Yearbook of English Studies* 24 (1994), pp. 180–92.

47. Edward S. Curtis, *The North American Indian: The Complete Portfolios* (Köln: Taschen, 1997), p. 36.

48. Curtis's obituary is reproduced at http://xroads.virginia.edu/~ma02/daniels/curtis/obituary.html.

49. Benita Eisler, *An American Romance: O'Keeffe and Stieglitz* (London: Penguin, 1991), p. 7.

50. Ibid., p. 183.

51. Quoted in Marcia Brennan, *Painting Gender*, p. 82.

52. Ibid., p. 83.

53. Eisler, *An American Romance*, p. 236.

54. Herbert J. Seligmann, 'A Photographer Challenges', *The Nation* (16 February 1921), p. 268.

55. See McGrath's 'Re-Reading Edward Weston: Feminism, Photography and Psychoanalysis', *The Photography Reader*, ed. Liz Wells (London: Routledge, 2003), pp. 327–37; and Susan Sontag, *On Photography* (London: Penguin, 2002).

56. Susan Fillin-Yeh, 'Dandies, Marginality and Modernism: Georgia O'Keeffe, Marcel Duchamp and other Cross-Dressers', *Oxford Art Journal* 18 (1995): pp. 33–44, p. 33.

57. See Susan Sontag, 'The Heroism of Vision', *On Photography*, pp. 83–112.

3. Fiction and Poetry

1. Theodore Dreiser, *Jennie Gerhardt* (London: Penguin, [1911] 1994), p. 125.
2. Ibid.
3. H. L. Mencken, 'On Being an American', *The Impossible Mencken: A Selection of His Best Newspaper Stories*, ed., Marion Elizabeth Rodgers (New York: Doubleday, 1991), pp. 21–5, p. 22.
4. Dreiser, *The Titan* (New York: Dell, [1914] 1959), p. 531.
5. H. L. Mencken, 'Theodore Dreiser' (1916), *The Vintage Mencken*, ed. Alistair Cooke (London: Vintage, 1955), p. 46.
6. See particularly Lee Clark Mitchell's *Determined Fictions* (New York: Columbia University Press, 1989), pp. vii–xvii.
7. DeWitt C. Wing, 'An Unreeling Realist', *The Little Review* (July 1914), pp. 49–51, p. 50.
8. Dreiser, *The Titan*, p. 25.
9. Carl Sandburg, 'Chicago', *The Complete Poems of Carl Sandburg* (San Diego: Harcourt, 1970), p. 3.
10. Margaret Anderson, *My Thirty Years' War* (New York: Horizon Press, 1969), p. 32.
11. Henry May, *The End of American Innocence: A Study of the First Years of Our Time* (New York: Columbia University Press, [1959] 1992), p. 106.
12. Wharton, *The Custom of the Country* (Oxford: Oxford World's Classics, [1913] 1995), p. 130.
13. Ibid., p. 131.
14. Debra Ann MacComb, 'New Wives for Old: Divorce and the Leisure-Class Marriage Market in Edith Wharton's The Custom of the Country', *American Literature* 68 (1996), pp. 765–97, p. 771.
15. Michael McGerr, *A Fierce Discontent: The Rise and Fall of the Progressive Movement, 1880–1920* (Oxford: Oxford University Press, 2003), p. 11.
16. *The Custom of the Country*, p. 159.
17. Ibid., p. 121.
18. Brian Lee and Robert Reinders, 'The Loss of Innocence: 1880-1914', *Introduction to American Studies*, ed. Malcolm Bradbury and Howard Temperley, 3rd edn (London: Longman, 1998), pp. 178–96, pp. 188–9.
19. Ellen Glasgow, *Virginia* (London: Virago, [1913] 1981), p. 154.
20. 'Farm Women Find Life Hard', *New York Times* (30 May 1915), p. SM14.
21. Willa Cather, *O Pioneers!* (London: Dover, [1913] 1993), pp. 5–6.
22. See, for example, *The Cambridge Companion to Willa Cather*, ed. Marilee Lindemann (Cambridge: Cambridge University Press, 2005); and Catherine Morley, 'Crossing the Water: Willa Cather and the Transatlantic Imaginary', *The European Journal of American Culture* 28.2 (2009): pp. 125–40.
23. Quoted in A. S. Byatt, 'Preface', *My Ántonia*, (London: Virago, [1918] 1993), n.p.
24. *My Ántonia*, p. 264.
25. Marilee Lindemann, 'It Ain't My Prairie: Gender, Power, and Narrative in My Ántonia', *New Essays on Cather's My Ántonia*, ed. Sharon O'Brien (Cambridge: Cambridge University Press, 1999), pp. 111–35, p. 114.

26. *My Ántonia*, p. 4.
27. Christine Bold, *Selling the Wild West: Popular Western Fiction, 1860 to 1960* (Bloomington: Indiana University Press, 1987), pp. 7–8.
28. Ibid., pp. 76, 93.
29. *The Nation* (1 October 1914), rpt. In *Tarzan of the Apes*, Edgar Rice Burroughs (New York: Barnes and Noble, 2006), p. 262.
30. See 'Introduction', Maura Spiegel, *Tarzan of the Apes*, p. xvi.
31. Ibid., p. xxi.
32. Gail Bederman, *Manliness and Civilization: A Cultural History of Gender and Race in the United States, 1880–1917* (Chicago: University of Chicago Press, 1995), p. 219.
33. *Tarzan of the Apes*, p. 6.
34. Ibid., p. 174.
35. Ibid., p. 249.
36. See Bederman, pp. 230–1.
37. Abraham Cahan, *The Rise of David Levinsky* (New York: Harper and Row, [1917] 1960), p. 530.
38. 'The Fat of the Land' (1919), in *Hungry Hearts* (London: Penguin, [1920] 1997), p. 128.
39. Claude McKay, 'America', in *The Norton Anthology of African American Literature*, eds Henry Louis Gates and Nellie Y. McKay (New York: Norton, 1997), p. 985.
40. Johnson, *The Autobiography of an Ex-Colored Man*, in *The Norton Anthology of African American Literature*, p. 861. Werner Sollors, *Neither Black nor White Yet Both: Thematic Explorations of Interracial Literature* (Cambridge MA: Harvard University Press, 1997), p. 249.
41. Rpt in *Winesburg, Ohio*, eds Charles E. Modlin and Ray Lewis White (New York: Norton, 1996), p. 163; Anderson, letter to George Freitag, rpt in *Winesburg, Ohio*, p. 150.
42. 'Sherwood Anderson: Looking for the White Spot', in T. J. Jackson Lears, *The Power of Culture: Critical Essays in American History*, eds Richard Wrightman Fox and T. J. Jackson Lears (Chicago: University of Chicago Press, 1993), pp. 3–37, pp. 14–15.
43. Anderson, *Winesburg, Ohio*, p. 34.
44. Ibid., p. 136.
45. Douglas Mao, 'Modern American Literary Criticism', in *The Cambridge Companion to American Literary Modernism*, ed. Walter Kalaidjian (Cambridge: Cambridge University Press, 2005), pp. 284–307, p. 285.
46. 'A Retrospect', *Literary Essays of Ezra Pound*, ed. T.S. Eliot (New York: New Directions), pp. 3–14, p. 4.
47. Ezra Pound, 'Patria Mia', in *Ezra Pound: Selected Prose*, pp. 99–141, p. 122.
48. Pound, 'Hugh Selwyn Mauberly', *Selected Poems 1908–1959* (London: Faber and Faber, 1975), p. 99.
49. George Bornstein, 'Ezra Pound and the Making of Modernism', *The Cambridge Companion to Ezra Pound*, ed. Ira Bruce Nadel (Cambridge: Cambridge University Press, 1999), pp. 22–42, p. 31.
50. Quoted in Mark Morrisson, *The Public Face of Modernism: Little Magazines,*

Audiences, and Reception, 1905–1920 (Madison: University of Wisconsin Press, 2001), p. 5.

51. See Morrisson, *The Public Face of Modernism*; and Karen Leick, 'Popular Modernism: Little Magazines and the American Daily Press', *PMLA* 123 (2008), pp. 125–39.

52. A. David Moody, *Ezra Pound: Poet, a Portrait of the Man and his Work*, Vol. I: *The Young Genius, 1885-1920* (Oxford: Oxford University Press, 2007), p. 319.

53. 'The Love Song of J. Alfred Prufrock', *T. S. Eliot: Collected Poems 1909–1962* (New York: Harcourt, Brace and World, 1970), p. 3.

54. T. S. Eliot, 'Tradition and the Individual Talent', *Selected Prose of T. S. Eliot*, ed. Frank Kermode (New York: Harcourt Brace, 1975), pp. 37–44, p. 38.

55. See, for example, Terry Eagleton in *Literary Theory: An Introduction*, 2nd edn (Oxford: Blackwell, 1996), pp. 33–5.

56. Moody, *Ezra Pound: Poet*, p. 317; Ann Douglas, *Terrible Honesty: Mongrel Manhattan in the 1920s* (London: Papermac, 1997), p. 7.

57. Ann Douglas, *Terrible Honesty*, p. 6.

58. Peter Jones, 'Introduction', *Imagist Poetry*, ed. Peter Jones (Harmondsworth: Penguin, 1985), p. 32.

59. Janet Lyon, 'Gender and Sexuality', in *The Cambridge Companion to American Modernism*, pp. 221–41, pp. 224–5.

60. Leick, 'Popular Modernism', p. 128.

61. *Sherwood Anderson/Gertrude Stein: Correspondence and Personal Essays*, ed. Ray Lewis White (Chapel Hill: University of North Carolina Press, 1972), p. 84, pp. 24–5; Mina Loy, 'Gertrude Stein', *The Lost Lunar Baedecker: Poems*, ed. Roger L. Conover (New York: Farrar, Straus and Giroux, 1996), p. 94.

62. Gertrude Stein, *Tender Buttons* (London: Dover, [1914] 1997), p. 30.

63. Gertrude Stein, 'Poetry and Grammar', *Look at Me Now and Here I Am: Writings and Lectures 1909–1945*, ed. Patricia Meyerowitz (London: Penguin, 1984), pp. 125–47, p. 142, p. 138.

64. Ibid, pp. 137, 141.

65. Peter Nicholls, *Modernisms* (London: Macmillan, 1995), p. 197.

66. Nicola Pitchford, 'Unlikely Modernism, Unlikely Postmodernism: Stein's *Tender Buttons*', *American Literary History* 11 (1999), pp. 642–67, p. 660.

67. *Tender Buttons*, p. 35.

68. Ibid., p. 29.

69. Pitchford, 'Unlikely Modernism', pp. 659–60.

70. Stein, 'Transatlantic Interview', quoted in '"Familiar Strangers": The Household Words of Gertrude Stein's "Tender Buttons"', Margueritte S. Murphy, *Contemporary Literature* 32 (1991), pp. 383–402, p. 387.

71. *Tender Buttons*, p. 27.

72. Malcolm Bradbury, *Dangerous Pilgrimages: Trans-Atlantic Mythologies and the Novel* (London: Penguin, 1996), p. 250.

73. Pound, 'Brief Note', *The Little Review* (August 1918), pp. 6–9, p. 7.

74. Pound, 'Patria Mia', p. 110.

75. Carl Sandburg, 'Halstead Street Car' (1916), *Chicago Poems*, in *The Complete Poems of Carl Sandburg* (New York: Harcourt, Brace, 1969), p. 6.

76. William Carlos Williams, *Spring and All*, in *The Collected Poems of William*

Carlos Williams, Volume I: *1909-1939*, eds A. Walton Litz and Christopher MacGowan (New York: New Directions, 1986), p. 207.

77. *The Selected Letters of William Carlos Williams*, ed. John C. Thirlwall (New York: New Directions, 1957), p. 227.

78. Frank Lentricchia, *Modernist Quartet* (Cambridge: Cambridge University Press, 1994), p. 107.

79. Frost, 'On Emerson', *Selected Prose of Robert Frost*, eds Hyde Cox and Edward Connery Lathem (New York: Holt, Rinehart, 1966), pp. 111–19, p. 112; Richard Gray, *American Poetry of the Twentieth Century* (London: Longman, 1990): p. 138.

80. Quoted in Seamus Heaney, 'Above the Brim', in *Homage to Robert Frost* (London: Faber, 1997), p. 71.

81. *Modernist Quartet*, pp. 101, 110.

82. Joseph Brodsky, 'On Grief and Reason', in *Homage to Robert Frost*, p. 7.

83. Bornstein, 'Ezra Pound and the Making of Modernism', p. 31; Lentricchia, *Modernist Quartet*, p. 85.

4. Performance and Music

1. Quoted in Lewis A. Erenberg, *Steppin' Out: New York Nightlife and the Transformation of American Culture, 1890–1930* (Chicago: University of Chicago Press, 1981), p. 146.

2. Ibid., p. 237.

3. Djuna Barnes, 'You Can Tango – a Little – at Arcadia Dance Hall' (June 1913), in *Djuna Barnes's New York*, ed. Alyce Barry (London: Virago, 1989), pp. 13–19, p. 15.

4. Ibid., pp. 18–19.

5. Kathy Peiss, *Cheap Amusements: Working Women and Leisure in Turn-of-the-Century New York* (Philadelphia PA: Temple University Press, 1986), p. 88.

6. David Nasaw, *Going Out: The Rise and Fall of Public Amusements* (New York: Basic Books, 1993), p. 104; Barnes, 'You can Tango', p. 18.

7. Report from the New York Committee on Amusements, quoted in Elisabeth I. Perry's '"The General Motherhood of the Commonwealth": Dance Hall Reform in the Progressive Era', *American Quarterly* 37 (1985), pp. 719–33, p. 728.

8. 'Wilson Banned Ball Fearing Turkey Trot', *New York Times* (21 January 1913), p. 3.

9. Elisabeth Marbury, 'Introduction', Vernon and Irene Castle, *Modern Dancing* (New York: Harper and Bros, 1914), p. 28; see also Julie Malnig, 'Athena Meets Venus: Visions of Women in Social Dance in the Teens and Early 1920s', *Dance Research Journal* 31 (1999), pp. 34–62, p. 39.

10. Erenberg, *Steppin' Out*, p. 113.

11. Lewis A. Erenberg, 'Everybody's Doin' It: The Pre-World War I Dance Craze, the Castles, and the Modern American Girl', *Feminist Studies* 3 (1975), pp. 155–70, p. 159.

12. Peiss, *Cheap Amusements*, p. 105.

13. Ibid., p. 8.

14. Erenberg, 'Everybody's Doin' It', p. 160.

15. Vernon and Irene Castle, *Modern Dancing*, p. 43.
16. Bill Harris, *The Hellfighters of Harlem* (New York: Carroll and Graf, 2002), p. 64.
17. Harris, *Hellfighters*, p. 63; Erenberg, 'Everybody's Doin' It', p. 163.
18. Vernon and Irene Castle, *Modern Dancing*, p. 134.
19. Eve Golden, *Vernon and Irene Castle's Ragtime Revolution* (Lexington: University Press of Kentucky, 2007), p. 10; Erenberg, 'Everybody's Doin' It', p. 161.
20. Erenberg, 'Everybody's Doin' It', p. 161.
21. Golden, *Vernon and Irene Castle's Ragtime Revolution*, pp. 114, 124, 93.
22. Frances Hackett, 'The Popular Hit', *The New Republic* (9 January 1915): p. 27.
23. *Modern Dancing*, p. 79.
24. Golden, *Vernon and Irene Castle's Ragtime Revolution*, p. 66.
25. Ibid., pp. 64–5.
26. See Malnig, 'Athena Meets Venus', especially p. 37.
27. Hackett, 'The Popular Hit', p. 27.
28. See Nasaw, *Going Out*, p. 113.
29. Ann Daly, *Done into Dance: Isadora Duncan in America* (Middletown CT: Wesleyan University Press, 1995), p. 9.
30. Ibid., pp. 16-17.
31. 'Maud Allen Dances Anew', *New York Times* (17 October 1916), p. 14.
32. Daly, *Done into Dance*, p. 6.
33. Jack Anderson, *Art Without Boundaries: The World of Modern Dance* (Iowa City: University of Iowa Press, 1999), p. 21.
34. Walter Lippmann, 'The White Passion', *The New Republic* (21 October 1916), pp. 293–5, p. 294.
35. Roger Copeland, ed., *What is Dance? Readings in Theory and Criticism* (New York: Oxford University Press, 1983), p. 265.
36. Joseph H. Mazo, *Prime Movers: The Makers of Modern Dance in America* (London: Adam and Charles Black, 1977), pp. 69–79.
37. Ibid., pp. 82–3.
38. J. E. Crawford Flitch's *Modern Dancing and Dancers*, quoted in Jane Desmond, *Dancing Desires: Choreographing Sexualities On and Off the Stage* (Madison: University of Wisconsin Press, 2001), p. 60.
39. Mazo, *Prime Movers*, p. 96.
40. See Bernard Hewitt, *Theatre U.S.A.: 1665 to 1957* (New York: McGraw-Hill, 1959), pp. 302–6; Mark Fearnow, 'Theatre Groups and Their Playwrights', *The Cambridge History of American Theatre*, Vol. II: *1870–1945*, eds Don B. Wilmeth and Christopher Bigsby (Cambridge: Cambridge University Press, 1999), pp. 343–77, pp. 345–8.
41. Adelle Heller, 'A New Theatre', *1915: The Cultural Moment*, eds Adelle Heller and Lois Rudnick (New Brunswick NJ: Rutgers University Press, 1991), p. 221; Mary C. Henderson, 'Against Broadway', *1915: The Cultural Moment*, p. 239.
42. Henderson, 'Against Broadway', p. 237.
43. Quoted in Hewitt, *Theatre U.S.A.*, p. 313.
44. See Ronald H. Wainscott, *The Emergence of the Modern American Theatre, 1914–1929* (New Haven, CT: Yale University Press, 1997), pp. 94–104.

45. Daniel J. Watermeier, 'O'Neill and the Theatre of his Time', *The Cambridge Companion to Eugene O'Neill*, ed. Michael Manheim (Cambridge: Cambridge University Press, 1998), pp. 33–50, p. 43.

46. 'Introduction', *The Provincetown Players: A Choice of the Shorter Works*, ed. Barbara Ozieblo (Sheffield: Sheffield Academic Press, 1994), pp. 12–13.

47. Quoted in Robert Károly Sarlós, *Jig Cook and the Provincetown Players: Theatre in Ferment* (Amherst: University of Massachusetts Press, 1982), p. 46.

48. Ibid., p. 36.

49. Heller, 'A New Theatre', p. 229.

50. Sarlós, *Jig Cook and the Provincetown Players*, p. 35.

51. Ozieblo, 'Introduction', p. 18.

52. Susan Glaspell, 'Trifles', in *The Heath Anthology of American Literature* vol. 2, eds Paul Lauter et al. (Lexington MA: D. C. Heath, 1990), pp. 1078–87, p. 1086.

53. An informative, short bibliographic essay on the range of feminist criticism these texts have attracted can be found in J. Ellen Gainor's *Susan Glaspell in Context: American Theater, Culture, and Politics, 1915–48* (Ann Arbor: University of Michigan Press, 2001), pp. 271–2.

54. Ozieblo, 'Introduction', pp. 25, 33.

55. Quoted in Sarlós, *Jig Cook and the Provincetown Players*, p. 141.

56. See Julia A. Walker, *Expressionism and Modernism in the American Theatre: Bodies, Voices, Words* (Cambridge: Cambridge University Press, 2005), p. 124.

57. Wainscott, *The Emergence of the Modern American Theater 1914–1929*, p. 56.

58. See John Frick, 'A Changing Theatre', in *The Cambridge History of American Theatre*, Vol. II, pp. 217–18; and Watermeier's 'O'Neill and the Theatre of his Time', p. 35.

59. J. Hartley Manners, *Peg O' My Heart* (New York; Samuel French, n.d.), p. 128.

60. Hewitt, *Theatre U.S.A.: 1665 to 1957*, p. 316.

61. Wainscott, *The Emergence of the Modern American Theater 1914–1929*, p. 191, p. 67.

62. George Jean Nathan, 'The Theatre', *Civilization in the United States*, ed. Harold E. Stearns (New York: Harcourt, 1922), pp. 243–53, pp. 244, 246.

63. 'Follies Begin Summer Capers', *New York Times* (2 June 1914), p. 11.

64. See Anthony Bianco, *Ghosts of 42nd Street: A History of America's Most Infamous Block* (New York: HarperPerennial, 2004), pp. 68–72.

65. Lois Banner, quoted in Malnig, 'Athena Meets Venus: Visions of Women in Social Dance in the Teens and Early 1920s', pp. 38, 52.

66. Bianco, *Ghosts of 42nd Street*, pp. 54, 73–4.

67. See Ronald Wainscott, 'Plays and Playwrights 1896–1915', in *The Cambridge History of American Theatre*, Vol. II, p. 266.

68. See Watermeier, *O'Neill and the Theatre of his Time*, p. 42.

69. Djuna Barnes, 'David Belasco Dreams', *I Could Never be Happy Without a Husband: Interviews by Djuna Barnes* (London: Virago, 1985), pp. 186–99, p. 192.

70. Charles Klein, 'What the Playwright is Up Against', *The Saturday Evening Post* (25 January 1913), p. 16.

71. Hewitt, *Theatre U.S.A.*, p. 301.

72. Ronald Wainscott, 'Plays and Playwrights 1896–1915', p. 285.

73. Brenda Murphy, 'Plays and Playwrights: 1915–1945', *The Cambridge History of American Theatre*, Vol. II: *1870–1945*, pp. 289–342; p. 315.

74. Waldo Frank, *Our America* (New York, Boni and Liveright, 1919), p. 213.

75. See Mel Gordon, 'The Yiddish Theatre in New York: 1900', *Theatre for Working-Class Audiences in the United States, 1830–1980*, eds Bruce A. McConachie and Daniel Friedman (Westport CT: Greenwood Press, 1985), pp. 69–73, p. 72.

76. A. Richard Sogliuzzo, 'Shakespeare, Sardou, and Pulcinella: Italian-American Working Class Theatre in New York, 1880–1940', *Theatre for Working-Class Audiences in the United States, 1830–1980*, pp. 75–86, p. 81.

77. Gordon, 'The Yiddish Theatre', p. 73.

78. See John Frick, 'A Changing Theatre', p. 221; http://www.actorsequity.org/aboutequity/historicaloverview.asp.

79. Michael Broyles, 'Art Music from 1860 to 1920', in *The Cambridge History of American Music*, ed. David Nicholls (Cambridge: Cambridge University Press, 1998), pp. 214–54, pp. 225, 229.

80. Ibid., p. 253.

81. For a discussion of this, see Joseph Horowitz, *Classical Music in America: A History of its Rise and Fall* (New York: Norton, 2005), pp. 265–70.

82. Charles Hamm, *Music in the New World* (New York: Norton, 1983), p. 432.

83. Philip Furia, *Irving Berlin: A Life in Song* (New York: Schirmer Books, 1998), p. 73.

84. See Adorno, 'On Popular Music', 1941, available at http://www.icce.rug.nl/~soundscapes/DATABASES/SWA/On_popular_music_1.shtml

85. Furia, *Irving Berlin: A Life in Song*, p. 41.

86. Ibid., p. 44.

87. See Charles Hamm, *Irving Berlin: Songs from the Melting Pot – The Formative Years, 1907–1914* (New York: Oxford University Press, 1997), p. 104.

88. Ibid., p. 90.

89. Jeffrey Magee, 'Ragtime and Early Jazz', *The Cambridge History of American Music*, ed. David Nicholls (Cambridge: Cambridge University Press, 1998), pp. 388–417, p. 394.

90. Charles Hamm assesses this controversy: see pp. 107–12.

91. Furia, *Irving Berlin*, pp. 49–50.

92. Ibid., p. 58.

93. Edward Jablonski, *Irving Berlin: American Troubadour* (New York: Henry Holt, 1999): p. 45; Charles Hamm, *Irving Berlin*, pp. 130–2.

94. *The Routledge Guide to Music Technology*, ed. Thom Holmes (London: Routledge, 2006): p. 323; p. 6.

95. Furia, *Irving Berlin*, p. 85.

96. See Jablonski, *Irving Berlin: American Troubadour*, p. 55.

97. Lead Belly is often referred to as Leadbelly on the covers of many of his releases; Lead Belly was his own favoured spelling, however, and is the usage on his headstone.

98. Langston Hughes, 'Songs Called the Blues', 1941, rpt in *The Collected Works of Langston Hughes*, Vol. 9, ed. Christopher C. De Santis (Columbia: University of Missouri Press, 2002), pp. 212–15, p. 213.

99. Giles Oakley, *The Devil's Music: A History of the Blues* (New York: Taplinger, 1976), p. 60.

100. Oakley, *The Devil's Music*, p. 60; William Barlow, 'The Music of the Dispossessed: The Rise of the Blues', in *America's Musical Pulse: Popular Music in Twentieth-

Century Society, ed. Kenneth J. Bindas (Westport CT: Praeger, 1992), pp. 53–62, p. 55.

101. See Oakley, *The Devil's Music*, p. 73; *The New Grove Gospel, Blues, and Jazz*, by Paul Oliver, Max Harrison, and William Bolcom (New York: Norton, 1986), p. 60.

102. Langston Hughes, *The First Book of Jazz*, in *The Collected Works of Langston Hughes*, Vol. 11, ed. Dianne Johnson (Columbia: University of Missouri Press, 2003), pp. 277–321, p. 290.

103. Barlow, 'The Music of the Dispossessed', p. 58.

104. See Buzzy Jackson, *A Bad Woman Feeling Good: Blues and the Women who Sing Them* (New York: Norton, 2005), pp. 12–21, p. 17.

105. Hazel Carby, 'Policing the Black Woman's Body in an Urban Context', *Critical Inquiry* 18 (1992), pp. 738–55, p. 755.

106. Burton W. Peretti, 'Emerging from America's Underside: The Black Musician from Ragtime to Jazz', in *America's Musical Pulse: Popular Music in Twentieth-Century Society*, pp. 63–82, p. 68.

107. Gunther Schuller, *Early Jazz: Its Roots and Musical Development* (New York: Oxford University Press, 1968), p. 137.

108. Ted Gioia, *The History of Jazz* (New York: Oxford University Press, 1997), p. 50.

109. Alyn Shipton, *A New History of Jazz* (New York: Continuum, 2007), p. 64.

110. Ibid., p. 63.

111. See Floyd Levin, 'Kid Ory's Legendary Nordskog/Sunshine Recordings', *Jazz Journal International* 46 (7) (July 1993), pp. 6–10; also available at http://www.doctorjazz.co.uk/page35.html.

112. Gioia, *The History of Jazz*, pp. 96–8.

113. Ibid., p. 71.

114. See David Horn's discussion of Chris Goddard's contention of this point; 'The Identity of Jazz', in *The Cambridge Companion to Jazz*, eds Mervyn Cooke and David Horn (Cambridge: Cambridge University Press, 2002), pp. 9–32, p. 27.

115. See 'Jazz in Scientific World', *New York Times* (16 November 1919), p. 8; 'Conspiracy of Silence Against Jazz', *New York Times* (21 September 1919), p. 84.

116. Brander Matthews, 'Professor C. Alphonso Smith Compiles a Dictionary of Temporary Words of Today', *New York Times Book Review* (9 November 1919), p. 1.

117. David Nasaw, *Going Out*, pp. 1–2.

118. Ibid., p. 239; Jesse Frederick Steiner, *Americans at Play: Recent Trends in Recreation and Leisure Time Activities* (New York: McGraw-Hill, 1933), p. 12.

5. The Great War and American Culture

1. Robert M. Zieger, *America's Great War: World War I and the American Experience* (Lanham MD: Rowman and Littlefield, 2000), p. 53.

2. Ibid., p. 37.

3. Gary Mead, *The Doughboys: America and the First World War* (London: Penguin, 2000), p. 4.

4. Ibid., pp. 347, 349.

5. Ibid., p. 358.

6. John T. Matthews, 'American Writing of the Great War', *The Cambridge Companion to the Literature of the First World War*, ed. Vincent Sherry (Cambridge: Cambridge University Press, 2005), pp. 217–42, p. 217.

7. Zane Grey, *The Desert of Wheat* (London: Hodder and Stoughton, 1919), p. 56.

8. Sherwood Anderson, *Letters to Bab: Sherwood Anderson to Marietta D. Finley, 1916–1933*, ed. William A. Sutton (Urbana: University of Illinois Press, 1985), p. 15.

9. Charles Reznikoff, 'Rhythms', *The Poems of Charles Reznikoff 1918–1975*, ed. Seamus Cooney (Boston MA: Black Sparrow, 2005), p. 6.

10. John T. Matthews, 'American Writing of the Great War', p. 221.

11. T. J. Jackson Lears, *No Place of Grace: Antimodernism and The Transformation of American Culture 1880–1920* (New York: Pantheon, 1981), p. 98.

12. Edith Wharton, *Fighting France: From Dunkirque to Belport* (New York: Scribners, 1917), pp. 219, 238, 234.

13. John T. Matthews, 'American Writing of the Great War', p. 226.

14. Henry James, *Within the Rim* (1915): available at http://www.archive.org/stream/withintherim00jamerich/withintherim00jamerich_djvu.txt

15. Alan Dawley, *Changing the World: American Progressives in War and Revolution* (Princeton: Princeton University Press, 2003), p. 2.

16. David M. Kennedy, *Over Here: The First World War and American Society* (New York: Oxford University Press, 2004), p. 39.

17. John Dewey, 'What America Will Fight For', *The New Republic* (18 August 1917), pp. 68–9; see also Kennedy, *Over Here*, pp. 50–3; Ronald Schaeffer, *America in the Great War: The Rise of the War Welfare State* (New York: Oxford University Press, 1991), pp. 109–26.

18. James R. Mock and Cedric Larson, *Words that Won the War: The Story of the Committee on Public Information 1917–1919* (Princeton NJ: Princeton University Press, 1939), p. 135; Gerald Herman, 'The Great War Revisioned: A World War I Filmography', in *Hollywood's World War I: Motion Picture Images*, eds Peter C. Rollins and John E. O'Connor (Bowling Green OH: Bowling Green State University Popular Press, 1997), pp. 245–82; p. 249.

19. Mock and Larson, *Words that Won the War*, p. 152.

20. Herman, 'The Great War Revisioned', p. 249.

21. Mark Crispin Miller, 'Introduction' to Edward Bernays, *Propaganda* (New York: Ig Publishing, [1928] 2005), pp. 9–12.

22. Mock and Larson, *Words that Won the War*, p. 4.

23. Zieger, *America's Great War*, p. 83.

24. Kennedy, *Over Here*, p. 47.

25. Ibid., p. 60.

26. Mock and Larson, *Words that Won the War*, pp. 66–74.

27. Ibid., p. 135.

28. Ibid., p. 147.

29. Ibid., pp. 98, 169.

30. See Kennedy, *Over Here*, p. 74.

31. Bernays, *Propaganda*, p. 37.

32. Interview with Henry James, *New York Times* (21 March 1915), p. SM3.

33. John Dos Passos, *One Man's Initiation: 1917* (Ithaca: Cornell University Press, [1920] 1969), p. 159.

34. James M. Welsh, 'The Great War and the War Film as Genre', in *Hollywood's World War I: Motion Picture Images*, pp. 7–38, p. 33.

35. Ibid.

36. Steven Ross, *Working-Class Hollywood: Silent Film and the Shaping of Class in America* (Princeton NJ: Princeton University Press, 1998), pp. 124–6.

37. Leslie Midkiff DeBauche, *Reel Patriotism: The Movies and World War I* (Madison: University of Wisconsin Press, 1997), p. 3.

38. Ibid., p. 118.

39. Richard Koszarski, *An Evening's Entertainment: The Age of the Silent Feature Picture, 1915–1928* (Berkeley: University of California Press, 1990), pp. 102–4.

40. Sheila Rowbotham, *A Century of Women: The History of Women in Britain and the United States* (London: Penguin, 1999), p. 104.

41. See Susan Douglas, *Inventing American Broadcasting 1899–1922* (Baltimore MD: Johns Hopkins University Press, 1987).

42. Ibid., p. 290.

43. Ibid., p. 280.

44. Wallace Irwin, 'Patrioteers: The Red War and the Pink', *The Saturday Evening Post* (16 March 1918), p. 16.

45. Daile Kaplan, *Lewis Hine in Europe: The Lost Photographs* (New York: Abbeville Press, 1988), p. 59.

46. Edward Jablonski, *Irving Berlin: American Troubador* (New York: Henry Holt, 1999), p. 80.

47. See Addams, 'Address of Miss Addams at Carnegie Hall', *The Jane Addams Reader*, ed. Jean Bethke Elshtain (New York: Basic Books 2002), p. 335; Zieger, *America's Great War*, p. 139.

48. Mark Van Wienen, ed. *Rendezvous with Death: American Poems of the Great War* (Urbana: University of Illinois Press, 2002), p. 80.

49. Jennifer Haytock, *At Home, At War: Domesticity and World War I in American Literature* (Columbus: Ohio State University Press, 2003), p. 31.

50. Ibid., p. 13.

51. As well as Haytock's *At Home, At War*, important books include Kimberly Jensen's *Mobilizing Minerva*, and the edited collections by Margaret Higonnet, listed under the further reading section.

52. Randolph Bourne, 'The History of a Literary Radical', in *Randolph Bourne: War and the Intellectuals, Collected Essays 1915–1919*, ed. Carl Resek (Indianapolis IN: Hackett, 1999), pp. 184–97, p. 197.

53. Casey Nelson Blake, *Beloved Community: The Cultural Criticism of Randolph Bourne, Van Wyck Brooks, Waldo Frank, and Lewis Mumford* (Chapel Hill: University of North Carolina Press, 1990), p. 3.

54. Ibid., p. 124.

55. Van Wyck Brooks, 'Toward a National Culture', *The Seven Arts* (March 1917), p. 547.

56. Thomas Bender, *New York Intellect: A History of Intellectual Life in New York City, from 1750 to the Beginnings of Our Own Time* (New York: Knopf, 1987), p. 241.

57. Blake, *Beloved Community*, p. 2.
58. Randolph Bourne, 'A War Diary', in *Randolph Bourne: War and the Intellectuals*, pp. 36–47, p. 40.
59. 'Twilight of Idols', in *Randolph Bourne: War and the Intellectuals*, pp. 53–64; p. 54.
60. 'John Dewey's Philosophy' [1915], *Randolph Bourne: The Radical Will, Selected Writings 1911–1918*, ed. Olaf Hansen (Berkeley: University of California Press, 1992), pp. 331–5, p. 331.
61. 'Twilight of Idols', p. 59.
62. Livingston observes that Bourne's 'arguments of 1917–18 inform every subsequent critique of pragmatism, from Van Wyck Brooks, Lewis Mumford, Harold Stearns, Waldo Frank, C. Wright Mills, and Christopher Lasch to Casey Blake, Robert Westbrook, John Diggins, Jackson Lears, Wilfred McClay, Peter Osborne, and Brian Lloyd. At some point in this lineage, probably in 1926, Bourne became a kind of talisman or totem, perhaps even a "fetish object", in the reiterations of the statement and the reproduction of the critique.' 'War and the Intellectuals: Bourne, Dewey, and the Fate of Pragmatism', *Journal of the Gilded Age and Progressive Era*, 2 (4) (2003), pp. 431–50, p. 440.
63. Bourne, 'Twilight of Idols', pp. 59, 64.
64. Bourne, 'A War Diary', p. 45.
65. Bourne, 'Below the Battle', *Randolph Bourne: War and the Intellectuals*, pp. 15–21, p. 21.
66. Bourne, 'A War Diary', p. 46.
67. Mark Van Wienen, *Partisans and Poets: The Political Work of American Poetry in the Great War* (Cambridge: Cambridge University Press, 1997), pp. 78, 89.
68. Kennedy, *Over Here*, p. 26.
69. Upton Sinclair, *Jimmie Higgins* (n.p. : Aegypan Press, [1919] 2007), p. 197.
70. See http://www.english.uiuc.edu/maps/poets/s_z/sandburg/war.htm; also Phillip R. Yanella, *The Other Carl Sandburg* (Jackson: University Press of Mississippi, 1996).
71. 'Four Brothers', in *Rendezvous with Death: American Poems of the Great War*, ed. Mark Van Wienen, pp. 196–201.
72. In Van Wienen, ed., *Rendezvous with Death*, p. 102.
73. Van Wienen, ed., *Rendezvous with Death*, pp. 3–4; also Mark Van Wienen, *Partisans and Poets: The Political Work of American Poetry in the Great War*.
74. *Rendezvous with Death*, p. 24.
75. Mark Van Wienen, 'Poetics of the Frugal Housewife: A Modernist Narrative of the Great War and America', *American Literary History* 7 (1995), pp. 55–91, pp. 67–8.
76. Ibid., pp. 69–70.
77. Theodore Kornweibel, *Seeing Red: Federal Campaigns Against Black Militancy, 1919–1925* (Bloomington: Indiana University Press, 1998), pp. 77–8.
78. Ibid., p. 37.
79. Bill Harris, *The Hellfighters of Harlem* (New York: Carrol and Graf, 2002): pp. 65–6.
80. Richard Slotkin, *Lost Battalions: The Great War and the Crisis of American Nationality* (New York: Henry Holt, 2005), p. 46.

81. See Harris, *The Hellfighters of Harlem,* pp. 55–78.
82. Ibid., p. 74.
83. Ibid., pp. 70–2.
84. Tyler Stovall, *Paris Noir: African Americans in the City of Light* (Boston: Houghton Mifflin, 1996), p. 21.
85. Jeffrey H. Jackson, 'Making Jazz French: The Reception of Jazz Music in Paris, 1927–1934', *French Historical Studies* 25 (2002), pp. 149–70.
86. Richard Slotkin, *Lost Battalions,* p. 405.
87. Higham, John, *Strangers in the Land: Patterns of American Nativism, 1860–1925* (New Brunswick NJ: Rutgers University Press, 2002), p. 251.
88. *Lewis Hine in Europe: The Lost Photographs,* p. 66.
89. David Lawrence, 'Americans for America', *Saturday Evening Post* (15 June 1918), p. 23.
90. David Kennedy, *Over Here,* p. 68.
91. Blanche Wiesen Cook, *Eleanor Roosevelt*: Volume One, *1884–1933* (New York: Viking Penguin, 1992), p. 239.
92. David Kennedy, *Over Here,* p. 92.

Conclusion

1. David Kennedy, *Over Here: The First World War and American Society* (New York: Oxford University Press, 2004), p. 363.
2. Edwin L. James, 'Throngs Hail Marchers', *New York Times* (19 September 1927), p. 1.
3. Ida B. Treat, 'Is this America?', *The Nation* (19 October 1927), p. 422.
4. Ernest Hemingway, *A Moveable Feast* (London: Arrow, [1936] 1994), p. 26.
5. Warren B. Susman, 'Culture and Civilization: The Nineteen-Twenties', in *Culture as History: The Transformation of American Society in the Twentieth Century* (Washington DC: Smithsonian, 2003), p. 114.
6. Harold Stearns, 'The Intellectual Life', in *Civilization in the United States* (New York: Harcourt-Brace, 1922), p. 135.
7. Ezra Pound, 'Hugh Selwyn Mauberly' (1920) in *Ezra Pound: Selected Poems 1908–1959* (London: Faber, 1975), p. 100.
8. Joel A. Rogers, 'Jazz at Home', *The New Negro,* ed. Alain Locke (New York: Simon and Schuster, [1925] 1997), pp. 216–24, p. 222, p. 224.
9. Malcolm Cowley, *Exile's Return* (New York: Compass Books, 1956), pp. 38, 97, 100, 73.
10. Ibid., p. 73.
11. Michael McGerr, *A Fierce Discontent: The Rise and Fall of the Progressive Movement, 1880–1920* (Oxford: Oxford University Press, 2003), p. 315.
12. See, in particular, Chip Rhodes's *Echoes of the Jazz Age: Mass Culture, Progressive Education, and Racial Disclosures in American Modernism* (London: Verso, 1998).
13. Walter Benn Michaels, *Our America: Nativism, Modernism, and Pluralism* (Durham NC: Duke University Press, 1995), p. 6.
14. Ibid., p. 8.
15. Douglas, *Terrible Honesty: Mongrel Manhattan in the 1920s* (London: Papermac, 1997), p. 199.

16. Ian Jarvie, 'Dollars and Ideology: Will Hays' Economic Foreign Policy 1922–1945', *Film History* 3 (1988), pp. 207–21, p. 211.
17. 'The Big Parade', *The Times* (22 May 1926), p. 10.
18. Kristin Thompson, 'National or International Films? The European Debate during the 1920s', *Film History* 8 (1996), pp. 281–96, p. 283.
19. Wyndham Lewis, 'Ernest Hemingway: The "Dumb Ox"', in *A Soldier of Humor and Other Writings*, ed. Raymond Rosenthal (New York: Signet, 1966), p. 287.
20. F. Scott Fitzgerald, 'Echoes of the Jazz Age', *The Crack-Up* (New York: New Directions 2009), pp. 13–22, p. 14.
21. David M. Kennedy, *Freedom From Fear: The American People in Depression and War* (New York: Oxford University Press, 2005).
22. McGerr, *A Fierce Discontent*, p. 317.
23. Michael Denning, *The Cultural Front: The Labouring of American Culture in the Twentieth Century* (London: Verso, 1997), p. 4.
24. Ibid., pp. 262–3.
25. Ibid., p. 199.
26. Ibid., p. 167.
27. John Dos Passos, *U.S.A.* (London: Penguin, [1938] 1981), pp. 1105–6.
28. Allan Ginsberg, 'America', (1956) *The Heath Anthology of American Literature*, Volume 2, 4th ed. (Boston: Houghton Mifflin, 2002), pp. 2305–6.
29. Walter Lippmann, 'Legendary John Reed', *The New Republic* (26 December 1914), p. 15.
30. For more on *Reds* see 'Thunder on the Left: The Making of *Reds*', Peter Biskind, *Vanity Fair*, March 2006, available at http://www.vanityfair.com/culture/features/2006/03/reds200603?currentPage=1; and A.O. Scott, 'Film on Revolution was Revolution Itself', *New York Times* (4 October 2006), available at http://www.nytimes.com/2006/10/04/movies/04reds.html.
31. See also Werner Sollors, '"Americans All:" Of Plymouth Rock and Jamestown and Ellis Island; or, Ethnic Literature and Some Redefinitions of "America"'. Available at http://www.nyupress.org/americansall/americansall2.html?$string, p. 2.
32. See, for example, Ali Behdad, *A Forgetful Nation: On Immigration and Cultural Identity in the United States* (Durham NC: Duke University Press, 2006), p. 77.
33. James Weldon Johnson, *Black Manhattan* (New York: Da Capo Press, [1930] 1991), p. 3.
34. James Baldwin, *Go Tell it on the Mountain* (London: Penguin, [1954] 1991), p. 189.
35. David Bordwell, 'Intensified Continuity: Visual Style in Contemporary American Film', *Film Quarterly* 55 (3) (Spring 2002), pp. 16–28: p. 24.
36. Robert H. Wiebe, *The Search for Order 1877–1920* (New York: Hill and Wang, 1967), p. 164.

Bibliography

General

Abrahams, Edward, *The Lyrical Left: Randolph Bourne, Alfred Stieglitz, and The Origins of Cultural Radicalism in America* (Charlottesville: University of Virginia Press, 1986).

Addams, Jane, *The Jane Addams Reader*, ed. Jean Bethke Elshtain (New York: Basic Books, 2002).

Allerfeldt, Kristofer, ed., *The Progressive Era in the USA: 1890–1921* (Aldershot: Ashgate, 2007).

Anderson, Margaret, *My Thirty Years' War* (New York: Horizon Press, 1969).

Bederman, Gail, *Manliness and Civilization: A Cultural History of Gender and Race in the United States, 1880–1917* (Chicago: Chicago University Press, 1995).

Blake, Casey Nelson, *Beloved Community: The Cultural Criticism of Randolph Bourne, Van Wyck Brooks, Waldo Frank, and Lewis Mumford* (Chapel Hill: University of North Carolina Press, 1990).

Bledstein, Burton J., *The Culture of Professionalism: The Middle-Class Development of Higher Education in America* (New York: Norton, 1976).

Brill, A. A., *Psychoanalysis: Its Theories and Practical Application* (Philadelphia PA: W. B. Saunders, 1912).

Brooks, Van Wyck, *Van Wyck Brooks: The Early Years*, ed. Claire Sprague (New York: Harper and Row, 1968).

Chauncey, George, *Gay New York: Gender, Urban Culture, and the Making of a Gay Male World, 1890–1940* (New York: Basic Books, 1995).

Cooper, John Milton Jr, *Pivotal Decades: The United States 1900–1920* (New York: Norton, 1990).

Crunden, Robert M., *American Salons: Encounters with European Modernism 1885–1917* (New York: Oxford University Press, 1993).

Dewey, John, *Democracy and Education: An Introduction to the Philosophy of Education* (New York: Macmillan, [1916] 1938).

Frank, Waldo, *Our America* (New York: Boni and Liveright, 1919).

Goldman, Emma, *Anarchism and Other Essays* (New York: Mother Earth, 1910).

Hale, Grace Elizabeth, *Making Whiteness: The Culture of Segregation in the South, 1890–1940* (New York: Vintage, 1999).

Heller, Adelle, and Lois Rudnick, eds, *1915: The Cultural Moment* (New Brunswick NJ: Rutgers University Press, 1991).

Higham, John, *Strangers in the Land: Patterns of American Nativism, 1860–1925* (New Brunswick NJ: Rutgers University Press, 2002).

Hofstadter, Richard, *The Age of Reform: From Bryan to F.D.R.* (New York: Knopf, 1955).

Jacobson, Matthew Frye, *Barbarian Virtues: The United States Encounters Foreign Peoples at Home and Abroad, 1876–1917* (New York: Hill and Wang, 2001).

Johnson, James Weldon, *Black Manhattan* (New York: Da Capo, [1930] 1991).

Kern, Steven J., *The Culture of Time and Space 1880–1918*, 2nd edn (Cambridge MA: Harvard University Press, 2003).

Lears, T. J. Jackson, *No Place of Grace: Antimodernism and the Transformation of American Culture, 1880–1920* (New York: Pantheon, 1982).

—, *The Rebirth of America 1877–1920* (New York: Harper's, 2009).

Lewis, David Levering, *When Harlem Was In Vogue* (New York: Oxford University Press, 1989).

Levine, Lawrence, *Highbrow/Lowbrow: The Emergence of Cultural Hierarchy in America* (New York: Oxford University Press, 1990).

Lippmann, Walter, *A Preface to Politics* (n.p.: Dodo Press, [1913] 2009).

—, *Public Opinion* (n.p.: Filiquarian Publishing, [1922] 2007).

McGerr, Michael, *A Fierce Discontent: The Rise and Fall of the Progressive Movement, 1880–1920* (Oxford: Oxford University Press, 2003).

McGovern, Charles F., *Sold American: Consumption and Citizenship, 1890–1945* (Chapel Hill: University of North Carolina Press, 2006).

May, Henry, *The End of American Innocence: A Study of the First Years of Our Own Time, 1912–1917*, new edn (New York: Columbia, 1992).

Ohmann, Richard, *Selling Culture: Magazines, Markets, and Class at the Turn of the Century* (London: Verso, 1996).

Painter, Nell Irving, *Standing at Armageddon: A Grassroots History of the Progressive Era* (New York: Norton, 2008).

Sanger, Margaret, *Woman and the New Race*, with a Preface by Havelock Ellis (New York: Brenatno's, 1920).

Schlereth, Thomas J., *Victorian America: Transformations in Everyday Life 1876–1915* (New York: HarperCollins, 1991).

Sklar, Martin, *The Corporate Reconstruction of American Capitalism, 1890–1916* (Cambridge: Cambridge University Press, 1988).

Watson, Bruce, *Bread and Roses: Mills, Migrants, and the Struggle for the American Dream* (New York: Penguin, 2005).

Watson, Steven, *Strange Bedfellows: The First American Avant-Garde* (New York: Abbeville Press, 1991).

Watts, Steven, *The People's Tycoon: Henry Ford and the American Century* (New York: Vintage, 2005).

Wiebe, Robert H., *The Search for Order 1877–1920* (New York: Hill and Wang, 1967).

Film and Vaudeville

Abel, Richard, *Americanizing the Movies and 'Movie-Mad' Audiences, 1910–1914* (Berkeley: University of California Press, 2006).

Allen, Michael, *Family Secrets: The Feature Films of D. W. Griffith* (London: BFI Publishing, 1999).

Bean, Jennifer M. and Diane Negra, eds, *A Feminist Reader in Early Cinema* (Durham NC: Duke University Press, 2002).

Bordwell, David, Janet Staiger and Kristin Thompson, *The Classical Hollywood Cinema: Film Style and Mode of Production to 1960* (London: Routledge, 1985).

Bowser, Eileen, *The Transformation of Cinema, 1907–1915* (New York: Scribner's, 1990).

Charney, Leo and Venessa L. Schwartz, eds, *Cinema and the Invention of Modern Life* (Berkeley: University of California Press, 1995).

Chude-Sokei, Louis, *The Last 'Darky': Bert Williams, Black-on-Black Minstrelsy, and the African Diaspora* (Durham NC: Duke University Press, 2006).

Cripps, Thomas, *Slow Fade to Black: The Negro in American Film, 1900–1942* (New York: Oxford University Press, 1977).

deCordova, Richard, *Picture Personalities: The Emergence of the Star System in America* (Urbana: University of Illinois Press, 1990).

Fields, Armond, and L. Mark Fields, *From the Bowery to Broadway: Lew Fields and the Roots of American Popular Theater* (Oxford: Oxford University Press, 1993).

Forbes, Camille L., *Introducing Bert Williams: Burnt Cork, Broadway, and the Story of America's First Black Star* (New York: Basic Civitas, 2008).

Gunning, Tom, *D. W. Griffith and the Origins of Narrative Film: The Early Years at Biograph* (Urbana: University of Illinois Press, 1991).

Keil, Charlie, *Early American Cinema in Transition: Story, Style, and Filmmaking, 1907–1913* (Madison: University of Wisconsin Press, 2001).

Kibler, M. Alison, *Rank Ladies: Gender and Cultural Hierarchy in American Vaudeville* (Chapel Hill: University of North Carolina Press, 1999).

Koszarski, Richard, *An Evening's Entertainment: The Age of the Silent Feature Picture, 1915–1928* (Berkeley: University of California Press, 1990).

Krasner, David, *A Beautiful Pageant: African American Theatre, Drama and Performance in the Harlem Renaissance, 1910–1927* (New York: Palgrave-Macmillan, 2002).

Lant, Antonia, and Ingrid Periz, eds, *Red Velvet Seat: Women's Writing on the First Fifty Years of Cinema* (London: Verso, 2006).

Lindsay, Vachel, *The Art of the Moving Picture* (New York: Modern Library-Random House, [1915] 2000).

Nasaw, David, *Going Out: the Rise and Fall of Public Amusements* (New York: Basic Books, 1993).

Rosenzweig, Roy, *Eight Hours for What We Will: Workers and Leisure in an Industrial City* (Cambridge: Cambridge University Press, 1983).

Ross, Steven J., *Working-Class Hollywood: Silent Film and the Shaping of Class in America* (Princeton NJ: Princeton University Press, 1998).

Singer, Benjamin, *Melodrama and Modernity: Early Pulp Cinema and the Social Contexts of Sensationalism* (New York: Columbia University Press, 2001).

Sklar, Richard, *Movie Made America: A Cultural History of American Movies* (London: Chappell and Co., 1978).

Stein, Charles W., ed., *American Vaudeville as Seen by its Contemporaries* (New York: Da Capo, 1984).

Thompson, Kristin, *Exporting Entertainment: America in the World Film Market 1907–34* (London: BFI Publishing, 1985).

Toll, Robert C., *On With the Show: the First Century of Show Business in America* (New York: Oxford University Press, 1976).

Ullmann, Sharon, *Sex Seen: The Emergence of Modern Sexuality in America* (Berkeley: University of California Press, 1997).

Visual Art and Photography

Bogart, Michele, *Artists, Advertising, and the Borders of Art* (Chicago: University of Chicago Press, 1995).

Brennan, Marcia, *Painting Gender, Constructing Theory: The Alfred Stieglitz Circle and American Formalist Aesthetics* (Cambridge MA: MIT Press, 2001).

Coppell, Stephen, *The American Scene: Prints from Hopper to Pollock* (London: The British Museum Press, 2008).

Corn, Wanda, *The Great American Thing: Modern Art and National Identity, 1915–1935* (Berkeley: University of California Press, 1999).

Crunden, Robert M., *American Salons: Encounters with European Modernism 1885–1917* (New York: Oxford University Press, 1993).

Doezema, Marianne, *George Bellows and Urban America* (New Haven CT: Yale University Press, 1992).

Eisinger, Joel, *Trace and Transformation: American Criticism of Photography in the Modernist Period* (Albuquerque: University of New Mexico Press, 1995).

Eisler, Benita, *An American Romance: O'Keeffe and Stieglitz* (London: Penguin, 1991).

Fagg, John, *On the Cusp: Stephen Crane, George Bellows, and Modernism* (Tuscaloosa: University of Alabama Press, 2009).

Frank, Waldo et al., *America and Alfred Stieglitz: A Collective Portrait*, eds Waldo Frank et al. (New York: Doubleday, 1934).

Gidley, Mick, *Edward S. Curtis and the North American Indian, Incorporated* (Cambridge: Cambridge University Press, 1998).

Hambourg, Maria Morris, *Paul Strand: Circa 1916* (New York: Metropolitan Museum of Art/Abrams, 1998).

Haskins, Jim, *James Van DerZee: The Picture-Takin' Man* (Trenton NJ: Africa World Press, 1991).

Henri, Robert, *The Art Spirit* (New York: Basic Books, [1923] 2007).

Hughes, Robert, *American Visions: Epic History of Art in America* (London: Harvill Press, 1999).

Huyssen, Andreas, *After the Great Divide: Modernism, Mass Culture, Postmodernism* (Bloomington: Indiana University Press, 1986).

Johnston, Patricia, *Real Fantasies: Edward Steichen's Advertising Photography* (Berkeley: University of California Press, 1997).

Kitch, Carolyn, *The Girl on the Magazine Cover: The Originals of Visual Stereotypes in American Mass Media* (Chapel Hill: University of North Carolina Press, 2001).

Kranzfelder, Ivo, *Edward Hopper: Vision of Reality* (Köln: Taschen, 2004).

Lears, T. J. Jackson, *Fables of Abundance: A Cultural History of Advertising in America* (New York: Basic Books, 1994).

Marin, John, *The Selected Writings of John Marin* (Whitefish MT: Kessinger Publishing, 2008).

Mundy, Jennifer, *Duchamp, Man Ray, Picabia* (London: Tate Publishing, 2008).

Naumann, Frances M. and Beth Venn, *Making Mischief: Dada Invades New York* (New York: Whitney Museum, 1996).

North, Michael, *Camera Works: Photography and the Twentieth-Century Word* (Oxford: Oxford University Press, 2005).

Orvell, Miles, *American Photography* (Oxford: Oxford University Press, 2003).

—. *The Real Thing: Imitation and Authenticity in American Culture, 1880–1940* (Chapel Hill: University of North Carolina Press, 1989).

Roberts, Pam, ed., *Camera Work: The Complete Illustrations, 1903–1917* (Köln: Taschen, 1997).

Rosenfeld, Paul, *Port of New York: Essays on Fourteen American Moderns* (New York: Harcourt, Brace and Co., 1924).

Sawelson-Gorse, Naomi, ed., *Women in Dada: Essays on Sex, Gender and Identity* (Cambridge MA: MIT Press, 2001).

Scott, William B. and Peter M. Rutkoff, *New York Modern: The Arts and the City* (Baltimore MD: Johns Hopkins University Press, 1999).

Shi, David E., *Facing Facts: Realism in American Thought and Culture, 1850–1920* (New York: Oxford University Press, 1996).

Sloan, John, *John Sloan's New York Scene*, ed. Bruce St John (New York: Harper and Row, 1965).

Stebbins, Jr., Theodore E. *The Photography of Charles Sheeler, American Modernist* (Boston MA: Bulfinch Press, 2002).

Stieglitz, Alfred, *Stieglitz on Photography: His Selected Essays and Notes*, ed. Richard Whelan (New York: Aperture, 2000).

Tallack, Douglas, *New York Sights: Visualizing Old and New New York* (Oxford: Berg, 2005).

Trachtenberg, Alan, *Reading American Photographs: Images as History – Matthew Brady to Walker Evans* (New York: Hill and Wang, 1990).

—, ed., *Classic Essays on Photography* (New Haven CT: Leete's Island Books, 1980).

West, Nancy Martha, *Kodak and the Lens of Nostalgia (Cultural Frames, Framing Culture)* (Charlottesville: University of Virginia Press, 2000).

Willis, Deborah, *Reflections in Black: A History of Black Photographers 1840 to the Present* (New York: Norton, 2000).

Zurier, Rebecca, *Picturing the City: Urban Vision and the Ashcan School* (Berkeley: University of California Press, 2006).

Fiction and Poetry

Altieri, Charles, *The Art of Twentieth-Century Poetry: Modernism and After* (Oxford: Blackwell, 2006).

Bederman, Gail, *Manliness and Civilization: A Cultural History of Gender and Race in the United States, 1880–1917* (Chicago: University of Chicago Press, 1995).

Bercovitch, Sacvan, ed., *The Cambridge History of American Literature*, Vol. Six: *Prose Writing, 1910–1950* (Cambridge: Cambridge University Press, 2002).

Bold, Christine, *Selling the Wild West: Popular Western Fiction, 1860 to 1960* (Bloomington: Indiana University Press, 1987).

Bradbury, Malcolm, *Dangerous Pilgrimages: Trans-Atlantic Mythologies and the Novel* (London: Penguin, 1996).

Cheyfitz, Eric, *The Poetics of Imperialism: Translation and Colonization from The Tempest to Tarzan* (New York: Oxford University Press, 1991).

Chu, Patricia, *Race, Nationalism, and the State in British and American Modernism* (Cambridge: Cambridge University Press, 2006).

Dreiser, Theodore, *Hey Rub-A-Dub-Dub: A Book of the Mystery and Terror of Life* (London: Constable, 1931).

Du Plessis, Rachel Blau, *Genders, Races, and Religious Cultures in Modern American Poetry, 1908–1934* (Cambridge: Cambridge University Press, 2001).

Dudley, John, *A Man's Game: Masculinity and the Anti-Aesthetics of American Literary Naturalism* (Tuscaloosa: University of Alabama Press, 2004).

Duffey, Bernard, *The Chicago Renaissance in American Letters: A Critical History* (Michigan: Michigan State University Press, 1956).

Dydo, Ulla with William Rice, *Gertrude Stein: The Language that Rises* (Evanston IL: University of Northwestern Press, 2003).

Fetterley, Judith and Marjorie Pryse, eds, *American Women Regionalists, 1850–1910* (New York: Norton, 1992).

Fox, Richard Wrightman and T. J. Jackson Lears, eds, *The Power of Culture: Critical Essays in American History* (Chicago: University of Chicago Press, 1993).

Kalaidjian, Walter, ed., *The Cambridge Companion to American Literary Modernism* (Cambridge: Cambridge University Press, 2005).

Kaplan, Amy, *The Social Construction of American Realism* (Chicago: University of Chicago Press, 1988).

Kenner, Hugh, *A Homemade World: The American Modernist Writers* (Baltimore MD: Johns Hopkins University Press, 1989).

—, *The Pound Era* (London: Faber, 1972).

Lentricchia, Frank, *Modernist Quartet* (Cambridge: Cambridge University Press, 1994).

McKible, Adam, *The Space and Place of Modernism: The Russian Revolution, Little Magazines, and New York* (New York: Routledge, 2002).

Michaels, Walter Benn, *Our America: Nativism, Modernism, and Pluralism* (Durham NC: Duke University Press, 1995).

—, *The Gold Standard and the Logic of Naturalism: American Literature at the Turn of the Century* (Berkeley: University of California Press, 1987).

Mitchell, Lee Clark, *Determined Fictions* (New York: Columbia University Press, 1989).

Morrisson, Mark, *The Public Face of Modernism: Little Magazines, Audiences, and Reception, 1905–1920* (Madison: University of Wisconsin Press, 2001).

Nelson, Cary, *Repression and Recovery: Modern American Poetry and the Politics of Cultural Memory, 1910–1945* (Madison: University of Wisconsin Press, 1989).

North, Michael, *The Dialect of Modernism: Race, Language, and Twentieth Century Literature* (New York: Oxford University Press, 1994).

O'Brien, Sharon, ed., *New Essays on Cather's My Ántonia* (Cambridge: Cambridge University Press, 1999).

Perloff, Marjorie, *The Dance of the Intellect: Studies in the Poetry of the Pound Tradition* (Evanston IL: Northwestern University Press, 1996).

Pound, Ezra, *Ezra Pound: Selected Prose*, ed. William Cookson (New York: New Directions, 1973).

Schneirov, Matthew, *The Dream of a New Social Order: Popular Magazines in America 1893–1914* (New York: Columbia University Press, 1994).

Slotkin, Richard, *Gunfighter Nation: The Myth of the Frontier in Twentieth-Century America* (Norman: Oklahoma University Press, 1998).

Sollors, Werner, *Beyond Ethnicity: Consent and Descent in American Culture* (Oxford: Oxford University Press, 1986).

Soto, Michael, *The Modernist Nation: Generation, Renaissance, and Twentieth-Century American Literature* (Tuscaloosa: University of Alabama Press, 2004).

Stein, Gertrude, *Look at Me Now and Here I Am: Writings and Lectures 1909–1945*, ed. Patricia Meyerowitz (London: Penguin, 1984).

Thompson, Stephanie Lewis, *Influencing America's Tastes: Realism in the Works of Wharton, Cather, and Hurst* (Gainesville: University Press of Florida, 2002).

Whalan, Mark, *Race, Manhood, and Modernism in America: The Short Story Cycles of Sherwood Anderson and Jean Toomer* (Knoxville: University of Tennessee Press, 2007).

Music, Theatre and Dance

Armstrong, Louis, *Satchmo: My Life in New Orleans* (New York: New American Library, 1955).

Baraka, Amiri, *Blues People: Negro Music in White America* (New York: W. Morrow, 1963).

Barker, Danny, *Buddy Bolden and the Last Days of Storyville* (London: Continuum, 2001).

Barnes, Djuna, *Djuna Barnes's New York*, ed. Alyce Barry (London: Virago, 1989).

Berlin, Edward, *Ragtime: A Musical and Cultural History* (Berkeley: University of California Press, 1984).

Bindas, Kenneth J., ed., *America's Musical Pulse: Popular Music in Twentieth-Century Society* (Westport CT: Praeger, 1992).

Block, Geoffrey Holden and Peter J. Burkholder, eds, *Charles Ives and the Classical Tradition* (New Haven CT: Yale University Press, 1996).

Castle, Irene, *Castles in the Air* (New York: Da Capo, 1980).

Castle, Vernon and Irene Castle, *Modern Dancing* (New York: Harper and Bros, 1914).

Charters, Samuel, *The Blues Makers* (New York: Da Capo, 1991).

Cooke, Mervyn and David Horn, eds, *The Cambridge Companion to Jazz* (Cambridge: Cambridge University Press, 2002).

Erenberg, Lewis A., *Steppin' Out: New York Nightlife and the Transformation of American Culture, 1890–1930* (Chicago: University of Chicago Press, 1981).

Feder, Stuart, *The Life of Charles Ives* (Cambridge: Cambridge University Press, 1999).

Flitch, John Ernest Crawford, *Modern Dancing and Dancers* (Philadelphia PA: Lippincott, 1912).

Gioia, Ted, *The History of Jazz* (New York: Oxford University Press, 1997).

Glaspell, Susan, *A Road to the Temple: A Biography of George Cram Cook*, ed. Linda Ben-Zvi (Jefferson NC: McFarland, 2005).

Hamm, Charles, *Music in the New World* (New York: Norton, 1983).

Hewitt, Bernard, *Theatre U.S.A.: 1665 to 1957* (New York: McGraw-Hill, 1959).

Holmes, Thom, ed., *The Routledge Guide to Music Technology* (London: Routledge, 2006).

Horowitz, Joseph. *Classical Music in America: A History of its Rise and Fall* (New York: Norton, 2005).

Jackson, Buzzy, *A Bad Woman Feeling Good: Blues and the Women who Sing Them* (New York: Norton, 2005).

Krasner, David, *A Beautiful Pageant: African American Theatre, Drama and Performance in the Harlem Renaissance 1910–1927* (New York: Palgrave Macmillan, 2004).

McConachie, Brice A. and Daniel Friedman, eds, *Theatre for Working-Class Audiences in the United States, 1830–1980* (Westport CT: Greenwood Press, 1985).

Mazo, Joseph H., *Prime Movers: The Makers of Modern Dance in America* (London: Adam and Charles Black, 1977).

Morton, Jelly Roll, *The Complete Library of Congress Recordings*, B000GFLE36, Rounder 2005.

Nathan, George Jean, *Another Book on the Theatre* (New York: Huebsch, 1915).

Nasaw, David, *Going Out: The Rise and Fall of Public Amusements* (New York: Basic Books, 1993).

Nicholls, David, ed., *The Cambridge History of American Music* (Cambridge: Cambridge University Press, 1998).

Oakley, Giles, *The Devil's Music: A History of the Blues* (New York: Taplinger, 1976).

O'Neill, Eugene, *Early Plays* (London: Penguin, 2001).

Peiss, Kathy, *Cheap Amusements: Working Women and Leisure in Turn-of-the-Century New York* (Philadelphia PA: Temple University Press, 1986).

Riis, Thomas A., *Just Before Jazz: Black Musical Theatre in New York, 1890–1915* (Washington DC: Smithsonian Institution Press, 1989).

Schuller, Gunther, *Early Jazz: Its Roots and Musical Development* (New York: Oxford University Press, 1968).

Shipton, Alyn, *A New History of Jazz* (New York: Continuum, 2007).

Steiner, Jesse Frederick, *Americans at Play: Recent Trends in Recreation and Leisure Time Activities* (New York: McGraw-Hill, 1933).

Walker, Julia A., *Expressionism and Modernism in the American Theatre: Bodies, Voices, Words* (Cambridge: Cambridge University Press, 2005).

Wainscott, Ronald H., *The Emergence of the Modern American Theatre, 1914–1929* (New Haven CT: Yale University Press, 1997).

Wilmeth, Don B. and Christopher Bigsby, eds, *The Cambridge History of American Theatre*, Vol. II: *1870–1945* (Cambridge: Cambridge University Press, 1999).

The Great War and American Culture

Barbeau, Arthur E., and Florette Henri, *The Unknown Soldiers: African-American Troops in World War I* (New York: Da Capo Press, 1996).

Bergonzi, Bernard, *Heroes' Twilight: A Study of the Literature of the Great War* (London: Carcarnet Press, 1996).

Buitenhuis, Peter, *The Great War of Words: British, American and Canadian Propaganda and Fiction, 1914–1933* (Vancouver: University of British Columbia Press, 1987).

Capozzolla, Christopher, *Uncle Sam Wants You: World War One and the Making of the Modern American Citizen* (New York: Oxford University Press, 2008).

Cooperman, Stanley, *The Great War and the American Novel* (Baltimore MD: Johns Hopkins University Press, 1970).

Dawley, Alan, *Changing the World: American Progressives in War and Revolution* (Princeton NJ: Princeton University Press, 2003).

DeBauche, Leslie Midkiff, *Reel Patriotism: The Movies and World War I* (Madison: University of Wisconsin Press, 1997).

Douglas, Susan, *Inventing American Broadcasting 1899–1922* (Baltimore MD: Johns Hopkins University Press, 1987).

Early, Frances H., *A World Without War: How U. S. Feminists and Pacifists Resisted World War I* (Syracuse NY: Syracuse University Press, 1997).

Ellis, Mark, *Race, War and Surveillance: African Americans and the United States Government During World War I* (Bloomington: Indiana University Press, 2001).

Goddard, Chris, *Jazz away from Home* (London: Paddington Press, 1979).

Haytock, Jennifer, *At Home, At War: Domesticity and World War I in American Literature* (Columbus: Ohio State University Press, 2003).

Higonnet, Margaret, ed., *Nurses at the Front: Writing the Wounds of War* (Boston MA: Northeastern University Press, 2001).

— ed., *Lines of Fire: Women Writers of World War I* (New York: Penguin, 1999).

—, Jane Jenson, Sonya Michel and Margaret C. Weitz, eds, *Behind the Lines: Gender and the Two World Wars* (New Haven CT: Yale University Press, 1987).

Jensen, Kimberly, *Mobilizing Minerva: American Women in the First World War* (Urbana: University of Illinois Press, 2008).

Keene, Jennifer, *Doughboys, the Great War, and the Remaking of America* (Baltimore MD: Johns Hopkins University Press, 2003).

Kennedy, David M., *Over Here: The First World War and American Society* (New York: Oxford University Press, 2004).

Kitch, Carolyn, *The Girl on the Magazine Cover: The Origins of Visual Stereotypes in American Mass Media* (Chapel Hill: University of North Carolina Press, 2001).

Krass, Peter, *Portrait of War: The U.S. Army's First Combat Artists and the Doughboys' Experience in WWI* (Hoboken NJ: John Wiley, 2007).

Mead, Gary, *The Doughboys: America and the First World War* (London: Penguin, 2000).

Mock, James R. and Cedric Larson, *Words Which Won the War: The Story of the Committee on Public Information 1917–1919* (Princeton NJ: Princeton University Press, 1939).

Rae, Patricia, ed., *Modernism and Mourning* (Lewisburg PA: Bucknell University Press, 2007).

Rollins, Peter C. and John E. O'Connor, eds, *Hollywood's World War I: Motion Picture Images* (Bowling Green OH: Bowling Green State University Popular Press, 1997).

Sherry, Vincent, *The Great War and the Language of Modernism* (New York: Oxford University Press, 2003).

Slotkin, Richard, *Lost Battalions: The Great War and the Crisis of American Nationality* (New York: Henry Holt, 2005).

Trout, Steven, ed., *Dictionary of Literary Biography*, Vol. 316, *American Prose Writers of World War I: A Documentary Volume* (Detroit MI: Thomson-Gale, 2005).

Van Wienen, Mark, *Partisans and Poets: The Political Work of American Poetry in the Great War* (Cambridge: Cambridge University Press, 1997).

—, ed., *Rendezvous with Death: American Poems of the Great War* (Urbana: University of Illinois Press, 2002).

Whalan, Mark, *The Great War and the Culture of the New Negro* (Gainesville: University Press of Florida, 2008).

Winter, Jay, ed., *The Great War and the Twentieth Century* (New Haven CT: Yale University Press, 2000).

Woodward, David R., *America and World War I: a Selected Annotated Bibliography of English-language Sources* (New York: Routledge, 2007).

Zieger, Robert M., *America's Great War: World War I and the American Experience* (Lanham MD: Rowman and Littlefield, 2000).

Index